HIGHER EDUCATION IN AFRICA: EQUITY, ACCESS, OPPORTUNITY

HIGHER EDUCATION IN AFRICA: EQUITY, ACCESS, OPPORTUNITY

EDITED BY SABINE O'HARA

This book is part of the African Higher Education Collaborative (AHEC), a project of the Institute of International Education's Council for International Exchange of Scholars, and received generous support from the Ford Foundation office in Egypt.

INSTITUTE OF
INTERNATIONAL
EDUCATION

New York

IIE publications can be purchased at: www.iiebooks.org

The Institute of International Education
809 United Nations Plaza, New York, New York 10017

© 2010 by the Institute of International Education
All rights reserved. Published 2010
Printed in the United States of America
ISBN-13: 978-0-87206-321-1

Library of Congress Cataloging-in-Publication Data

Higher education in Africa : equity, access, opportunity / edited by Sabine O'Hara.
   p. cm.
  "Part of the African Higher Education Collaborative (AHEC)."
  ISBN 978-0-87206-334-1
1. Education, Higher--Africa. 2. Higher education accessibility--Africa. I. O'Hara, Sabine.
  LA1503.H525 2010
  378.6--dc22
                       2010043627

Series editors:
Daniel Obst, Deputy Vice President for International Partnerships, IIE
Sharon Witherell, Director of Public Affairs, IIE

Managing Editor: Andrew Ricketts, Program Officer, IIE
Assistant Editor: David Somers, Founder, Brevity Inc.
Copy Editor: Amy Ruttenberg, Council for International Exchange of Scholars, IIE
Cover and text design: Pat Scully Design

TABLE OF CONTENTS

FIGURES AND TABLES

FOREWORD

BY ALLAN E. GOODMAN, PRESIDENT AND CHIEF EXECUTIVE OFFICER
INSTITUTE OF INTERNATIONAL EDUCATION

The Institute of International Education's programs in Africa are working to develop a highly skilled workforce on the continent and to build the next generation of national and global leaders. Working closely with businesses, governments and non-governmental organizations in the region, IIE's offices in Ethiopia and Cairo have implemented initiatives to build leadership capacity and expand access to higher education across the continent.

We are especially pleased that IIE's programs in Africa, made possible through public and private investments, are helping to address many of the challenges identified in this publication by the Africa Higher Education Collaborative. This project was managed by the Institute of International Education's Council for International Exchange of Scholars, with generous support from the Ford Foundation office in Egypt.

In line with the call to address gender imbalance in higher education, the Ethiopian Women's Leadership Program, funded by the David and Lucile Packard Foundation, creates champions of women's health, education and economic empowerment. In an effort to help develop and retain the next generation of African academics, the Institute is partnering with the Carnegie Corporation of New York's Higher Education and Libraries in Africa (HELA) program on a November 2010 conference in Nairobi, Developing and Retaining the Next Generation of African Academics: Excellence, Retention, and Sustainability, to unite academic leaders from a variety of African higher education institutions. We are also proud of our role in administering the South African Education Program (SAEP) from 1979 to 2001, which enabled over 1,600 black South African students to attend U.S. universities to obtain the knowledge and skills to become leaders in a post-apartheid society.

To date, more than 1,300 Africans have participated in the Hubert Humphrey Fellowship program, funded by the U.S. Department of State, which brings accomplished mid-career professionals from the public and private sector to the United States for a year of advanced study and related professional experiences. The program provides a basis for lasting ties between U.S. citizens and their professional counterparts in other countries. Thousands of African students and scholars have come to the United States through the Fulbright Program, which IIE has the honor to administer on behalf of the U.S. Department of State. Fulbright is one of the most effective and responsive components of U.S. public diplomacy, continuously encouraging new ways of thinking and preparing a new generation of global leaders.

By creating and administering exchange and training programs, IIE helps develop the talent and human resources needed to address the shared challenges facing the world community. We would like to thank our partners in these endeavors, and we applaud the good work that is being done throughout the continent to improve access and equity in African higher education.

Allan E. Goodman

Introduction

IMPROVING EQUITY AND ACCESS TO AFRICAN HIGHER EDUCATION: LESSONS FOR FUTURE DIRECTIONS

BY SABINE O'HARA

Introduction

In February 2008, a group of 20 scholars from Egypt, Kenya, Nigeria and South Africa convened in Cairo to launch the Africa Higher Education Collaborative (AHEC). The focal point for the collaborative remains a crucial one for the African continent: *improving equity and access to higher education in Africa.* The purpose of AHEC quickly encompassed the following: to exchange information; pursue research; identify strategies for addressing barriers to higher education equity and access; and serve as a think tank and repository of information for policy makers, scholars and practitioners of higher education across Africa.

Prior to the first meeting of the AHEC scholars a second focus also emerged: the need to increase *collaboration* among African scholars. Thus, AHEC sought to also contribute to building a network of African scholars steeped in African higher education and familiar with the acute needs of Africa's over-extended and under-resourced higher education systems.

AHEC was initially conceptualized by the Institute of International Education (IIE)'s Council for International Exchange of Scholars (CIES) and its then-executive director, Dr. Pattie McGill Peterson; by IIE's Middle East-North Africa Office in Cairo; and by the Ford Foundation office in Egypt, which funded the program. The selection of the AHEC topic was determined through consultation with higher education experts from throughout Africa, as well as U.S. scholars with extensive experience in African higher education.

Why Equity and Access to Higher Education?

The critical importance of initiatives that improve equity and access to higher education in Africa is undisputed. The 1998/99 *World Development Report: Knowledge for Development* clearly documents the strong link between higher education and economic development, particularly in the knowledge-based economies of the 21st century. However, despite much effort, progress in expanding higher education access has been slow on most of the African continent. With the exception of Egypt and South Africa, which have participation rates in higher education of 30 and 15 percent respectively, participation rates on the rest of the continent remain disappointingly low at less than five percent.

Much of the pressure on Africa's higher education systems stems from the continent's steep increase in demand that continues to outpace supply. By way of population, Africa is a young continent and, as a result, faces significant demographic pressures on education at every level from primary to graduate education. Added demand for tertiary education comes from so-called, non-traditional learners who show a heightened need and interest in access to advanced knowledge associated with the post-manufacturing, modern knowledge economy. In this new knowledge economy, inadequate access to higher education seriously constrains Africa's future. Increased access to quality higher education thus remains the continent's ticket to future prosperity, global competitiveness and, more indirectly, to improved public health, social stability and sustainable development.

Numerous reports have outlined the connection between advanced education and economic progress and improvements in the quality of life. The 1998/99 World Development Report emphasizes four key strategies that for a successful transition to the new knowledge economy: an appropriate economic and institutional regime, a strong human capital base, a dynamic information infrastructure, and an efficient national innovation systems. All four strategies are inextricably linked to a strong higher education system (Salmi, 2009).

A decidedly African perspective on the subject can be found in the New Program for African Development (NEPAD). NEPAD seeks to advance two key objectives: (1) to eradicate poverty and assist African countries in advancing sustainable growth and development and (2) to combat the exclusion of the African continent from the international development arena. Many of the initiatives outlined in NEPAD speak directly to the need for improved education as a basis for transforming the brain drain, which has stifled development across the African continent, into a brain gain. The report identifies increased knowledge in health care, agriculture, environmental protection, science and technology as particularly urgent needs. It also stresses the need for the continued expansion of education-related ICT initiatives and it points to the critical importance of protecting and encouraging indigenous knowledge systems that are unique to the African context.

Research in regional economics shows similar connections between economic development and human capital and information technology. Education, health, social amenities and civic engagement, environmental quality and information infrastructure have been termed the five pillars of economic development (O'Hara and Vazquez, 2006).

The consensus emerging from these and other development reports is that increased access to education and educational quality are essential prerequisites for Africa's success in the global knowledge economy society and its increasingly global labor market, which is characterized by worldwide competition and mobility. The educational challenge for Africa's universities then is two-fold: (1) they must provide increased access to the knowledge and skills necessary to succeed in the new innovation-driven, global knowledge economy; and (2) they must produce the skills and expertise necessary to build the capacity of Africa's public and private sector and to close the human resources gap that is so critical for the development success of Africa's relatively new democracies. Meeting this dual challenge requires first and foremost that education is relevant and that universities embrace their new educational objectives of straddling different academic fields, straddling the classroom and the community and straddling the knowledge of credentialed experts and that of non-credentialed experts with in-depth local and regional knowledge.

Meeting the demands of this new kind of relevant knowledge requires more than increased higher education capacity. It requires increased attention to learning outcomes and educational quality at all levels, from primary to tertiary to post-graduate to continuing and lifelong education. Furthermore, for higher education in today's fast-paced knowledge societies, it is challenging enough to address access, but to also address the need for improved quality and cost containment seems impossible.

The chapters contained in this volume address this challenging triad of access, quality and cost. Yet they also offer more than that; they bring vivid detail to the higher education access and equity debate by giving voice to the specific contexts and experiences of the authors in Africa's varied higher education institutions. They also reflect the focus of the four working groups that formed within the group of AHEC participants based on the specific interests of the AHEC scholars themselves: a focus on financial mechanisms and funding options to improve equity and access to higher education; a focus on educational institutions and the services they must provide to improve learner success; a focus on delivery systems, including distance learning, that are responsive to the needs of diverse groups of learners; and a focus on various kinds of marginalization that exacerbate inequity and exclusion, including gender and populations with disabilities.

Peliwe Lolwana's chapter compares the higher education systems of Kenya, Nigeria and South Africa, and argues that higher education across the continent is in crisis due to the prevailing conditions of severe excess demand and under supply. Given the critical importance of higher education as the basis for Africa's future development, Lolwana argues that Africa must pay attention to its higher education systems and must be committed to increasing higher education access by embracing higher education as a public good. Sabiha Essack, too, focuses on the need to increase participation in higher education. Yet she adds a focus on the quality aspects of higher education and raises the question how higher education institutions can improve the learning outcomes and success of their students. Expanded access, she argues, is counterproductive if students cannot succeed.

The chapter by Gerald Ouma, a Kenyan scholar who now teaches in South Africa, offers a comparison of the two countries' higher education funding policies and mechanisms. As Ouma shows, they reflect significant differences in the two countries' higher education systems, histories and political and socio-economic contexts. These differences in context invariably influence government policies, with Kenya reflecting significant external influences such as the World Bank and the IMF, and South Africa reflecting primarily internal influences and policies shaped by the political considerations of the new post-apartheid democracy. Adedeji, Baraka, Dugga and Odebero focus on an aspect of higher education financing that is quickly growing in importance across the African continent, namely the role of private sector education and of endowment funding. The chapter examines the institutional models and regulations impacting the fast-growing private higher education sector in Egypt, Kenya and Nigeria, and the role endowment funds play as a source of non-governmental funding.

Ibrahim Oanda Ogachi and Lilian-Rita Akudolu discuss the persistent gender imbalance in higher education access and success in Sub-Saharan Africa. Their analysis shows that despite several initiatives designed to alleviate gender inequities, enrollments of female students remain disproportionately low. Inequalities are especially apparent among socio-economically disadvantaged females and among those who seek enrollment in fields of study that are traditionally considered male domains, such as science and technology. Michael Cross and Haroon Mahomed offer another perspective on the topic of exclusion. Their chapter discusses the increased differentiation in higher education that is reflective of the needs of an increasingly diverse student body. While the challenge associated with increased diversity has been primarily an issue in high-access countries, Cross and Mahomed argue that they are facing Africa as well, albeit at a far smaller scale. If improvements in access and equity are to succeed, then attention must be given to the needs of learners who do not meet the standard characteristics of the traditional, privileged learner profile. A more diverse student body calls for more diversified forms of educational delivery, pedagogy and epistemologies. The authors argue that prevailing practices and norms continue to selectively enable the successful participation of some to the exclusion of others. The chapter discusses the social and academic resources that university students draw on in the South African context and points to potential pedagogical and social improvements in students' university experience that can improve the success of a more diverse student body.

A student population that often faces discrimination and exclusion is students with disabilities. Violet Wawire, Helen Mwanza and Nadia Elarabi offer a comparative study of students with disabilities in Kenya and Egypt. The chapter also provides an overview of broadly accepted conventions for students with disabilities, as well as data obtained from surveys. It concludes with recommendations for strategies to address some of the identified problems that students with disabilities face. Felix Kayode Olakulehini offers a specific strategy to overcome access barriers for student populations with disabilities, namely distance learning and its potential for addressing the needs of populations with various types of disabilities.

Beyond the specific content perspectives offered by the African higher education professionals whose work is assembled in this volume, the chapters also reflect the second dimension of AHEC—the acute need to increase collaboration among African scholars.

Why a Collaborative?

Using joint publications as an indicator, it is evident that collaboration among African scholars is relatively rare. To date, scholarly collaborations have taken place primarily between scholars in the United States and Europe. Collaborations with Asian scholars are on the rise and have led the way to a growing number of collaborations between scholars in the United States and Europe and those on other continents, including scholars in the so-called developing world. Yet little collaboration has taken place among scholars in the south and most especially among African scholars.

This lack of collaboration on the African continent is clearly limiting. Many of the higher education challenges facing Africa are context-specific and demand context-specific solutions. AHEC therefore, recognized that one of its contributions was to develop a network of African scholars who are steeped in African higher education and are familiar with the acute need for increased equity and access in light of Africa's over-extended and under-resourced higher education systems.

Why is an African collaborative so important? In his opening remarks to the constituting meeting of AHEC in Cairo, Dr. Akilagpa Sawyerr, former secretary general of the Association of African Universities and lead facilitator of AHEC, made an articulate case for increasing collaborations among African scholars. He pointed out that effective collaboration has some important prerequisites, including a general appreciation for the history of higher education in Africa and openness to context-specific conditions that cannot serve as a barrier, but must be acknowledged as a basis for effective analysis. Pan-African collaborations among scholars who bring an informed, context-aware perspective to the debate about the opportunities and needs facing Africa's universities are therefore vital for identifying practical solutions that will advance higher education access and success. Collaboration and networking promote the exchange of ideas, encourage information sharing and create an environment of trust where solutions can be tested and where open deliberation occurs about what works where and how.

Africa is no monolith; the four African countries represented in AHEC range from $580 (Nigeria) to $5,400 (South Africa) per year in national income per capita. They also span a human development index from 112 for Egypt to 158 for Nigeria. Just as the sustainable development debate has pointed to the importance of context-specific social, cultural and environmental conditions and of the local knowledge perspectives that carry them, so too does the higher education debate benefit from a focus on and awareness of context-specific social, cultural, environmental and economic conditions (O'Hara, 1999). Context-specific perspectives are the very basis for advancing productive discourse and for bringing diverse knowledge to the analysis of viable solutions to pressing development problems.

The result of such collaborative efforts will invariably be new ways of thinking and of re-framing solutions that can assist policy makers and practitioners. Moreover, collaborations offer mentoring opportunities and support to the participating scholars; the more diverse the participants, the more effective can be the collaboration. Yet collaborations also offer encouragement and support to those who must address the barriers standing in the way of increased insights and better solutions. These can range from a lack of data to intentional information barriers, to marginalization and exclusion to outright opposition to the policies and strategies proposed by scholars.

A great debt of gratitude is due to Dr. Akilagpa Sawyerr, Dr. Pundi Pillay, Dr. Olive Mugenda, and Dr. Hoda El Sada, who served as resource persons, facilitators and presenters during the AHEC program. Their impact on the participating scholars and their work is evident in these pages and in various other country-based and comparative initiatives that originated in the AHEC program. Drs. Dina El Kawara and John Butler Adams from the Ford Foundation offices in Egypt and South Africa also deserve thanks for their support and interest throughout the collaboration. In addition, several guest speakers brought important perspectives to the AHEC process. They include Abdul-Monem Al-Mashat, Cheryl DelaRay, Bakary Diallo, Jonathan Jensen, Silas Lwacambamba, Alphonse Maindo and Barney Pityana. All offered their valuable insights as experienced higher education researchers and practitioners who are committed to relevance and accountability, while some also offered their perspectives as public scholars and higher education advocates. A special word of thanks also goes to David Somers of Brevity, Inc. for his superb editing assistance and ability to maintain the rich voices of this book's many authors.

And last but not least, sincere thanks and appreciation are due to the AHEC participants themselves. They are the scholars from Egypt, Kenya, Nigeria and South Africa who devoted time and energy to participate in an 18-month collaborative process of face-to-face meetings, discussions, exchange of data, feedback on research ideas and numerous presentations. It is their engagement that molded the collaborative itself. They are Nadia Ahmed, Boshra Awad, Pakinaz Baraka, Ahmed S.H. Hassan, and Mohamed Nabih (Egypt); Helen Mwanzi, Ibrahim Oanda Ogachi, Stephen Odebero, Gerald Ouma, and Violet Wawire (Kenya); Segun Adedeji, Lilian-Rita Akudolu, Felix Olakulehin, and Victor Samson (Nigeria); and Narend Baijnath, Michael Cross, Sabiha Essack, Peliwe Lolwana, and Haroon Mahomed (South Africa). Drs. Adedeji, Baijnath, Essack, and Mahomed also served as facilitators of the four working groups the scholars formed, and three of the scholars, Drs. Akudolu, Essack, and Oanda Ogachi, also brought graduate students into the AHEC project and into their collaborative research. This speaks well for the future of the collaborations begun and the connections made during the AHEC program.

The recent interest in African higher education adds further encouragement to future scholarly work on the topic of improving access and equity in African higher education. After decades during which attention was almost exclusively devoted to primary education and literacy, two undeniably important issues, higher education and the indispensible role it plays in economic development, is finally gaining attention. Yet the growing attention also raises questions about the role of African scholars and African scholarship, appropriate solutions, degrees of intervention, implementation capacity at African universities and among their faculty and staff, and the context specific direction and balance of new higher education initiatives. Finding the proper balance will depend on effective collaborations between African and international higher education bodies and scholars, and most certainly between regional and pan-African ones. Thanks to its collaborators and supporters, AHEC may have made a contribution to this important balancing process of shaping African higher education based on African voices, perspectives, and experience.

Sabine O'Hara[1]

August 2010

NOTES

[1] Dr. Sabine O'Hara served as Executive Director of the Council for International Exchange of Scholars and Vice President of Scholar Programs for the Institute of International Education from 2007 to 2010. In this capacity she oversaw the design and implementation of the AHEC program in close collaboration with the AHEC facilitators.

REFERENCES

NEPAD. 2001: The New Partnership for Africa's Development. http://www.uneca.org/nepad/Media-Dialogue/NEPAD_Framework_Document.pdf. Abuja, Nigeria.

O'Hara, S. 1999: Economics, Ecology and Quality of Life: Who Evaluates? Feminist Economics. Vol. 5(2): 83-89.

O'Hara, S. and Vazquez, J. 2006: The Five Pillars of Economic Development: A Study of Best Practices for the Roanoke Valley. Research Report. Roanoke College, Salem, VA.

Salmi, J. 2009: The Challenge of Establishing World-Class Universities. Direction in Development. The World Bank. Washington DC.

World Bank. 1999: World Development Report 1998/99: Knowledge for Development. http://www.worldbank.org/wdr/wdr98/contents.htm. Washington DC.

Chapter One
MAKING HIGHER EDUCATION A PUBLIC AND SOCIAL GOOD IN AFRICA

BY PELIWE LOLWANA, COUNCIL FOR QUALITY ASSURANCE IN GENERAL AND FURTHER EDUCATION AND TRAINING IN SOUTH AFRICA

Introduction

Africa at the beginning of the 21st century clearly lags far behind developed countries and developing countries on other continents in its provision and availability of higher education. In 2003, with its 54 countries, Africa had no more than 300 institutions which fit the definition of a university (Teferra and Altbach, 2003). The scarcity of higher education has not only dwarfed the educational outputs of the continent, but has become an important contributor to the sluggishness of the continent's economic and political development (Teferra & Altbach, 2003; Saint et al. 2003; Ng'ethe et al. 2008; Fehnel, 2003).

While African higher education participation rates are small, demand for post-secondary options has been growing; in fact, demand far outstrips the supply. For example, enrollment in Egypt for undergraduate studies grew from 484,206 in 1988-89 to 1,167,891 in 1998-99; in Kenya the number of undergraduates increased from 31,630 in 1990 to 97,107 in 2008; in Nigeria enrollment grew from 6,707 in 1965 to 411,347 in 1998; and in South Africa enrollment increased from 303,000 to 736,000 students in 2006 (Said, 2003; Ngome, 2003; Jibril, 2003; Bunting & Cloete, 2007; Mugenda, 2009). Yet, Africa's growth is relative and dwarfed by the growth experienced in other countries. For example, Clancy, et al. (2007), reported a staggering increase of up to two-thirds of age cohorts in the admission rates of many countries. What is it that stunts African higher education? There are many factors that seem to inhibit growth in the continent's higher education system, and some of these will be explored in this chapter in order to better understand what interventions would help correct such a situation.

Indeed, the size of the current higher education system is a deterrent to higher participation rates in African higher education. Size is a function of both the number who qualify to enter higher education, as well as the space available in African higher education institutions. Unfortunately, the sector has not grown significantly over a long period. Fehnel (2003) compared Ghana and Korea, countries which were similar in the 1960s in terms of their investments in education. Korea, on the one hand, made a long-term commitment to increase access to education at all levels. Ghana, on the other hand, continued on its same trajectory, and the development plot of the two countries diverged dramatically.

In Africa, educational opportunities diminish as one advances in the system. This dwindling of opportunities is worrisome since only a few, and typically the wealthier, continue to access higher levels of education. Still, education is key to re-creating a new social order despite inaccessibility to levels beyond primary education for many children, the inability of the African higher education systems to offer places for a wide range of students in higher education, and the absence of strategies that draw the marginalized (e.g. adults, rural people, workers, etc.) back to higher education (Bregman, 2004; Fehnel, 2003). Education might just be the only currency that can be distributed in order to improve equity in a given society.

This chapter does not present a full and comprehensive study of all 54 African countries. Instead, it chooses Kenya, Nigeria and South Africa as points of reference for its arguments. Although the information available even about these few countries is scant, the absence of data should not weaken the argument that African higher education is in crisis.

African countries have no option for their developmental trajectory but to pay attention to the development and growth of their higher education systems. This chapter examines the throughputs of students below higher education, presents the shape and size of higher education in Kenya, Nigeria and South Africa, and discusses how higher education in other countries has been developing. Lastly, it offers some suggestions on possible efforts to grow higher education in Africa.

Post-Primary Education in Some African Countries

For a long time now, international donors have been preoccupied with the acquisition of primary education in Africa. For example, UNESCO's focus on Universal Primary Education (UPE) has had a dual impact on African education. On one hand, UPE has encouraged African countries, sometimes aided by international donors, to aggressively meet the Millennium Goals of providing primary education for all and, according to Bregman (2008), Africa is passing the test with flying colors. On the other hand, the success of primary education in Africa has revealed the deficiencies or inadequacies of the post-primary education system. Both secondary education and post-secondary education systems are inadequate to meet the educational demands of the young and the old in most African countries.

Throughputs from Senior Secondary School

Secondary education systems have recently come to the attention of major influencers of public education in Africa, namely the World Bank and UNESCO, and African secondary education systems are recognized as the least developed in the world (Bregman, 2008; Lolwana, 2008). At the dawn of the 21st century, Sub-Saharan Africa (SSA) is still experiencing a population boom (Mahajan, 2008), which means, in contrast to the high and medium income countries, SSA has the record number of young people to educate. While EFA and other attempts to meet Millennium Development Goals (MDGs) have resulted in unprecedented growth of primary education in SSA, secondary schooling still remains limited (King, 2007; Bregman, 2004). Lack of secondary education in the SSA is detrimental for the region's ability to meet the MDGs, compete globally and support growing democratic trends.

Bregman (2008) observes that patterns of secondary education system in Africa still reflect the traditional structures inherited from England and France. Its structure of primary, junior secondary and senior secondary cycles is a key factor in a small secondary education system (Lolwana, 2008; Kelleghan & Greaney 2003; Bregman, 2004). In addition, there are great inefficiencies within the school system caused by poor teaching, non-differentiated curricula, size limitations and rigorous selection. Bregman (2008) further notes that the net effect is that only one in four or five African youth completes secondary education.

TABLE 1.1: PARTICIPATION RATES IN THE EDUCATION SYSTEM

2005	Kenya	Nigeria	South Africa
Primary education enrollment (%)	112.2	102.9	104.1
Secondary education enrollment (%)	48.8	34.2	93.4
Tertiary education enrollment (%)	2.8	10.2	15.3

Source: African Higher Education Collaborative: Country Data (2009)

Table 1.1 clearly shows the education system's limitations with accommodating many people who earnestly start at the primary level with high hopes to advance. Traditionally, post-primary education is designed for a smaller, elite group of African children. Further, geographical disparities compound access problems in most African countries (Mugenda, 2009), with rural and informal settlements least represented in higher levels of education.

Shape and Size of Post-Secondary Education

Most African countries still have just one institution of higher education, a national university. According to Fehnel, this type of institution was created shortly after independence as a symbol of freedom from a colonial past. Although few higher education institutions exist among the countries in this study, the types of institutions are illustrative. The following information is collected from various sources (AHEC country data, 2008; Ng'ethe, 2008; Teferra, D. & Altbach, 2003; Mugenda, 2009).

TABLE 1.2: NUMBER OF HIGHER EDUCATION INSTITUTIONS IN KENYA, NIGERIA AND SOUTH AFRICA

Institutions	Kenya	Nigeria	South Africa
Population	34,3	131,5m	47,4m
Public Universities	7	50	23
Private Universities	14	23	350[1]
Public Polytechnics	5	97	0
Private Polytechnics	0	11	0
Public Post-Secondary Colleges	38	63	50
Private Post-Secondary Colleges	0	9	350[1]

Source: African Higher Education Collaborative: Country Data (2009)

The University System

Ng'ethe (2008) states that African higher education exists in the absence of debates about its size and shape, with the exception of South Africa. What he fails to understand is that the South African debate was driven by an agenda that includes a need to redirect a previously racially oriented higher education system. South Africa deracialized its system and reduced the number of institutions from 32 to 23, giving the country three types of higher education institutions: universities, universities of applied technologies, and comprehensive universities. This is, of course, a theoretical classification, because in practice all institutions seem to be doing the same thing; isomorphism has suddenly crept in as predicted by Ng'ethe (2008). Discussions with the National Board for Technical Education in Nigeria as recent as 2008 confirm the country's intention to convert the polytechnics in that country to universities, and the board is referencing the South African changes, which they are emulating. The *University World News* (2009) reports that Kenya has also embarked on plans to convert some of the country's polytechnics to degree-granting institutions. It must be noted, however, that these moves are similar to those that took place in the United Kingdom up to 1992.

Some would argue that even though African higher education systems face pressures for expansion, they have unfortunately delivered 'more of the same' (University World News, 2008). Ng'ethe (2008) attributes this phenomenon to a lack of direction that would create African higher education institutions and programs that matriculate. As a result, there might be more institutions, but they are doing almost the same things. Ng'ethe concludes that the kind of differentiation that seems to exist in

African higher education is horizontal, where there are different types of knowledge fields, not different types of institutions. This is in contrast to the OECD institutions, where there has been a focus on mission expansion and the development of different institutions with different missions, and this seems to have been instrumental in improving access to higher education (Garrod & Macfarlane, 2009).

Lastly, African countries do not seem to have effectively capitalized on the growing private higher education sector, but instead seem to be treating these institutions as a problem that will soon go away. In some cases, public higher education is closely protected and as it becomes the pride of the nation, the best students who have gone to the best private secondary schools are the first to gain admissions into an elite public higher education; the poorer students who have attended poor public schools end up having poor, unregulated, private higher education as their only option for post-secondary education.

The College System

The other institution that provides post-school education in Africa is a college. There are different types of colleges found in the space between secondary and higher education. Some colleges have a single purpose (e.g. teaching, nursing, agriculture, etc); others have multiple purposes, especially technical or further education and training colleges. The technical or further education and training colleges evolved from colleges that primarily supported the apprenticeship system which produced trade artisans for the major industries in Africa. Predominantly, most technical colleges were always located at the secondary school level, and it would be through this route that those who did not complete their secondary education could gain an alternative secondary school qualification. The qualification was different because, unlike the school qualification, these learners could only proceed to polytechnics or technikons[2].

However, single-purpose colleges have acquired a similar status to technikons or polytechnics as post-secondary institutions, but not higher education. In South Africa, where many single-purpose colleges have been eliminated, no institutions have replaced them as easily accessible post-secondary institutions. In Kenya and Nigeria, these colleges still continue as post-secondary education institutions and are commonly known as tertiary institutions, but not of the same status as polytechnics and universities.

Many technical colleges in South Africa offer post-secondary education programs whose role in the tertiary sector is dubious. It must be said that as time has passed, the technical colleges have drawn more and more from the ranks of those students who passed the senior secondary education examinations, albeit weakly, but either did not satisfy the admission requirements for university entrance or did not have the resources required to be admitted in the university system.

Post-Secondary Education on the Move

Higher education publications make clear that post-secondary education is on the move. In fact, Garrod & Macfarlane (2009), quoting from the Organisation for Economic Co-operation (OECD), believe, "the higher education expansion witnessed all over OECD countries reflects a widening of access to new groups of students that have historically been excluded from post-secondary education and the changing needs of a global, knowledge-based economy (p.3)."

The two needs Garrod and Macfarlane identified are seen in the differentiation of higher education institutions increasingly found in OECD countries. For example, Norway has established what is known as 'third generation' higher education institutions (University World News, 2008); further education colleges in the United Kingdom now offer foundational degrees; and Korea and Singapore have expanded their higher education systems through a junior college system (Ng'ethe, 2008). The emergence of other institutions in higher education has not only brought about a diverse system, but it has also essentially done away with the exclusivity of elite pathways from school to higher education. Garrod and Macfarlane (2009) remind us that Eton College in England, for example, still dominates Oxford and Cambridge admissions. But because there are a range of institutions to accommodate a range of learners in the system, as well as different routes to access higher education, this elite exclusivity is no longer an issue. Students who go to junior or community colleges are different from those who go straight to universities (Townsend & Dougherty, 2006; Cohen & Brawer, 2003).

Ng'ethe (2008) considers a system of differentiation in programs and institutions to be key in expanding higher education. To this end he says,

"A system of elite higher education without the balancing force of mass higher education would not be politically or socially viable, and a system of mass higher education without the academic models and values of elite institutions would be unsound educationally and politically (p. 10)."

Also, in many countries with a reasonably sized higher education system, there is a conscious attempt to embrace private higher education. Kim, et al. (2007), argue convincingly that there is no higher education system that has succeeded in massifying without treating the private component of its system as an integral part of the whole system.

The need to have different types of institutions that provide post-secondary education is one way of increasing access to higher education. The other way is to target those who are considered to be non-traditional students and bring them back to higher education. Indeed, nations are challenged by the notion of promoting economic prosperity and egalitarian societies, and they widely acknowledge that education for the young is not enough for them to meet adequately the socio-economic challenges in the world. This challenge has become more and more pronounced since the collapse of the Cold War, blurring the boundaries and needs between developed and underdeveloped states (Sall, 2003). In other words, the need for continuing education seems to be growing in both developing and developed countries as the world's political and economic systems continue to be thrown into doubt by an increasingly international society. Those countries experiencing most changes can expect to also experience a greater need to increase their provision for everyone in order to prepare their citizens to deal effectively with a changing world.

In countries where education is broadly offered, post-secondary education institutions are not only comprehensive or multi-purpose in nature, but they also tend to target students in their communities. One example is the United States' community college system, where institutions provide a range of programs including academic development, work preparation, community development, continuing education, general education or liberal arts education for talented scholars, entrepreneurship and transfer courses to degree-awarding programs at university (Townsend & Dougherty, 2006; Vaughan, 2000). Specifically, community colleges are institutions that are accessible and located in communities to serve their educational needs.

Upsizing the African Higher Education System

The African education system is facing challenges that other developing countries have faced. Consider the example of Korea and Ghana, cited at the beginning of this chapter, which made different choices resulting in totally different scenarios in their education systems (Fehnel, 2003). What's important for African countries is to understand the relationship of primary, secondary and tertiary education systems; when one level expands, increased inequality can be expected on the next level (Clancy, 2007). Also, no country in the 21st century can afford to treat higher education as an elite system designed only for the select few, which means that expanding the higher education system is no longer an option only for rich countries. Global imperatives demand this of each and every country. Lastly, in spite of the suggested massification of African higher education, countries need to be aware of what unbridled expansion might do to the system and what steps they might take to guard against a negative impact.

An Expanded Secondary Education System

The fact that the senior secondary education system is relatively small in most African countries has already been highlighted. In fact, Bregman (2004) has defined the problem as being one of finding solutions to "cope with the success of primary education" in Africa. However, the policy landscape and the resources available for education in the different countries make it difficult to have a "one-size-fits-all" prescription for the urgent need to transform the education system (Lewin, 2006). It is for this reason that an expansion strategy in African education systems must be found. This will include huge investments to build the needed infrastructure, improvements in teacher education, a diversified curriculum and fewer selection and promotion policies (Lewin, 2006; Lolwana, 2008).

Despite evidence of growth in secondary education, something still drives students away from secondary schools, because the number of students who qualify for higher education remains painfully small. A possible limitation in secondary education makes advancement unattractive to young people. Muller (2003) attributes this limitation to the sectoral interest of the university sector. Most countries that have succeeded in massifying the secondary school system seem to have done so through a greater diversification of curriculum to meet the educational needs of different groups (Holsinger & Cowell, 2000). But many of Africa's secondary education systems are scholarly and discourage those who are less academically inclined.

Solving problems with higher education or with any part of the formal education system must involve dealing with young people who have left the school system. Colonization left Africa with massive backlogs in literacy, which did not change with independence (Gebremarian, 2001; Maruatona, 2006). The low literacy levels in Sub-Saharan Africa are perpetuated by both the low capacity in secondary schools and the absence of opportunities for young adults to continue with their education. Young adults soon become adults and parents who lack the ability to assist their children in their own education. As Gebremarian (2001) notes, "Primary education is a means to adult education and is hardly ever an end in itself (p.98)."

The lost potential of many young adults, who could still contribute actively in the economy of their countries, is a serious indictment. Therefore, it is not enough to develop a vibrant and thriving education system for the young and full-time learners without a corresponding system for adults outside of the formal system. Many adult education programs tend to be limited to basic literacy or primary school levels, which does not raise standards of education for the whole population (Lolwana, 2007).

A Differentiated Post-Secondary Education System

The differentiated institutional types with distinct academic and career foci have been blurred in many African countries (Ng'ethe, 2008). The result is problematic and what Ng'ethe terms 'institutional isomorphism,' whereby there is a gradual adoption of a single set of institutional characteristics within the higher education system. The problem with size of African higher education stems primarily from the fact that it is defined only in terms of universities. The vibrant polytechnic sector, where mostly academically and financially weaker students landed, and where the thrust has been vocationally oriented programs, is gone or dying.

The polytechnic sector provided a post-secondary education system that made it possible for many individuals to eventually enter the 'proper' higher education system. Although there was never a clear articulation between the college system and universities, except by arrangement (Kruss, 2008), polytechnics and technikons provided a place for many students to mature and gain confidence. They also led directly to employment opportunities that allowed individuals to pay for their further studies. Most disadvantaged students are destined for a less demanding institution that accepts lower entrance requirements, and they are drawn to shorter and vocationally oriented courses. Consequently, Africa's higher education system calls for a differentiated post-secondary education system in which colleges, career-focused institutions and private provision are part of an expanded system.

There is a clear need for a new institution to enter the post-secondary provision space. It is time for post-secondary colleges in Africa, both public and private institutions, to respond and deal with increased demand for higher education or post-secondary education. Expansion is not going to come from the current university system because the current system is stretched to its limits (Bunting & Cloete, 2008). The inequality of access to post-secondary education is one reason for calling for another institution to enter in the higher education system in order to expand the size of the higher education. Clancy, et al. (2007) also have this wise counsel about the benefits of an expanded higher education system:

> "…in the absence of growth in educational systems, there will be no distribution of educational opportunity among social classes. Growth will enhance the educational chances of formerly disadvantaged groups mainly through the principle of non-selection, whereby more and more students pass on to advanced levels of education (p.47)."

Adding another type of institution will provide more diversity, which is needed. This does not mean that these institutions become universities; rather, adding a new type would ensure that there is a wide range of institutions that could be accessible to learners of different abilities, conditions and readiness. Ng'ethe (2008) describes students of these institutions as "requiring a high degree of specific skill; people with practical abilities but little theoretical inclination; late starters; second-chancers or adult learners; working students; disabled students; and parents with childcare responsibilities (p.7)."

Lastly, African countries have to reconsider their admission policies into higher education. Admission policies from school to higher education have remained unchanged in many African countries for a long time, and this is partly the reason why a rather constant number of students flow through the school system to higher education. Kenya, Nigeria and South Africa rely heavily on their end of the secondary school examination results in admitting students to higher education, in spite of the low completion rate of schooling. None of these countries seems to have comprehensive[3] alternate admission routes. In this light then, admission policies should be reconstructed so that those who do not achieve the traditional university admission requirements nevertheless still have the possibility of accessing higher education.

In an environment where there is a heterogeneous pool of students and new types of institutions, success will be underpinned by comprehensive support services in the entire system, as they are likely to be the home for students who need the most support. Institutional support services seem to be particularly weak in colleges at this point and comprise two facets: 1) regulating student behavior in order to maintain the institutional order and 2) helping students to navigate the bureaucracy and to link all college functions (Cohen and Brawer, 2003). These two facets have been found to be key in the effectiveness of any college system, due to the nature of its diverse programs, as well as diverse student intake. In fact, some would proclaim that in a college, support services are the hub, the core, around which the whole enterprise moves.

Articulation, Regulating and Capacity Building

While colleges should be the main vehicle for expanding the higher education system in Africa, certain fundamentals would have to be considered in order to make this institution a useful addition to higher education system. These fundamentals have to do with diversification; differentiation, articulation, regulating and capacity building.

As soon as different types of institutions belong to one system, isomorphism tends to creep in (Ng'ethe, 2008). What would prevent non-university, post-secondary institutions from mimicking universities or developing isomorphism? While varied institutional types address horizontal differentiation, program variations will speak to vertical differentiation (World Bank, 2000). Program differentiation is informed by a detailed content analysis, as well as the stipulation of qualifications that would be awarded in one institutional type as opposed to another institution type. Ng'ethe (2008) accurately states that program differentiation requires different analytical methods. Many non-university institutions award certificates and diplomas rather than degrees, which would have significant recognition in higher education if they provide genuine transferability of achievements into degree-awarding programs. This is when differentiation can be seen to be articulating successfully.

Besides diversity, differentiation and program articulation, regulatory and funding mechanisms are two other elements that would make the inclusion of the college sector in higher education successful. Internally or within the system, it is important to have regulatory tools that will make a college institution belong to and behave like higher education institutions. For example, in the United States model, all post-secondary education institutions are considered part of its higher education system (Ng'ethe, 2008; Richardson, et al. 1999).

Second, a key feature of a massified higher education system is the strength of its quality assurance system. Higher education institutions all over the world defend their autonomy and, therefore, it becomes necessary to engender a quality regulatory system. The tension between differentiation and quality assurance in the Africa higher education system has been aptly demonstrated by Ng'ethe (2008). He believes that the more differentiated the system is, the more likely the quality will be negatively affected because the different institutions bring different sets of institutional and programmatic characteristics. This is going to be a challenge but one that has to be confronted. Quality assurance is an important and necessary function that will ensure the credibility of programs and institutions in a differentiated system.

The third requirement has to do with governance. Richardson, et al. (1999) believe that the performance of a higher education system is influenced by government policy, as well as the interface of government and higher education institutions. African governments have been increasingly moving toward a centralized governance of higher education institutions by using a funding mechanism that allows and disallows institutions to do certain things. However, the university sector has a long history of institutional autonomy, and most institutions have built adequate capacity within to manage this regulation and its requirements. However, the college system is very far from having such capacity; any serious considerations to include this institution in the higher education system must be accompanied by a serious commitment to build its governance structure and, in particular, the interface between institutions and government. In addition, caution must be taken not to use funding as a steering mechanism that makes all institutions behave the same. Instead, funding must be geared toward promoting mission diversity and differentiation.

Lastly, building capacity for the new types of institutions is key to unlocking their potential. It is clear from the literature of other countries that capacity building will succeed only with university involvement. Although different countries adopt different models, from state-wide higher education systems (e.g., United States) to a federation plan (e.g., UK) and to a single university system (e.g., Hong Kong), what is common in all these models is the central involvement of the university sector in developing the capacity of lecturers and leadership in the college system, as well as producing the research that becomes the basis for the knowledge about the sector and further planning. Therefore, the universities will have to see themselves as drivers of this growth and not as competitors.

Conclusion

Knowledge produced in higher education has become the most important factor for economic development in the 21st century. Saint, et al. (2003) demonstrate this point by comparing the research and development investments in OECD countries with those in developing countries like China, India and Brazil, as well as the rest of the world. There seems to be a proportionate relationship between research and development investments and economic development. Therefore, if Africa is going to catch up, it has to grow its knowledge outputs and, consequently, the continent must grow its higher education size by increasing access to higher education.

African higher education is at a crossroads, and in order to make all education a public and social good, questions in relation to the size and shape of the whole education system have to be raised. These include the under-performance of the secondary education system for those in and out of school, the small size of the current higher education sector, and the continued exclusion of the adult and disadvantaged population from higher and continuing education.

Alongside these three concerns is an imperative to find ways of improving the efficacy of the secondary education system. In addition, looking at what works in systems that have successfully massified their higher education systems and also managed to redistribute educational opportunities to all social classes, it is evident that the most logical intervention is adding another institution like a junior college at the bottom end of the higher education system. This intervention does three things: 1) it expands post-secondary education institutions and programs that are available in the system; 2) it allows the system to reach those students who get automatically excluded by an elite system; and 3) it targets the middle level skills production of a country which is often constricted by a university-only higher education system.

As countries question the divide between higher and further education institutions, a continuum of post-school provision seems to be on the rise and blurs what has traditionally been considered as higher education. This blur of institutional types and expansion of different institutional missions should be considered to be good for a whole lot of reasons including the increased capacity and diversification that this brings. Whether or not seamless higher education systems will ever be achieved or should this be a goal for these systems is a moot question. Instead, African higher education systems have to be on the move in increasing their higher education capacity.

Lastly, this chapter highlighted the dynamics that would ensue when a different institution, like a college, is added to a higher education system. In particular, this chapter emphasized the difficulties in diversified and differentiated programs and institutions. One important element is articulation of programs so that students can easily navigate the higher education system. Of course, the regulatory requirements and capacity development of such a system cannot be underscored enough. More importantly, the interface between these institutions and government is crucial, especially for the new generation of institutions.

NOTES

[1] Government reports do not discriminate between the university and non-university private institutions.

[2] Term used in South Africa in reference to what is known as Polytechnics in the UK and in most Anglophone countries.

[3] The existing discretionary policies that allow universities to admit students who have not satisfied the traditional requirements are not designed for large pipelines but smaller exceptions.

REFERENCES

AHEC Country Data 2009: http://www.cies.org/Programs/AHEC/CountryData.htm sourced on 24th July 2009.

Bregman, J. 2004: What's next: how to cope with the success of primary Education For All? Paper presented the workshop of donor agencies in October 15, 2004.

Bregman, J. 2008: Beyond Primary education: Challenges and approaches to expanding learning opportunities in Africa. Paper presented at the Biennial on Education in Africa: Maputo, Mozambique, May 5-9.

Bunting, I. & Cloete, N. 2008: Governing Access to Higher Education-Country Report: South Africa. Unpublished paper

Clancy, P.; Eggins, H.; Goastellec, G.; Guri-Rosenblit, S.; Nga Nguyen, P. & Yizengaw, T. 2007: Comparative Perspectives on Access and Equality. In Altbach, P. & McGill Peterson, P. (Eds.) Higher Education in the new century: Global challenges and Innovation ideas. Rotterdam: Sense Publishers in cooperation with UNESCO.

Cohen, M. & Brawer, F. B. (4th ed.) 2003: The American Community College (4th edition). San Francisco: Jossey Bassey.

Fehnel, R. 2003: Massification and Future Trends in African Higher Education. In Teferra, D. & Altbach (Eds.) African Higher Education: An International Reference Handbook. Indiana University Press: Bloomington.

Garrod, N. & Maxfarlane, B. 2009: Challenging Boundaries: Managing the Integraton of Post-secondary education. New York and London: Routledge Taylor & Francis Group.

Gebremariam, K. 2001: Democratization and Adult Education in Africa. In Ntiri, D. (Ed.) Models for Adult and Lifelong Learning: Politicization and Democratization of Adult Education (Volume 3). Office of Adult and Lifelong Learning Research: Wayne State University, Detroit, Michigan.

Holsinger, D. B. & Cowell, R. N. 2000: Positioning Secondary School Education in Developing Countries. International Institute for Educational Planning / UNESCO: Paris. P.7 -92.

Jibril, M. 2003: Nigeria. In Teferra, D. & Altbach (Eds.) African Higher Education. Indiana University Press: Bloomington.

Kelleghan, T. & Greaney, V. 2003: Monitoring Performance: Assessment and Examinations in Africa. Association for the Development of Education in Africa (ADEA) Biennial Meeting Dec 3 – 6, 2003 (grand Bale, Mauritius).

Kim, S.; Gilani. Z.; Landoni, P.; Musis, N.B.; & Teixeira, P. 2007: Rethinking the Public –Private Mix in Higher Education: Global Trends and National Policy Challenges. In Altbach, P. & MacGill Peterson, P. (Eds.) Higher Education in the New Century: Global Challenges and Innovative Ideas. Sense Publishers: Rotterdam.

King, K. 2007: Balancing Basic and Post-Basic Education in Kenya: National Versus International Policy Agendas. In *International Journal of Educational Development*, 27 (4) 358-370.

Kruss, G. 2008: Teacher Education and Institutional Change in South Africa. HSRC Press: Cape Town.

Lewin K. M. 2006: Seeking Secondary Schooling in Sub-Saharan Africa; Strategies for Sustainable Financing. Africa Region Human Development; Secondary Education in Africa

Lolwana, P. 2007: Developing Higher Education through a Second Chance and Post-Secondary Education Systems in South Africa. An unpublished draft paper.

Lolwana, P. 2008: Improving the Efficacy of Assessment, Certification and Curriculum in the African Education Systems. Paper presented at the Biennial on Education in Africa: Maputo, Mozambique, May 5-9.

Mahajan, V. 2008: Africa Rising: How 900 million African Consumers Offer More than You Think. Texas: Wharton School Publishing.

Mugenda, O.M. 2009: Higher Education in Kenya: Challenges and Opportunities. Unpublished paper presented at the AHEC meeting in Nairobi, 30th March 2009.

Muller, J. 2004: Assessment, Qualifications and the National Qualifications Framework in South African Schooling. In Chisholm, L. (2004) (Ed.) *Changing Class: Education and Social Change in Post-Apartheid South Africa*. Cape Town: HSRC press p.247-265.

Maruatona, T. 2006: Adult Literacy and Empowerment in Africa: Problems and Prospects. In Merriam, S. B.; Courtenay, B. C. & Cervero, R. M. (Eds.) *Global Issues and Adult Education: Perspectives from Latin America, Southern Africa, and United States*. San Francisco: Jossey-Bassey. p.344 -355.

Ng'ethe, N.; Subotzky, G. & Afeti, G. 2008: Differentiation and Articulation in Tertiary Education Systems: A Study of Twelve Countries. World Bank Publishers: Washington D.C.

Ngome, C. 2003: Kenya. In Teferra, D. & Altbach (Eds.) African Higher Education. Indiana University Press: Bloomington.

Richardson, Jr., R.; Bracco, K.R.; Callan, P. M. & Finney, J. E. 1999: Designing State Higher Education Systems for a New century. Arizona, U.S.A: Oryx Press.

Sall, A. 2003: Africa 2025: What Possible Futures for Sub-Saharan Africa? Pretoria: Unisa Press.

Said. M.E. 2003: Egypt. In Teferra, D. & Altbach (Eds.) African Higher Education. Indiana University Press: Bloomington.

Saint, W.; Hartnett, T.A. & Strassner, E. 2003: Higher Education in Nigeria: A Status Report. *Higher Education Policy*, 16, pp. 259 -281.

Teferra, D. & Altbach (Eds.) 2003: African Higher Education: An International Reference Handbook. Indiana University Press: Bloomington.

Townsend, B. K. & Dougherty, K. J. 2006: Community College Missions in the 21st Century. San Francisco: Jossey-Bass.

University World News 2008: Africa Edition. January edition.

University World News 2009: Africa Edition.

Vaughan, G.B. 2000: The Community College Story (2nd ed.) Community College Press, Washington, D.C.

World Bank, 2000: Higher Education in Developing Countries: Peril and Promise. Task Force on Higher Education and Society, Washington, D.C.

Chapter Two

Translating Equitable Access into Retention and Success in African Higher Education: The Role and Responsibility of Individual Institutions

BY SABIHA Y. ESSACK, UNIVERSITY OF KWAZULU-NATAL

Introduction

The African Union (AU) and its program, The New Partnership for Africa's Development (NEPAD), explicitly prioritize education. The AU (2006a) has identified human resources development by "education" as the major means of attaining its vision of an integrated, peaceful, prosperous Africa, driven by Africans and affirming its place in the knowledge economy and global community. Its plan of action for the "Second Decade of Education for Africa" names tertiary education as one of seven focus areas, i.e., the "complete revitalization of higher education, with the emergence of strong and vibrant institutions profoundly engaged in fundamental and development-oriented research, teaching, community outreach and enrichment services to the lower levels of education; and functioning in an environment of academic freedom and institutional autonomy, within an overall framework of public accountability (AU, 2006a, 1)."

This focus is echoed in the AU's Priority Programme 19 (2006b), which states objectives of socio-economic development by partnering with youth for the promotion of human resource development, capacity development and science and technology as tools. The AU (2004) also prioritizes education in its Millennium Development Goals with the success indicators of promoting gender equality and empowerment of women y attention are participation rates, access, retention and success in higher education.

Participation

Participation is defined as the proportion of the total population of the relevant age cohort enrolled for education, and it is often stratified by different categories of people who access education. Participation at all levels of education in Sub-Saharan Africa is not only the lowest globally, but is also gender-biased in favor of males, as shown in Table 2.1 extracted from the *Education for All Global Monitoring Report 2009*.

Of particular relevance to this chapter is the weighted average of people accessing secondary and tertiary education, cited as 32 percent and 5 percent in 2005, respectively. Even greater disparity exists when the participation rates are stratified by gender, with the weighted average of women in higher education cited as a little more than a third (UNESCO, 2008).

TABLE 2.1:   PARTICIPATION RATES IN SUB-SAHARAN AFRICA

		Gross Enrollment Rates (GERs) - %			Gender Parity Indices (GPIs)		
Pre-primary Education	GER/GPI	14	109	0.8	0.97	1.79	0.49
	Year	2006	2006	2005	2006	2006	2005
	Country	All¹	Seychelles	Chad	All¹	Lesotho	Chad
Primary Education	GER/GPI	97	138	47	0.89	1.06	0.66
	Year	2005	2005	2005	2005	2004	2005 (UIS est.)
	Country	All¹	Madagascar	Niger	All¹	Gambia	CAR
Secondary Education	GER/GPI	32	105	9	0.79	1.26	0.33
	Year	2005	2005	2005	2005	2005	2005
	Country	All¹	Seychelles	Niger	All¹	Lesotho	Chad
Tertiary Education	GER/GPI	5	17	0.4	0.62	1.27	0.15
	Year	2005	2005	2004	2005	2005	2004
	Country	All¹	Mauritius	Malawi	All¹	Lesotho	Eritrea

¹ Average for countries for which data was available
Source: Education for All Global Monitoring Report 2009

These rates have not changed significantly over the last 40 years, as reflected in Figure 2.1, where participation in higher education in Ghana is compared with that of Korea.

TRANSLATING EQUITABLE ACCESS INTO RETENTION AND SUCCESS IN AFRICAN HIGHER EDUCATION

Key: Grey=Primary Education, Black=Secondary Education, White=Higher Education.

Interventions to increase participation rates require comprehensive engagement with cultural, educational, political, religious, socio-economic and tribal issues, as discussed in previous chapters.

Access

Access to higher education began as a paradigm of inherited merit, where a select group of academically proficient students were admitted solely on the basis of their socio-economic and educational backgrounds. It has progressed to equal rights, where demographic, economic, political and ideological imperatives have influenced the massification of higher education such that it represents a national diversity. Higher education has been made accessible to large numbers of the population irrespective of socio-economic and educational status, ultimately resulting in equity or equality of opportunity and providing equal opportunity of access to a variety of academic fields and disciplines and to postgraduate education (Clancy and Goastellec, 2007 and Council for Higher Education, 2004b). Equity of access thus relates to an institution's initiatives in making the full complement of its educational offerings accessible to a diversity of students, particularly marginalized groups (Council for Higher Education, 2004a).

Although the definition of "marginalized" and the prioritization of marginalized cohorts (where more than one exist) varies from country to country, the definition usually encompasses one or more of the following:

• Gender – gender bias against women, especially in certain fields of study.

• Geography – students from peri-urban and rural areas.

- Education – poor quality of the secondary education experience and the subsequent level of preparedness for higher education.
- Economic status – less affluent students with limited ability/inability to self-fund/co-fund higher education.
- Language – students with a mother tongue different from that used in the higher education institutions.
- Minority/race/ethnicity – minorities, races or ethnic groups marginalized by political regimes (Jones et al. 2008 and Waetjen, 2006).

Matching equity of access to equity of outcome by successful participation and completion necessitates several pivotal, holistic and innovative strategies for pre- and post-student admission.

Pre-Admission Strategies

Pre-admission strategies largely relate to student selection using tools predictive of student success. Merit-based student selection for marginalized groups, whether considering performance at secondary school level or in merit-based selection tests, such as the traditional intellectual assessments and aptitude tests, has engendered worldwide criticism. Widening access to marginalized groups has thus involved a range of student selection tools *inter alia* developing flexible entry requirements, assessments for the recognition of prior learning, program-specific admissions tests and alternative admissions tests (Council for Higher Education, 2004a).

Many of these tests have evolved from a purely quantitative exercise to personal interviews and psychological profiling, and many have been augmented by broader criteria, such as a student's rank rather than performance in school as an indicator of ability. Others use proxy indicators such as attitude, commitment to learning, leadership qualities, motivation, personality and psychological self-efficacy (Jones et al. 2008; Coughlan, 2006; McLaughlin et al. 2007) as evidenced by the following selected case studies of aptitude tests, interactive assessments and psychological profiling.

- The Alternative Access Research Project (AARP) developed by the University of Cape Town in South Africa consists of a battery of admissions tests with the aim of identifying academically talented students with the potential to succeed. The battery has six components: the academic and quantitative literacy test, the mathematics test, the placement test in English for educational purposes (PTEEP), the mathematics comprehension test, the mathematics achievement test and the reasoning test.[2] Visser and Hanslo (2005) reported on different statistical methods employed to relate AARP tests scores to performance and retention.

  The project initially used correlations and regression analyses relating AARP test scores to student performance largely at first year level and survival analyses relating AARP test scores to outcome whether completion, graduation, academic exclusion or drop-out. They used such parameters as the survival function, which is the probability that a student will remain longer than the minimum time for a particular program, and the hazard function, which is the probability that a student is excluded at a particular time. Decreasing sample sizes in subsequent years precluded the use of these statistical methods, which were further confounded by academic development programs and course interventions.

- The PTEEP test consists of a combination of multiple choice questions and productive pieces including aspects of teaching, modeling and practice. It was found to provide additional information regarding the risk of exclusion and dropout only among marginalized cohorts of students with similar secondary education examination performances.

Shochet (1994) contended that sub-optimal performance of marginalized students in intellectual assessments or aptitude tests was attributed to minimal exposure to mediated learning experiences and that a true reflection of learning potential was attainable by an interactive assessment model or the "test-teach-retest" method where students are actively coached or subjected to mediated learning during test administration. His research conducted at the University of Natal (now KwaZulu-Natal) in South Africa showed an inverse relationship between cognitive modifiability and predictability of intellectual assessments or aptitude tests ultimately advocating cognitive modifiability as a moderator of traditional predictors and not necessarily predictive of success (Shochet, 1994).

McLaughlin, et al. (2007), in a study conducted among nursing students at a university in the United Kingdom, related academic performance to a questionnaire-based evaluation of occupational and academic self-efficacy. The study also related academic performance to personality and ascertained extraversion (characterized by sensation seeking, assertiveness, sociability and constant stimulation), neuroticism (characterized by low self-esteem, depression, shyness, moodiness and anxiety) and psychoticism (characterized by aggressiveness, tough-mindedness, apathy, impulsiveness and recklessness), believed to be partially hereditary and partially physiological, among a first-year cohort of nursing students. It was found that psychoticism and extraversion were negatively associated with academic performance, while occupational self-efficacy related to motivation and learning was statistically, significantly and positively associated with academic performance.

Despite the fact that alternative access mechanisms, whether quantitative or qualitative, have met with mixed success and show limited predictive value in marginalized student cohorts, they nevertheless provide an important body of work facilitating the access of marginalized students. While research to optimize alternative access criteria is ongoing, it is imperative that institutions acknowledge that alternative access mechanisms inherently assess learning potential and the potential to succeed on the express proviso of the availability and accessibility to adequate and appropriate academic and other support.

<u>Post-Admission Strategies</u>

Equity of outcome may be achieved by implementing pivotal, holistic and innovative post-admission strategies. These include *inter alia* curriculum interventions such as separate or bridging, semi-integrated or foundational and holistic and integrated models together with contextualized and relevant curriculum content. These are found in competency-based education (CBE), outcomes-based education (OBE) and participative pedagogies, such as peer-led team learning (PLTL), problem-based learning (PBL) and cased-based curricula (CBC), in tandem with additional academic support by supplemental instruction (SI), structured learning assistance (SLA), and psycho-social student support by means of mentorship, student counseling centers and a range of other student services.

- **Curriculum**—Curriculum intervention is aimed at adapting curricula to assist in developing a student's general academic and cognitive skills, language proficiency and capacity for self-directed learning (Council for Higher Education, 2004a). It provides contextualized and relevant curriculum content, and it ensures relevant learning outcomes commensurate with international reference points[3] developed in consultation with stakeholders. These stakeholders include but are not limited to faculty, students, alumni, employers, government ministries, private and public national and international higher education institutions, consultants and specialists, mentors and coaches, assessors and moderators, higher education quality assurance bodies, professional bodies, advisory bodies, research institutions and the broader society (Meyer and Bushney, 2008).

  The graduate is ideally an intellectual, a professional and a critical citizen able to think theoretically, analyze rigorously and process empirical data with a deep social commitment to addressing the developmental needs of Africa (Badat, 2005). This learner-centeredness requires curriculum design and content relevant and contextual to the learners' life experiences and the use of appropriate teaching, learning and assessment methodologies (Koch et al. 2001; Venter et al. 2001). Curriculum intervention thus focuses on curriculum design, content and pedagogy.

  Curriculum design to facilitate the retention and success of marginalized students has progressed from a "more time, more tuition" separate or bridging approach and semi-integrated or foundational approach to the integrated and holistic approach (Crosling et al. 2009; Kloot et al. 2008). Separate or bridging approaches provide academic support and aim to improve an inadequate secondary education. Semi-integrated or foundational approaches additionally provide academic development laying the necessary foundations for further study by developing cognitive, communication and study skills. The integrated and holistic approach integrates academic development in mainstream programs instilling cognitive, practical reasoning and thinking and conceptual, critical thinking, language, communication, and life and study skills through disciplinary content (Kloot et al. 2008). Horizontal and vertical integration are essential components of curriculum design with the former encompassing the contextualization of academic and life skills within a disciplinary field and relating cognate disciplines as opposed to teaching in silos. The latter involves the convergence of academic development with mainstream curricula (Jones et al. 2008). While holistic integrated approaches may be best practice, circumventing the stigmatization of marginalized cohorts, separate and semi-integrated approaches are useful preliminary interventions allowing natural progression to holistic and integrated approaches.

It is imperative that the curriculum content discourse in African higher education, in terms of relevance and context, focuses on indigenous knowledge defined as "an idea or system of thought peculiar to the [inhabitants] of a particular geographical location of socio-cultural environment (le Grange, 2008, 817)." Le Grange (2008) contends that although knowledge systems differ in epistemology, pedagogy, logic, cognitive structures and socio-economic and socio-cultural contexts, all systems inherently share "localness" and their own knowledge space/place.

Africanization "relates to Africans upholding African aspirations, descent, cultural heritage, own ideas, rights, interests and ideals, self-concept and own rationality in intercultural context (Botha, 2007, 205)," as well as non-Africans respecting and facilitating Africans' efforts to do so. Africanization in the university context necessitates the relevance of African universities to Africa by promoting unique African philosophies and organizational cultures, by addressing the needs and expectations of developing, largely third-world African countries and by focusing on the needs, circumstances and aspirations of Africans; in essence relating to the continent, philosophy, culture, countries and people of Africa (Botha, 2007).

Notwithstanding the importance of including the African and non-African international components (Botha, 2007), the generation and dissemination of indigenous knowledge in African higher education is critical to addressing the challenges of Africa. So too, is the shift from "pure disciplinary, homogenous, expert-led, supply driven, hierarchical, peer-reviewed and [largely] university based" knowledge to "applied, problem-centered, transdisciplinary, heterogeneous, hybrid, demand-driven, entrepreneurial and network-embedded" knowledge (le Grange, 2008, 821).

- **Pedagogy**—The delivery of contextualized curricula with integrated academic development requires a shift from the traditional concept of knowledge as a product delivery system transmitted by the lecturer/teacher who imparts factual, discipline-oriented information with necessary guidance on assessment, but which results in minimal learning and no opportunity for exploration and problem solving (Venter, 2001) to interactive pedagogies based on the connectivism and constructivism learning theories, both of which create "rich environments for active learning (REALs) (Kilfoil, 2008, 1023)."

Connectivism explains the dynamics of networks, environments and ecologies related to accretion, which defines learning as a continuous embedded function of the environment and at the point of need (real life). Connectivism is based on these principles:

- that learning and knowledge lie in a variety of diverse opinions;
- that learning is a process of connecting specialized information sources;
- that the capacity to know where to source knowledge is superior to knowing "what" and "how";
- that nurturing and sustaining connections is critical to continual learning,
- that the ability to connect diverse disciplinary fields, ideas and concepts is a fundamental skill;
- that the acquisition and/or construction of current cutting edge knowledge is the central tenet; and
- that decision-making is in itself a learning process.

Similarly constructivism promotes learning and investigation within authentic contexts; fosters the development of student responsibility, initiative, decision-making and intentional learning; engenders collaboration among students and faculty; uses dynamic, interdisciplinary, generative learning activities that facilitate critical thinking processes to assist students to develop comprehensive and complex knowledge structures; and evaluates student progress in content and learning skills within authentic contexts using real life examples (Kilfoil, 2008). The student is "an active participant in the learning process constructing knowledge through social interaction, negation and cooperation (Dlodlo and Beyers, 2009, 427)." Personal experiences of students enrich learning and facilitate the construction of individual knowledge while engendering problem-solving abilities; a positive attitude to learning; greater self-esteem; greater confidence to attempt new and cognitively-demanding tasks; and an appreciation for socio-cultural differences and inculcating teamwork skills, such as listening, encouragement, empathy and conflict resolution (Dlodlo and Beyers, 2009).

Integral to connectivism and constructivism are collaborative learning, cooperative learning and learning communities as evident in pedagogies such as supplemental instruction (SI), structured learning assistance (SLA) and accelerated learning groups (ALGs), which are adjunct, and the emerging scholars program (ESP), video-based supplemental instruction (VSI) and peer-led team learning (PLTL), which are embedded (Arendale, 2005).

SI facilitates the mastery of content in the process of developing and integrating learning and study skills in high risk courses and aims to improve student performance, retention and completion/graduation rates (Arendale, 2005). SI is peer-assisted study sessions; they are regularly scheduled, informal review sessions where students compare notes, discuss readings, develop organizational tools, and predict test items. Sessions are facilitated by SI leaders who are students who have previously done well in the course and who attend all lectures, take notes and act as model students. There is no remedial stigma attached to SI because it is a voluntary, non-remedial approach to learning and targets high-risk courses. It does not target high-risk students with varying levels of academic preparedness and diverse socio-cultural backgrounds.[4] SLA assists students in developing the basis required to engage with the course content and to develop and apply the learning strategies most suited to the content. This also focuses on high risk courses and it is usually mandatory for all students to attend until mastery is demonstrated by high marks in examinations (Arendale, 2005). Learning strategies such as note taking, listening, study habits and test taking are skills inculcated in addition to content mastery. SLA is mediated by facilitators who act as role models to engender student responsibility and commitment to tasks[5]. ALGs are designed to meet the needs of students with significant skill and knowledge deficiencies that preclude participation in SI or SLA. An individual education plan is combined with peer-led, small group learning activities and formative assessment by a learning skills specialist. Adequate progress in ALGs allows progression to SI or SLA.

ESP builds a cohort community of first-year students from marginalized groups that are academically oriented and can serve as a source of peer support. The cohort is provided with extensive orientation and academic mentorship, while their academic progress and adjustment to the environment is actively monitored. Independent learning is developed by ongoing supplementary instruction, and there is strong advocacy for their interests (Arendale, 2005).

VSI differs from SI in that students are issued all didactic presentations on videotape. Students do not attend lectures but engage with the video material supported by specially designed facilitator and student manuals. VSI students, led by a trained facilitator, start and stop the presentations at stipulated intervals. When required, VSI incorporates periodic, small group assignments to ascertain concept mastery. Feedback on tasks completed under the supervision and guidance of the facilitator allows students to construct and confirm their understanding (Arendale, 2005).

PLTL is where peer-leaders guide the activities of small groups in workshop format, providing an active learning experience, creating a leadership role at undergraduate level and engendering faculty development in a creative dimension of instruction[6]. Students cooperatively solve challenging problems guided by peer leaders trained to ensure that students actively and productively engage with the material and each other. The supportive format facilitates conceptual understanding by encouraging discussions. Students learn to work in teams and communicate more effectively, while peer leaders acquire teaching and group management skills (Arendale, 2005).

Curriculum and pedagogy that engenders student engagement (described as a student's commitment and application) and the quality of student effort and learning (evidenced by time and energy devoted to academic and learning activities and the meaning and understanding achieved by learning) are significant factors in student retention and success. Engendering engagement is the mutual responsibility of the student and the institution. The institution is responsible for creating environments that facilitate engagement and learning by developing student-responsive curricula with authentic content, challenging tasks relevant to students' life experiences, adequate and appropriate orientation and induction and the integration of learning and other skills together with active and interactive learning paradigms and formative assessments for academic development (Crosling et al. 2009).

The choice of learning support programs should be dictated by the learning-related student needs. It requires faculty development, because it is imperative that faculty have an excellent command of the disciplinary subject matter in the African context and they are proficient in learner-centered curriculum development and pedagogies. They must also have the personal attributes of creating a supportive and affirming learning environment by being able to "recognize individual potential, teaching with passion, relating to and motivating the student, validating different points of view, encouraging interaction and building [productive] relationships (Cross et al. 2009, 34-35)."

Student Mentoring and Support Services

The academic interventions described above should be augmented by "appropriate guidance, emotional support, encouragement, financial and academic assistance in a caring, nurturing and non-alienating environment (Laden, 2004, 16)." They should be mediated and facilitated by faculty, career and guidance counselors (Laden, 2004) and a total student counseling and welfare service that comprises academic development, psycho-social and health services to provide comprehensive and holistic support for marginalized groups which have a particular set of needs related to their unique, pre-higher education experiences.

- **Peer Mentoring**—Peer mentoring may be described as a process by which a more experienced or able student instructs, counsels, guides and facilitates the personal and intellectual development of a less experienced student (Holmes et al. 2007), facilitating the transition from secondary school and enabling the navigation of and integration into higher education. Peer mentoring has been advocated as a transformation strategy in higher education (Blunt and Conolly, 2006) as has been its integration into the broader context of student learning and development (van Wyk and Daniels, 2004). Peer mentors facilitate the induction and retention of students and enable them to realize their potential by providing psycho-social guidance and support. They serve as positive, encouraging and affirming role models (Blunt and Conolly, 2006) and demonstrate the principles of accessibility, inclusivity, recognition of diversity in its many forms, adaptability and networking (Granados and Lopez, 1999). Peer mentoring is encapsulated in SI, SLA, ALGs, PLTL, ESP and VSI, all of which allow the creation of learner communities, enabling learners to share across the curriculum and shape a collective, coherent educational experience via a supportive peer group (Favish, 2005).

Mentorship between faculty and student is another option, and it requires a cadre of faculty who are considered realistic role models, who provide inclusive academic and personal advice, who monitor academic progress, who display sympathy and empathy and who play an affirming and advocacy role in terms of each student's unique academic, career and personal issues. Such faculty serves as mentors; they provide professional contacts and advice, and they lead by example. They serve as academic coaches providing tutoring and encouragement, and they facilitate the fulfillment of academic potential. They serve as advocates tabling student issues with relevant stakeholders and as counselors listening to academic and personal problems. In short, they provide support and sound advice (Guiffrida, 2005).

The subscription to and subsequent success of mentoring programs requires a well-designed organizational structure and implementation framework. Programs should, in addition, enjoy credibility among mentors and mentees, and they should be mentee-centered with due consideration given to factors such as race, gender, ethnicity, etc. when assigning mentors to mentees (Page et al., 2005).

- **Student Welfare Services**—The Student Counseling Service (SCS) is vital to student retention and success in higher education especially because of the growing enrollment of students from marginalized groups with diverse ethnic, social and educational backgrounds, many of whom have had inadequate secondary school preparation and thus encounter several and diverse learning barriers (Morrison et al. 2006 and Botha et al. 2005). Morrison, et al. (2006) cited many studies that report on the positive impact of one or more components of the SCS on retention rates, on student learning and achievement of academic targets, on students in stressful situations, on students at risk of dropout, as well as on positive personal outcomes, such as improvement of self-esteem, anxiety and motivation. According to the International Association of Counseling Services, the SCS has three roles: (1) a holistic approach to student welfare, (2) facilitating the acquisition of learning skills and (3) personal counseling and/or psychotherapeutic services related to difficulties with integration, psycho-social problems and career counseling. Other functions include consultation with faculty, advocacy for student needs, program development, retention activities and initiatives to enhance the campus environment. SCS participates in a variety of institutional forums, provides feedback on student counseling-related needs, and initiates and contributes to student policy development and review. Referral to faculty and tutors for academic aspects, other social support structures internal and external to the institution and health-care services is implicit in the SCS. The role of a counselor is thus four-fold: educational support including the psychometric assessment of potential, career planning assistance, assistance with personal and emotional difficulties and referral to allied support structures, as appropriate (Morrison et al. 2006).

Research on the value of the SCS is, however, largely on students who independently make use of the services and not necessarily those who should use the services but do not access them for reasons of stigmatization, unawareness, cultural underpinnings, etc. The SCS should thus be proactive, integrated and offer a range of services informed by comprehensive consultation with relevant stakeholders (such as executive management, faculty, departments responsible for student recruitment, student housing and student finance, student bodies, parents, potential employers, funders, professional associations and the wider University communities) and commensurate with the needs of an institution's diverse student cohorts, ensuring that it reaches the target student cohorts and is marketed as integral to the mission and goals of the institution (Morrison, et al. 2006).

Conclusion

Developing and implementing a holistic model to translate equity of access into equity of outcome in marginalized groups requires the following adapted from Laden (2005):

- Create a receptive, non-alienating environment that welcomes and celebrates diversity and integrates it into the institution's organizational culture.

- Provide appropriate programs, curriculum, pedagogy and student welfare services by collaboration between faculty and student services personnel to facilitate and enhance students' abilities to achieve academic and career aspirations.

- Orient and induct students to facilitate the transition from secondary school and enable successful navigation of and integration into the higher education system using mechanisms and/or resources, such as extended orientation programs, writing centers, tutoring centers, peer mentors, etc.

- Implement a monitoring and early alert system that identifies students who are encountering academic and other difficulties and allows prompt intervention.

- Ensure that all initiatives and interventions are informed by relevant stakeholders, especially the very student cohorts for whom they are developed.

Higher education institutions thus require adequate numbers of appropriate human resource cadres including, but not limited to, peer mentors, student counselors and academic staff skilled with the ability to deliver learner-centered teaching and learning programs, equipped with the knowledge, skills and attitudes to provide holistic student care, development and support to translate equity of access into equity of outcome.

NOTES

[1] http://www.nepad.org/2005/ files/inbrief.php (Accessed 23 September 2009)

[2] http://www.aarp.ac.za/uct/tests.htm (Accessed 23 September 2009)

[3] http://www.ond.vlaanderen.be/hogeronderwijs/bologna/conference/documents/

[4] http://web2.umkc.edu/cad/SI/overview.html (Accessed 23 September 2009)

[5] http://www.ferris.edu/htmls/academics/sla/PI_Our_Program.htm (Accessed 23 September 2009)

[6] http://www.pltl.org/WhatIsPLTLDefinition.php

REFERENCES

African Union. 2006a. Second Decade of Education for Africa (2006-2015) Plan of Action. African Union, Addis Ababa, Ethiopia.

African Union. 2006b. Strategic Plan of the Commission of the African Union Volume 3: 2004-2007 Plan of Action. African Union, Addis Ababa, Ethiopia.

African Union. 2004. Strategic Plan of the African Union Commission Volume 1: Vision and Mission of the African Union. African Union, Addis Ababa, Ethiopia.

Arendale, D. R. 2005. Postsecondary Peer Cooperative Learning Programs: Annotated Bibliography. General College University of Minnesota, Minneapolis, MN.

Badat, S. 2005. South Africa: Distance Higher Education Policies for Access, Social Equity, Quality, and Social and Economic Responsiveness in a Context of the Diversity of Provision. *Distance Education 26* (2): 183-204.

Bank, T. W. (2009). Accelerating Catch-up: Tertiary Education for Growth in Sub-Saharan Africa, The World Bank, Geneva, Switzerland.

Bloom, D., Canning, D. and Chan, K. 2005. Higher Education and Economic Development in Africa. Harvard University, Massachusetts.

Blunt R.J.S and Conolly, J. 2006. Perceptions of Mentoring: Expectations of a Key Resource for Higher Education. *South African Journal of Higher Education 20* (2): 195-208.

Botha, M.M. 2007. Africanizing the Curriculum: An Exploratory Study. *South African Journal of Higher Education 21* (2): 201-216.

Botha, H.L., Brand, H.J., Cilliers, C.D., Davidow, A., de Jager A.C. and Smith, D. 2005. Student Counseling and Development Services in Higher Education Institutions in South Africa. *South African Journal of Higher Education 19* (1): 655-678.

Clancy, P. and Goastellec, G. 2007. Exploring Access and Equity in Higher Education: Policy and Performance in a Comparative Perspective. *Higher Education Quarterly 61* (2): 136-154.

Coughlan, F. 2006. Access for success. *South African Journal of Higher Education 20* (2): 209-218.

Council for Higher Education. 2004a. Improving Teaching and Learning Resources. Council for Higher Education, Pretoria, South Africa.

Council for Higher Education. 2004b. South African Higher Education in the First Decade of Democracy. Council for Higher Education, Pretoria, South Africa.

Council for Higher Education. 2001. Developing African Higher Education. Council for Higher Education, Pretoria, South Africa.

Crosling, G., Heagney, M. and Thomas, L. 2009. Improving Student Retention in Higher Education. *Australian Universities' Review 51* (2): 9-18.

Cross, M., Shalem, Y., Backhuse, J. and Adam, F. 2009. How Undergraduate Students 'Negotiate' Academic Performance within a Diverse University Environment. *South African Journal of Higher Education 23* (1): 21-42.

Dlodlo, N. and Beyers, R.N. 2009. The Experiences of South African High School Girls in a Fab Lab Environment. Proceedings of the World Academy of Science, Engineering and Technology 37: 423-430.

Favish, J. 2005. Equity in Changing Patterns of Enrolment, in Learner Retention and Success at the Cape Technikon. *South African Journal of Higher Education 19* (2): 655-678.

Granados, R. and Lopez, J.M. 1999. Student-run Support Organizations for Under-represented Graduate Students: Goals, Creation, Implementation, and Assessment. *Peabody Journal of Education 74* (2):135–149.

Guiffrida, D. 2005. Othermothering as a Framework for Understanding African American Students' Definitions of Student-Centered Faculty. *The Journal of Higher Education 76* (6): 701-723.

Holmes, S. L., Land, L. D. and Hinton-Hudson, V. D. 2007. Race Still Matters: Considerations for Mentoring Black Women in Academe. *The Negro Educational Review 58* (1-2): 105-129.

Jones, B., Coetzee, G. and Bailey, T. 2008. Factors that Facilitate Success for Disadvantaged Higher Education Students. Rural Education Access Programme, Cape Town, South Africa.

Kilfoil, W.R. 2008. A Model for Learning Development. *South African Journal of Higher Education 22* (5): 1019-1028.

Kloot, B., Case, J.M. and Marshall, D. 2008. A Critical Review of the Educational Philosophies Underpinning Science and Engineering Foundation Programmes. *South African Journal of Higher Education 22* (4): 799-816.

Koch, E., Foxcroft, C. and Watson, A. 2001. A Development Focus to Student Access at the University of Port Elizabeth: Process and Preliminary Insights in Placement Assessments. *South African Journal of Higher Education 15* (2): 126-131.

Laden, B. V. 2004. Serving Emerging Majority Students. New Directions for Community Colleges 127: 5-19.

Le Grange, L. 2008. Challenges for Enacting an Indigenous Science Curriculum: A Reply to Ogunniyi and Ogawa. *South African Journal of Higher Education 22* (4): 817-826.

McLaughlin, K., Moutray, M. and Muldoon, O.T. 2007. The Role of Personality and Self-efficacy in the Selection and Retention of Successful Nursing Students: A Longitudinal Study. *Journal of Advanced Nursing 61* (2):211-221.

Meyer, M.H. and Bushney, M.J. 2008. Towards a Multi-stakeholder-driven Model for Excellence in Higher Education Curriculum Development. *South African Journal of Higher Education 22* (6): 1229-1240.

Morrison, J.M., Brand, H.J. and Cilliers, C.D. 2006. Assessing the Impact of Student Counseling Service Centers at Tertiary Education Institutions: How Should it be Approached? *South African Journal of Higher Education 20* (5): 655-678.

Page, B.J. Loots, A. and du Toit D.F. 2005. Perspectives on a South African Tutor/Mentor Program: The Stellenbosch University Experience. Mentoring and Tutoring 13(1): 5-21.

Shochet, I.M. 1994. The Moderator Effect of Cognitive Modifiability on a Traditional Undergraduate Admissions Test for Disadvantaged Black Students in South Africa. *South African Journal of Psychology 24* (4): 208-215.

UNESCO. 2008. Education for All Global Monitoring Report 2009. UNESCO, Paris, France.

Van Wyk, J-A and Daniels, F. 2004. An Integrated Mentoring Strategy for Service Learning in Higher Education. *South African Journal of Higher Education 18* (2): 359-370.

Venter, E. 2001 A Constructivist Approach to Learning and Teaching. *South African Journal of Higher Education* *15*(2): 86-92.

Venter, I.M., Blignaut, R.J. and Stoltz, D. 2001. Research Methodologies Explored for a Paradigm Shift in University Teaching. *South African Journal of Higher Education 15* (2): 162-169.

Waetjen, T. 2006. Measures of Redress: Defining Disadvantage in a University Access Programme. *South African Review of Sociology 37* (2): 200-216.

Chapter Three

IMPROVING ACCESS TO HIGHER EDUCATION THROUGH FINANCIAL MECHANISMS: THE CASE OF SOUTH AFRICA AND KENYA

BY GERALD WANGENGE-OUMA, UNIVERSITY OF THE WESTERN CAPE

Introduction

Kenya and South Africa (SA) are interesting national contexts against which to compare higher education funding policies and mechanisms. As this chapter reveals, their funding policies and mechanisms are circumscribed by generally dissimilar historical, political and economic contexts. Kenya's higher education funding mechanisms are typical of many African post-colonies, where recent policy shifts have generally been coercively or normatively influenced mainly by external pressures issuing especially from supranational institutions (mainly the World Bank and the International Monetary Fund) and their pursuit of neo-liberalism as the de facto economic policy framework (Ouma, 2007; Wangenge-Ouma, 2008b). On the other hand, South Africa's system is both different and unique, not just in the African context, but globally. The country's apartheid past and its post-apartheid transformation agenda play a huge role in both the understanding and construction of higher education funding mechanisms (Ouma, 2007).

The size and shape of higher education in the two countries is also dissimilar. Kenya has seven public universities; the University of Nairobi (UoN) is the oldest and attained full-fledged university status in 1970. Kenya is also home to about 23 private universities. Enrollment in Kenya's public universities currently stands at about 90,000 students and the participation rate is about 3 percent. On the other hand, SA has 23 public universities and about 78 private institutions offer university-level programs.

Public universities in post-apartheid SA are divided into three types: 11 traditional universities, e.g. University of Cape Town, University of Fort Hare and Rhodes University; six universities of technology, which offer practically-oriented diplomas and degrees in technical fields, e.g., Cape Peninsula University of Technology, Tshwane University of Technology and Central University of Technology; and six comprehensive universities, which offer a combination of both types of qualification, e.g., University of Johannesburg and Nelson Mandela Metropolitan University. Distance learning has for a long time been the forte of the University of South Africa, one of the oldest distance learning universities in the world (Ouma, 2007).

Since 1994, and especially in 2004 and 2005, the shape and size of SA's higher education has undergone tremendous transformation. The higher education system has shifted from the apartheid-era binary system, characterized by two mutually exclusive types of institutions—universities and technikons—and administered by disparate authorities, to a single, coordinated higher education system composed of universities. The unitary system has resulted from recent mergers and incorporations which reduced the number of universities and technikons from 36 to 23. About 735,000 students are enrolled in SA's public universities, while enrollment in private institutions is relatively small and the participation rate currently stands at about 16 percent (Bunting & Cloete, 2008).

It is important to point out that during Apartheid (1948—1994), higher education in SA was characterized chiefly by racial and ethnic exclusivity. Universities were established for the exclusive use of the various population groups. Universities established for whites, such as the University of Cape Town, University of Pretoria and Rhodes University, are generally referred to as Historically Advantaged Universities (HAUs) or Historically White Universities (HWUs), and those that were established for the exclusive use of blacks (consisting of Africans, Indians and coloureds), such University of Fort Hare and University of the Western Cape, are generally referred to as Historically Disadvantaged Universities (HDUs) or Historically Black Universities (HBUs).

Higher Education Funding Policies

The complex question of how universities should be financed suggests various solutions, which can be abstracted into two disparate models. The first model is that of absolute state subsidization, and the second model is privately financed universities without state assistance. Until fairly recently, variants of the first model were in vogue in most African countries, many developing countries and in the industrialized world, especially in Europe. The second model applies mainly in the case of proprietary, for-profit universities. These two extreme funding models hardly exist in a pure form. The second is obviously not available to public universities. It has been argued, especially for public universities, that the 'correct' funding model lies somewhere between the two extremes, i.e., from both public and private sources (Gravenir, et al. 2006).

Within the two polar approaches of financing higher education, three models emerge: **free** (tuition) **higher education, cost sharing** and **marketization and commercialization**. Various rationales inform the higher education funding models. The policy of *free higher education* assumes that higher education is a public good with a wide variety of and significant benefits to society, such as technological advancement, development of skilled labor, reduction in crime and poverty and fostering a culture of tolerance and social justice (HESA, 2007). Thus, providing free higher education is essential in expediting the achievement of the immense social benefits associated with higher education.

The intrinsic merit of higher education is yet another rationale advanced for its free provision. This rationale assumes that people may be ignorant of the benefits of higher education, they may not appreciate the value of higher education or they may not foresee the implications of their investment decisions in higher education, and so they may be unwilling to invest in higher education (Tilak, 2004). This argument holds that governments have better information than individuals or families regarding the value of higher education to society; they are wiser and better able to foresee the future. Thus, governments should make higher education free to promote its consumption.

The *cost sharing model* opposes free higher education. It is based mainly on the premise that higher education is both a public good and a private benefit, and therefore the cost of provision should be shared between the state and individual beneficiaries. Cost sharing, as described by Johnstone (2006), may take the form of tuition fees, either being introduced where they did not hitherto exist or being rapidly increased where they already do. It may also take the form of public institutions charging nearly breakeven or full cost fees for accommodation, books and other costs of student living that the government may formerly have funded.

Another rationale for cost sharing is higher education's need for non-governmental revenue made necessary by (1) the increasing social demand for higher education and increasing per student costs and (2) the decreasing state funding of higher education (Johnstone, 2006; Melck, 1990). It has also been argued that cost sharing as a higher education funding policy enhances efficiency and responsiveness by higher education institutions (Barr, 2004; Johnstone, 2006; Melck, 1990). It is assumed that the payment of some tuition fees will make students and their families more discerning consumers and the universities more cost conscious and responsive providers (HESA, 2008; Melck, 1990).

Lastly, equity has also been advanced as an important rationale for cost sharing, based on the following premises (HESA, 2008, p.32):

- "Free" higher education isn't truly free. It is actually paid for by all citizens, including the permanently poor through indirect taxes, whether or not they know that they have been taxed.

- A significant percentage of the beneficiaries of higher education are from wealthy families who are able to pay a portion of the costs of instruction. Thus, a policy of free higher education, in effect, benefits this category of students. Such a policy has negative equity implications such that resources are transferred to affluent families. In other words, through taxation, the poor pay for the education of the rich.

- A portion of the tuition fees collected could be used to fund grants and loans for students likely to be excluded from higher education.

- Even if students are poor while at university, they are likely to earn higher-than-average incomes after graduating. This imbalance in lifetime earnings and expenditures can be corrected by a loan program without providing free education to those who will be able to pay later (at the expense of services to the permanently poor; e.g., health services and primary education).

Other than free higher education and cost sharing, *marketization and commercialization* have recently emerged in the higher education discourse as possible ways of funding higher education, especially in a context of declining state financial support. Marketization is a notion that refers to income generation from market sources (e.g., the university's many publics such as students, industry, alumni and governmental and non-governmental entities), especially to mitigate resource dependence arising mainly from declining state financial support (Slaughter & Leslie, 1997, Wangenge-Ouma, 2008b). It has been argued that since public universities now compete for resources in a market context, they are forced to adopt practices that are consistent with private business practice. Public universities are thus forced to act as though they were private entities, with a greater orientation to the student as a "consumer" or customer, university education as a "product," "market niches," "pricing" and aggressive marketing (Johnstone, 1998).

The foregoing discussion has broadly mapped out the various ways in which higher education is funded, providing a theoretical context against which to understand various higher education funding policies. Subsequent sections examine the various ways in which Kenya and South Africa fund higher education. An attempt is made also to identify the historical context of various funding policies and mechanisms.

Funding Kenya's Public Higher Education

Since Kenya's attainment of political independence in 1963, its higher education policies have generally been characterized by a combination of full state subsidization and some variation of cost sharing.

Free higher education

Public higher education in Kenya was historically free, with the public purse covering both tuition and living allowances. The rationale for state subsidization of higher education (as in many other African post-colonies) was based, among other things, on the country's desire to create highly skilled labor that could replace the departing colonial administrators and also to ensure equity of access. In the welfare-dominated, post-colonial period, it was argued that unless the state subsidized the highly expensive higher education, many students would be unable to benefit from it (Sanyal, 1998; Wangenge-Ouma, 2008b) and that human resource development would be compromised. Free provision was therefore seen as the surest way for the state to guarantee equality of opportunity.

For the university to achieve its role of stimulating social and economic development, it was argued that generous funding be provided. By offering highly subsidized education, free of any direct charges, the government hoped to increase access to university education (Ouma, 2007; Wangenge-Ouma, 2008b). Thus, the university was viewed as the key engine for development and, therefore, levying fees would unnecessarily obstruct the attainment of this goal (Ouma, 2007; Wangenge-Ouma, 2008b). As Banya & Elu (2001) point out, in the immediate post-independence period, many African governments held the view that economic transformation of the continent was to follow from university education. Kenya was no exception.

The policy of free higher education lasted from 1963 to 1974 when a student loan program was established. During this period, university education was financed almost entirely by the state. Other than provision of funds to cover both capital development and re-current expenditures, the government met tuition fees and provided other allowances to keep the students 'comfortable.'

However, a 1964–1970 development plan shows that the Kenyan government acknowledged the need to involve students in meeting higher education costs. The plan stated that

> It will be Government policy to move increasingly towards loans as a method of financing students in secondary and higher education. [...]. The provision of a revolving loan fund would in time reduce the recurrent expenditure of the Government on bursaries and thus shift this burden from the general tax payer to the segment of society which benefits more directly (RoK 1964, p.105).

At this point, it may be argued that both the social benefit and private benefit rationales for funding higher education were persuasive to the then young government. The question of establishing a student loan system was again revisited in a subsequent development plan (1970–1974). In this plan, the government proposed to withdraw the grants allocated to students at university in favor of loans. This proposal took effect in the 1974-75 academic year, when a student loan program was introduced.

Each loan, however, was meant to cover only the cost of personal expenses, such as accommodation, meals, textbooks and stationery, travel and other effects, leaving the burden of funding tuition to the government. Getting this loan was automatic; it did not matter whether one was from an advantaged background or otherwise. As the loan only covered extra academic expenses, university education remained, in effect, tuition free (Ouma, 2007; Wangenge-Ouma, 2008b). The development plan that proposed the introduction of the loan program made it clear that "[t]he *principle of free tuition will be maintained* [added emphasis]. The loan system will apply to accommodation and personal allowances (RoK 1973, p.72)." Consequently, the idea of making the beneficiaries pay for their education did not make sense.

It is not clear why the government maintained tuition-free higher education, while most of the reasons it advanced for introducing the loan program were sufficient for introducing some form of tuition fees. When introducing the loan program, the government (RoK 1973) argued that:

(a) the income-earning prospects of university graduates were far better than those of people whose education has not reached this level. "Yet university students at present pay nothing for their education, while lower down the system fees are paid. In other words, the benefits derived from education are inversely related to the costs to the individual… (RoK 1973:72);"

(b) the loan system would encourage students to spend part of their time living independently, since accommodation costs would eventually have to be paid by students. This, the government reasoned, would reduce the pressure for more government-built student accommodation;

(c) it would eventually reduce the costs of university education borne by the government; and,

(d) it would discourage students from entering over-subscribed courses since they would no longer be able to live free at the government's expense.

It appears that charging fees was not politically feasible. Higher education was viewed as a public service, and universities held a social function whose attainment would be compromised if fees were introduced.

Yet it was not long before it became impossible to continue with free higher education. In the years subsequent to Kenya's political independence, the social demand for higher education soared (Ouma, 2007). In 1964, 1980 and 1990, the number of university students—i.e. undergraduate, postgraduate and diploma—grew from 571 to 5,411 to 26,092, respectively (Wangenge-Ouma, p. 221).

Unfortunately, this rising demand was taking place at a time when the country's economic performance was plummeting, worsened by the world economic recession of the 1980s. Externally, higher education (especially in Africa) had become an increasingly unpopular public investment mainly because of the World Bank's (1988, 1994) arguments for reduced public investment in the sub-sector. Also globally, a new development paradigm took root that disapproved of free state provision of social services. Therefore, it was becoming increasingly difficult for the state to continue providing free higher education.

Cost-sharing

As already mentioned, cost sharing was, in principle, introduced in Kenya's higher education system in 1974, even though higher education essentially remained free. It was not until the 1991-92 academic year that the Kenyan government re-introduced cost sharing in which students paid tuition fees. Payment of boarding, food, other supplies and pocket allowances was also terminated. The new form of cost sharing thus required students or their parents to cover both tuition and the cost of maintenance.

Free higher education was no longer possible due to, among other factors, the rapid growth of university enrollments coinciding with rising constraints in the public budget, resulting in the state's inability to adequately fund social services such as (higher) education (Ouma, 2007). The Kenyan government argued that "the combination of increased enrollments and budget constraints ... *distorted* [added emphasis] public budget allocations to the various education and training sub-sectors (RoK 1998, p.96)." It was further argued that there was clear evidence that rapid expansion of enrollments led to a more rapid rise in public expenditure on university education than the rise in the total budgetary allocation to the entire education sector (RoK 1998).

The introduction of the new form of cost sharing was also a consequence of the introduction of structural adjustment programs (SAPs) with the coercive influence of international financial institutions (IFIs), mainly the World Bank and the International Monetary Fund (IMF). While the World Bank insisted that Kenya introduce cost sharing (World Bank 1988, 1994), it is reported that the Kenyan government's request for US $55 million from the World Bank to finance higher education precipitated the Bank's demands. In other words, as is characteristic of World Bank loans to poor countries, strings were attached; i.e., new financing strategies for higher education which actually referred to cost-sharing (Kiamba, 2005, Nafukho, 2004).

Wangenge-Ouma (2008b) points out that the shift from free higher education to cost sharing (1991-92) did not herald any major financial responsibilities on the part of students and their parents. He expounds:

> "Cost sharing went hand-in-hand with heavy subsidization of the system and low-level cost recovery. Heavy subsidization, which still applies to date, covers all students admitted through the Joint Admissions Board (the Board admits students who receive a government subsidy that covers, inter alia, tuition and accommodation), irrespective of their ability or inability to pay. For a long time, government-subsidized students have paid Ksh. [Kenya shillings] 16,000 (approx. US$229) as tuition fees, irrespective of their study programs" (Wangenge-Ouma, 2008b, p.223).

As the quotation implies, although the Kenyan government allowed public universities to start charging tuition fees, the fees were set by government (Ksh. 16,000, approximately US$229) and were undifferentiated. This means that students paid a flat, nationally set rate. The flat fees applied to all undergraduate study programs across the public higher education system. This model obviously denied individual universities the autonomy to set fees, and it ignored the actual costs of higher education for its various programs.

Therefore, even though public universities started levying tuition fees and fees for extra academic services, such as food and accommodation, the charges were significantly below market prices meaning the universities had difficulty meeting their financial obligations. The most affected universities were those that offered mainly science-oriented programs, such as the University of Nairobi, Moi University and Jomo Kenyatta University of Agriculture and Technology.

Financial challenges resulting mainly from declining government funding and the insufficient revenue from the nominal fees paid by government-subsidized students called for rethinking the way higher education was financed (Ouma, 2007; Wangenge-Ouma, 2008b). As a result, a variant to the existing cost sharing policy was introduced—the dual track, tuition fee model.

Dual track, tuition fee model

The dual track, tuition fee model is characterized by a highly restricted, "merit based" entry to free, low cost or government-subsidized higher education (the so-called Module 1 track), with other applicants, who are not admitted to this track, permitted entry on a full fee-paying basis (Module 2 track). Therefore, in this model, institutions are allowed to enroll 'extra' students over and above those whose fees are subsidized by government. The 'extra' students are usually charged full cost recovery fees (HESA, 2008, p. 22). Other than Kenya, the dual track, tuition fee model is also found in countries such as Uganda, Tanzania, Egypt, Malawi and Australia.

The dual track, tuition fee policy in Kenya is mainly characterized by programs generally referred to as 'parallel programs.' Although Kenyatta University was the first one to experiment with the dual track, tuition fee model in the early 1990s through its school-based programs,[1] UoN is generally credited with the introduction of the present architecture of parallel programs in 1998. Students enrolled in parallel programs do not receive a government subsidy; they are full, fee-paying students who generally attend lessons in the evenings and on weekends. All other charges for parallel students are pegged at market rates. Increasingly, parallel students attend lessons on a full-time basis. In some universities, attempts have been made to integrate parallel students with those who are government-subsidized. Almost all the universities have also established campuses to accommodate parallel students.

As a result of the dual track, tuition fee model, the campuses of Kenya's public universities now have two types of students: those who receive a government subsidy and pay nominal fees and those who do not receive a government subsidy and pay market-related fees.

The emerging trends in policy and financing of public university education in Kenya assumes what could be described as a mixture of both welfare and market approaches. The welfare approach is a continuation of the post-independence, free provision of university education. The market approach is mainly characterized by the dual track, tuition fee model. Thus, from the perspective of funding, there is a segment of students in Kenya's public universities whose education is treated as a 'public good,' hence highly subsidized by government, and another segment whose education is treated as a 'private good,' and who must pay market-related fees.

Mechanisms for Allocating Funds

In a number of countries, governments use specific funding formulae or mechanisms for allocating public funds to universities. In Kenya, although it is officially claimed that a unit-cost system is used to allocate funds to public universities, it is apparent the Kenyan government employs a sector-wide strategy. Therefore, the country's higher education funding mechanism must be understood in the context of the financing of the whole education sector.

The most important feature of the process is that there are no set formulae shaping allocations within the sub-sector. All public universities are required to submit a budget to the Ministry of Education; however, the submitted budgets do not appear to influence the allocations approved by the Ministry in any significant way, as illustrated by Figure 3.1. Instead, allocations take into account, albeit inconsistently, the size of the institution, its needs and its historical allocations. The allocations are thus not based on projections of actual need (RoK 1998). Comprehensive needs-based criteria for planning university budgets have not been fully developed. It is not uncommon for vice-chancellors to lobby the minister of education for enhanced allocations.

FIGURE 3.1: JOMO-KENYATTA UNIVERSITY OF AGRICULTURE AND TECHNOLOGY'S BUDGET SUBMISSIONS, GOVERNMENT ALLOCATIONS AND SHORTFALLS, 1998 – 2005 (MILLION KSH)

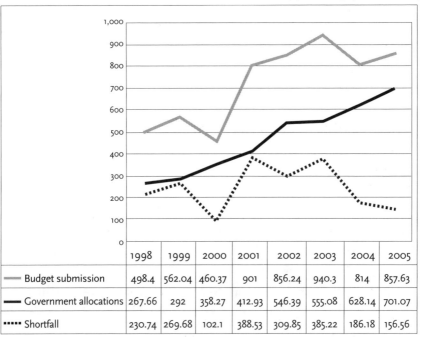

	1998	1999	2000	2001	2002	2003	2004	2005
Budget submission	498.4	562.04	460.37	901	856.24	940.3	814	857.63
Government allocations	267.66	292	358.27	412.93	546.39	555.08	628.14	701.07
Shortfall	230.74	269.68	102.1	388.53	309.85	385.22	186.18	156.56

Source: JKUAT (Ouma, 2007)

Allocations are made using a line item budget, i.e., in the form of block grants (lump sums). Although this affords universities some discretion on how they allocate these funds, the line item approach is unsatisfactory as it fails to take into account the varying needs of different programs (RoK 1998). Also, the approved funds are usually released one month in arrears, resulting in what some public universities have described as serious effects on cash flow, a hindrance to efficient administration of finances and running of programs (Ouma, 2007). In the public expenditure review (PER) reports which universities submit annually to the Ministry of Education, universities have argued for the release of government grants on a quarterly basis (Ouma, 2007). The PER reports prepared by all public universities usually show how government grants plus funds generated by the universities are spent, support budget proposals and make a case for government funding based on the figures (estimates) provided.

Although there exists a unit cost for higher education that supposedly guides government funding of public universities, as indicated above, the manner in which grants are allocated makes it impossible to determine how the unit cost is applied. The line item budget used to allocate funds to public universities does not show how much government allocates per student. The historical figure of Ksh. 120,000 arrived at in 1991 does not seem to apply.

By and large, the approach employed by the Kenyan government to allocate funds to public universities could be described as negotiated funding. It is an approach that neither considers the cost of higher education nor the outputs of the higher education system. In this funding approach, "individual allocations are usually based on those of the previous year, perhaps augmented by across-the-board incremental increases (Ziderman & Albrecht, 1995, p.108)."

Funding South Africa's Public Higher Education

Funding public higher education in SA has historically been predicated on the philosophy of shared costs where both the state and students make a contribution. This sets SA apart from many African countries, which until recently offered free higher education. Thus, the funding of higher education in SA has always, to a large extent, been predicated on the understanding that higher education is both a public good and a private benefit. This cost-sharing model attempts to ensure an appropriate balance between the public and private costs and benefits of investment in higher education.

Van Harte (2002) points out that SA, even before it became a republic in 1961, charged tuition fees at those post-secondary institutions that over time fully evolved into the modern universities of today. However, there were provisions made for some students to attend for free (Cape of Good Hope Ordinance 11 of 1837, cited in Van Harte 2002). In 1922, Van Harte (2002) reports, an amendment was passed that set into motion a system that continues today in which charging tuition fees is acceptable, and in which government signals its support of public higher education by providing financial support to it. Thus, the overriding principle in public higher education funding is that costs must be shared between society, as the recipient of public benefits, and students, as the recipients of private benefits.

During apartheid, government did fully fund both the tuition and living costs of students studying for careers deemed to be for the public benefit, e.g., police officers, nurses and teachers, through direct government allocations or through bursaries directly to the students (Van Harte, 2002). All the programs in this category were offered in the college sector. The dominant thinking regarding higher education funding emphasized private investment. In some cases, where public benefit was deemed to surpass private benefit, government met all the costs of higher education training.

Funding Policies and Mechanisms

Government funding of higher education in SA has shifted from the apartheid-era formula that primarily used enrollment-driven calculations to produce an institutional funding amount to a new formula that is intended to address the country's new policy goals of equity, redress and efficiency.

- **Funding during the apartheid era**—Bunting (2006a) has discussed the manner in which the South African government funded higher education during the apartheid era (prior to 1994). He identified two broad types of government funding that were in place. These were negotiated budgets associated with HBUs and technikons and formula funding associated initially with HWUs. The funding systems were instruments used in the implementation of the government's so-called 'separate but equal' policy. As expected, the apartheid-era funding systems "explicitly rejected the principles of equity and redress, holding that it was not the business of the higher education system to deal with social inequalities which affected either individuals or institutions (Bunting, 2006b, p.84)." Following the regime shift in 1994, a change in the manner in which higher education was funded became a priority and was inevitable. The apartheid-era funding framework was inconsistent with the new government's policies of equity, redress and development.

- **Funding in post-apartheid South Africa**—The apartheid-era formula funding adopted by all HBUs and technikons by 1988 remained in use up to 2003 (NCHE, 2004). The continued use of the funding formula, which was principally FTE-driven, occasioned financial difficulty to a number of HBUs (Bunting, 2006b).

The new post-apartheid regime did not, however, wait until a new funding framework was in place to address issues of social transformation (individual redress), i.e., enhancing the participation of disadvantaged students in higher education. In 1996, the National Student Financial Aid Scheme (NSFAS) was established. The Scheme's main goal is to assist academically-able students who are financially challenged to pursue higher education studies.

Both the Education White Paper 3: A Program for the Transformation of Higher Education, 1997 (DoE, 1997) and the 2001 National Plan for Higher Education in SA (MoE, 2001) emphasized the need for a new higher education funding framework that could serve as an effective steering mechanism for the attainment of transformation goals of the post-apartheid state. In 2003, as reported in the Government Gazette of 9 December 2003 (Vol. 462, no 25824), a new funding framework was published (DoE, 2005).

New Funding Framework

Government funding of higher education has recently (2004) shifted from the apartheid-era funding formula that primarily used enrollment-driven calculations to produce an institutional funding amount to a new formula that is intended to address the post-apartheid state's key policy goals of equity and redress. A basic feature of the new funding framework (NFF) is that it links the awarding of government higher education grants to national and institutional planning. This funding/planning link makes the new framework essentially a goal-oriented mechanism for the distribution of government grants to individual institutions, in accordance with (a) national planning and policy priorities, (b) the quantum of funds made available in the national higher education budget and (c) the approved plans of individual institutions (MoE, 2004). The new funding framework is, accordingly, an important steering mechanism for achieving pre-established policy priorities.

The national budget for higher education institutions (HEIs) is divided into three components: block grants, earmarked funds and institutional restructuring funds. Block grants constitute the bulk of total allocations to universities (cf. Table 3.1) and are teaching input grants generated through a formula which considers approved FTE students weighted against predetermined teaching input indicators or criteria (course material, course level and instruction-delivery mode). They are also teaching output grants which depend on the institution's actual number of non-research graduates and diplomates and a normative total of non-research graduates and diplomates which it should have produced in terms of national benchmarks. These totals produce different grants for an institution.

Since 2004, the distribution of funds against the three broad funding categories has shifted as shown in Table 3.1 below:

TABLE 3.1: DISTRIBUTION OF GOVERNMENT GRANTS TO PUBLIC HIGHER EDUCATION
INSTITUTIONS, 2004 – 2008

	2004	2005	2006	2007	2008	2008*
Block grant allocation	87%	85%	85%	82%	80%	80%
Earmarked grants	8%	10%	10%	13%	16%	20%
Institutional restructuring	5%	5%	5%	5%	4%	0%

* projected
Source: Stumpf (2008)

An institution's research output grant depends on actual totals of research graduates, research publication units and a normative total, which the institution should have produced in terms of national benchmarks. Institutional factor grants are for institutions with a large proportion of disadvantaged students. Setting aside funds for institutions with large proportions of disadvantaged students aligns with one of the priorities set by the National Plan for Higher Education (NPHE): increasing "the participation, success and graduation rates of black students in general and African and coloured students in particular (MoE, 2001, p. 35)." For the purposes of this grant, disadvantaged students are deemed to be African and coloured students who are South African citizens. The institutional factor grant operates by adding an amount to the teaching input grants of institutions, which depend on the proportion of disadvantaged students (MoE, 2004). There are also institutional factor grants allocated based on the size of institutions.

Actual allocations for the various grants are determined after an elaborate process that involves a series of calculations. The various indicators or criteria for the various grant allocations are weighted differently; the weightings are made by instruction-delivery mode, funding group and course level.

The previous discussion on funding policies and mechanisms for SA's higher education reveals several important points, the key one being the shifts in the mechanisms for allocating public funds. It has been pointed out that for most of the apartheid era, there were different funding mechanisms for HWUs, HBUs and technikons. The funding mechanisms for HBUs were consistent with the logic of apartheid, which did not encourage large-scale access to higher education by the black population. The new higher education funding mechanism introduced in 2004 retains the two main components of the SAPSE framework: block grants and earmarked funding for specific purposes. However, it differs from the SAPSE model in its policy underpinnings. The new funding framework does not provide institutional set-up as the old formula did. However, it does provide addressing historical institutional disadvantage by means of two factors applicable to institutions with large proportions of (formerly) disadvantaged students (African and coloured students). Thus, unlike the apartheid funding formula, the new formula seeks to encourage and support equity of access, which is in line with the new government's agenda of transformation.

Comparative Analysis

The approaches and mechanisms employed by the two countries are based on two different philosophies. Unlike Kenya, where higher education is largely considered a public service and whose funding has historically been predicated on the social returns argument on investment in higher education, the funding of higher education in South Africa has always, to a large extent, been predicated on the private returns argument on investment in higher education. Thus, the principal higher education funding policy in South Africa is cost-sharing. Although Kenya twice introduced some forms of cost-sharing, until the introduction of the dual track, tuition fee policy, the contribution of students and their families was generally nominal. The cost-sharing practiced in South Africa is geared toward substantial cost-recovery, and not unlike the dual track system in Kenya, generates income. Therefore, even though both countries have a cost-sharing policy, the manner of implementation exhibits variations.

Even though SA has consistently pursued the policy of cost-sharing, pressure has been mounting for a free higher education system (HESA, 2008). The arguments for free higher education in SA bear similarities with those advanced in Kenya after independence. The apartheid system deliberately discriminated against the black population group and especially the black African group. As a result, the majority of the country's black African group remains both economically and educationally marginalized. For instance, the participation of the black African population group stood at 12 percent in 2005, compared to 61 percent for the white population group and 51 percent for the Indian population group (Bunting and Cloete, 2008). Charging tuition fees has variously been cited as a cause of educational marginalization and an obstacle to the attainment of the post-apartheid state's transformation agenda.

Regarding mechanisms for allocating funds to universities, the two countries' systems fundamentally differ. Officially, allocations to Kenya's public universities are made on the basis of an undifferentiated unit cost of Ksh. 120,000, but the foregoing discussion shows that this is not the case. Instead, the negotiated funding system seems to apply. In the South African case, the funding formula rewards both the inputs and outputs of the higher education system. Allocations are made not just on the basis of the number of students enrolled, but also for teaching and research outputs. Furthermore, the South African funding formula, unlike the Kenyan system, recognizes the differentiated nature of higher education costs.

An important observation is that the two countries' higher education funding policies are generally linked to national policies. This is more pronounced in the case of South African. Whereas the apartheid-era funding systems served as instruments for the implementation of the government's so-called 'separate but equal' policy, the

809 United Nations Plaza
New York, New York 10017

DIRECT 212.984.5367
FAX 212.984.5496
EMAIL membership@iie.org

INSTITUTE OF INTERNATIONAL EDUCATION

Celebrating Over 90 Years of
Opening Minds to the World®

Membership Services

December 2010

Dear IIENetwork Members,

I am pleased to send you this complimentary copy of *Higher Education in Africa: Equity, Access, Opportunity*. This book is part of the African Higher Education Collaborative (AHEC), a project of the Institute of International Education's Council for International Exchange of Scholars. It received generous support from the Ford Foundation office in Egypt.

The enclosed book addresses the challenging triad of access, quality and cost in African higher education, with a special attention on four countries: Egypt, Kenya, Nigeria and South Africa. The book gives voice to the specific contexts and experiences of authors from Africa's varied higher education institutions, bringing vivid

financial mechanisms and funding options to improve equity and access to higher education; another chapter focuses on the services that educational institutions must provide to improve learner success; another chapter focuses on delivery systems such as distance learning that can respond to the needs of diverse groups of learners; yet another chapter focuses on the various kinds of marginalization that exacerbate inequity and exclusion by gender or among populations with disabilities.

For more information on the origins of this book, or the African Higher Education Collaborative (AHEC) itself, please visit http://www.africahighered.org/. I trust the new IIE publication will prove a valuable resource to your work.

Sincerely,

Daniel Obst
Deputy Vice President
Institute of International Education

visit us online at www.iie.org

new funding formula is intended to help address the country's new policy goals of equity and redress. In the case of Kenya, the funding/national planning or policy link was more explicit immediately after independence when the free higher education policy was expressly intended to expedite human resource development to replace the departing colonial administrators. Subsequent funding policies have not in any clear way been linked to national goals or priorities.

Conclusion

This chapter has discussed the various higher education funding policies and mechanisms of two Sub-Saharan African countries with different histories and political economies. The chapter has shown how different national contexts have produced different approaches to the funding of higher education. The two countries' higher education funding frameworks are generally circumscribed by two dissimilar political, social and economic contexts. These contexts invariably influence government policies with regard to funding; the processes are both local and global or external, especially for Kenya, and mainly local for SA. In Kenya's case, the changes (especially the shift to cost-sharing) were primarily a result of the coercive influence of the World Bank and IMF. The new policy was part of these institutions' neo-liberal project (and the SAPs) imposed on many debtor countries. On the contrary, changes in SA have been driven in the first instance by local and political considerations.

Overall, as the comparative discussion has shown, higher education funding policies have significant implications for important policy goals such as access, equity and even quality. Further, both the funding policies and the mechanisms used to disburse funds are important to the higher education enterprise, especially with regards to the institutions' financial health.

NOTES

[1] The term 'school based programs' refers to programs where serving teachers studying for degrees attend sessions at the university during the August, December and April school holidays.

REFERENCES

Banya, K. & Elu, J. (2001). 'The World Bank and Financing Higher Education in Sub-Saharan Africa', *Higher Education,* Vol. 42 (1): 1 – 34.

Barr N. (2004). 'Higher Education Funding', *Oxford Review of Economic Policy* 20 (2), 264 - 283.

Bunting, I. (2006a). "Funding." In N. Cloete, R. Fehnel, P. Maassen, T. Moja, T. Gibbon and H. Perold (Eds.) *Transformations in Higher Education: Global Pressures and Local Realities.* Springer, Dordrecht. Pg. 73–94.

Bunting, I. (2006b). "Students." In N. Cloete, R. Fehnel, P. Maassen, T. Moja, T. Gibbon, and H. Perold (Eds.) *Transformations in Higher Education: Global Pressures and Local Realities.* Springer, Dordrecht. Pg. 95–111.

Bunting, I. and Cloete, N. (2008). "Governing Access to Higher Education in South Africa." Unpublished paper.

Department of Education (1997). "Education White Paper 3: A Program for the Transformation of Higher Education. General Notice 1196 of 1997." Pretoria.

Department of Education (2005). "Data on Higher Education Funding". Available: http://www.education.gov.za/. (June 20 2005).

HESA (2008). Tuition fees: Higher Education Institutions in South Africa. HESA.

Johnstone D.B. (2006). *Financing Higher Education: Cost Sharing in International Perspective.* Rotterdam: Sense Publishers.

Johnstone, D.B. (1998). *The Financing and Management of Higher Education: A Status Report on Worldwide Reforms.* Washington, DC: World Bank.

Kiamba, C. (2004). 'Privately Sponsored Students and Other Income Generating Activities at the University of Nairobi', *Journal of Higher Education in Africa,* Vol. 2 (2): 53 – 74.

Kiamba, C. (2005). Entrepreneurialism and Adaptability in Kenyan Universities in the Face of Declining Donor and Government Support. Paper Presented at Nuffic Conference 'A Changing Landscape', The Hague, 23-25 May.

Gravenir, F. Q., Wangenge-Ouma, G., Mse, G. S. and Mukirae, N. (2006). "Re-thinking the Financing of Kenya's Higher Education: Options for Enhancing Equity, Access, and Quality." *The African Symposium,* Vol. 6 Nos. 3 & 4: 35–45.

Merisotis, J.P. and Gilleland, D.S. (2000). *Funding South African Higher Education: Steering Mechanisms to Meet National Goals.* The Institute for Higher Education Policy, Washington, D.C.

Melck A.P. (1990). Who Should Pay for Education? Inaugural Lecture. University of South Africa.

Ministry of Education (2001). National Plan for Higher Education in South Africa. Pretoria.

Ministry of Education (2004). A New Funding Framework: How Government Funds are Allocated to Public Higher Education Institutions. Pretoria.

Nafukho, F. M. (2004). The Market Model of Financing State Universities in Kenya: Some Innovative Lessons. In Zeleza, P.T. & Olukoshi, A. (Eds). *African Universities in the Twenty-first Century.* Volume I. Pretoria: UNISA Press. Pg. 126–139.

National Council on Higher Education (2004). *South African Higher Education in the First Decade of Democracy.* Council on Higher Education, Pretoria.

Ouma, G. (2007). "Reducing Resource Dependence on Government Funding: The Case of Public Universities in Kenya and South Africa." Ph.D. dissertation, University of Cape Town.

Republic of Kenya (RoK) (1964). *Development Plan, 1964-1970.* Nairobi: Government Printer.

Republic of Kenya (1973). *Development Plan, 1974-78.* Draft Chapter on Education. Nairobi: Government Printer.

Republic of Kenya (1998). *Master Plan on Education and Training, 1997-2010.* Nairobi: Jomo Kenyatta Foundation.

Republic of Kenya (2001). *Totally Integrated and Quality Education and Training. Report of the Commission of Inquiry into the Education System of Kenya.* Nairobi: Government Printer.

Sanyal, B. (1998). *Diversification of Sources and the Role of Privatisation in Financing Higher Education in the Arab States Region.* Paris: UNESCO-IIEP.

Slaughter, S. & Leslie, L. L. (1997). *Academic Capitalism and the Entrepreneurial University.* Baltimore: John Hopkins University Press.

Stumpf, R. (2008). "Funding for the Improvement of Higher Education: Changes and Challenges." Paper presented at the Institute for International Research's Higher Education Summit. Johannesburg, July 28–30.

Tilak, J.B.G. (2004). Higher Education Between the State and the Market. UNESCO Forum Colloquium on Research and Higher Education Policy, 1-3 December.

Van Harte, M. (2002). "Can Student Loan Schemes Ensure Access to Higher Education? South Africa's Experience." The International Comparative Higher Education Finance and Accessibility Project, Graduate School of Education, University of Buffalo.

Wangenge-Ouma, G. (2008a) 'Higher Education Marketisation and its Discontents: The Case of Quality in Kenya'. *Higher Education,* 56, 457–471.

Wangenge-Ouma, G. (2008b). 'Globalisation and Higher Education Funding Policy Shifts in Kenya.' *Journal of Higher Education Policy and Management,* Vol. 30 (3), 215-229.

World Bank (1988). *Education in Sub-Saharan Africa: Policies for Adjustment, Revitalization, and Expansion.* Washington, DC: World Bank.

World Bank (1994). *Higher Education: The Lessons of Experience.* Washington, DC: World Bank.

Ziderman, A. & Albrecht, D. (1995). *Financing Universities in Developing Countries.* Washington, D.C.: The Falmer Press.

Chapter Four

PRIVATE FINANCING AS A MEANS TO IMPROVE ACCESS TO HIGHER EDUCATION IN AFRICA

BY SEGUN ADEDEJI, UNIVERSITY OF IBADAN; PAKINAZ BARAKA;
VICTOR S. DUGGA, UNIVERSITY OF JOS; AND STEPHEN O. ODEBERO,
MASINDE MULIRO UNIVERSITY OF SCIENCE AND TECHNOLOGY

Introduction

Despite strong enrollment growth, most African tertiary institutions are not generating enough graduates and many of the institutions lack the ability to support national economic and social development in the 21st century.

Over the past two decades, tertiary enrollment has generally increased far more quickly than tertiary budgets. In fact, enrollment more than tripled between 1991 and 2005, expanding 8.7 percent for one of the highest regional growth rates in the world (World Bank, 2008: 11). But at the same time, tertiary public financing, which averaged US$6,800 per student annually in 1980, dropped to just US$981 in 2005 for 33 low-income African countries (World Bank, 2008: 11). Indeed, as the number of tertiary students surged, the funds available to educate each student decreased drastically and both educational quality and relevance suffered as a result (World Bank, 2008: 11).

In many African countries, a private tertiary education sector is developing rapidly in response to limited access and declining quality in the public sector and in response to the labor market's needs. Since 1990, private colleges, universities and tertiary-level professional institutions have been established at a faster rate than public ones. While public universities doubled from roughly 100 to nearly 200 between 1990 and 2007, the number of private tertiary institutions increased during the same period from 24 to around 500 (World Bank, 2008: 13).

However, insufficient regulatory frameworks for investment, accreditation and quality assurance and lack of incentives through competitive funding for research and innovations have hindered the ability of private institutions to compete on a level playing field with public institutions and to broaden their role in economic and social development (World Bank, 2008: 13).

This chapter is divided into three major sections. The first examines the nature and extent of private higher education in Egypt, while the second does the same for Kenya. The third examines three aspects of the Nigerian higher education system: the growth of private universities, household expenditure on higher education and endowments, which are an important source of non-governmental funding.

Egypt

Until recently, higher education was considered a primarily public sector issue in Egypt. However, with the increased attention being paid to privatization and markets since the fall of the Berlin Wall, private higher education has grown significantly in Egypt, as it has in many other developing countries (UNESCO, 2009:7). Despite this growth, private higher education in Egypt still absorbs only 3 percent of total higher education enrollment. It should be noted also that—as is the case in other North African countries—private higher education in Egypt is mostly planned and promoted by government, often in partnership with European, United States and other donor support (UNESCO, 2009:11).

Characteristics of Private Higher Education

Heterogeneity characterizes the provision of private higher education across developed and developing countries (see for example, Levy, 2006: 61-143). Levy suggests that the dominant typology in most developing countries has been framed around elite, religious and demand-absorbing provisions. This typology remains pertinent in Egypt, although there is a significant "for-profit" component to private education. Another type of higher education provision that has recently emerged in Egypt is that of public-private partnerships.

However, it is worth noting that the largest growth area in private higher education is among "non-elite" and mostly "demand-absorbing" institutions. Secondary students who fail to get high scores in the national graduation examinations are denied access to the public system and have no choice but to attend a private university or other tertiary education institution.

The Tertiary Education System

Egypt operates two parallel education systems: the secular system and the religious, or Al-Azhar, system. By law, education is free at all levels of education. However, in response to declining government expenditures, public higher institutions have recently introduced special programs with full fees, especially in applied sciences. Other public tertiary institutions remain free of charge or charge nominal fees.

The tertiary system comprises 18 public universities (including Al-Azhar University), along with six branches which will soon become independent universities; 20 private universities; 13 public non-university institutions (including eight technical colleges); and 96 non-university private institutions. In addition, there are 11 non-university institutions established by other governmental entities (not the Ministry of Higher Education) or under special agreements and two private, foreign institutions: the American University in Cairo (AUC), established in 1919, and the Arab Academy for Science and Technology and Maritime Transport (AASTMT), established in 1972 (Johnstone 2009:11). Table 4.1 shows the diversified nature of higher education in Egypt.

TABLE 4.1: NUMBER AND TYPE OF TERTIARY EDUCATION INSTITUTIONS IN EGYPT

Type	Number
Public university	18
Private university	20
Public, non-university institutions	13
Private higher institutions	96
Other non-university institutions	11
Foreign institutions	2
Total	**157**

Growth of Private Higher Education

Law 101 for the year 1992 was the first law issued allowing the establishment of private universities in Egypt. In 1996, four private universities were established and started to operate. In ten years, the number of private universities increased steadily each year to reach 15 universities by the end of 2006. During the last three years, the number of private universities increased at a faster rate to reach 20 universities by the end of 2009. Today, the total number of students enrolled in private universities is 70,383.

Types of Private Higher Education Institutions

Private universities can be divided into two main categories. The first consists of highly prestigious and extremely expensive private universities. According to Levy (2007), these can be labeled as *elite* universities. They have generally been established under a specific agreement between the Egyptian government and the government of another country or a partnership between Egyptian investors and a prestigious, non-Egyptian university. The second category consists of less expensive and lower-quality universities, or *non-elite*.

Ownership and Management

Private higher education institutions have been established chiefly by individuals or family groups and depend on tuition fees because they are financially independent. This phenomenon is not unique to Egypt. According to Altbach (2005: 10-12), the emergence of such family-style higher education institutions is a worldwide phenomenon. In such institutions, the family maintains direct involvement in the administration, governance, financial control and direct and/or indirect ownership of the institution. These are de jure, not-for-profit institutions; however, they exhibit several characteristics of the private, for-profit institutions found elsewhere in the world.

Tuition Fees and Academic Programs

Tuition fees in private universities range from 5,000 to 60,000 £E (Egyptian Pound, currently 1US$= £E 5.35) per year depending on the type of program chosen, students' scores required by the university and field of specialization. The American University in Cairo, the oldest private university in Egypt, for example, charges the highest fees, ranging from 30,000 to 80,000 £E for 12 credit hours per semester. Private universities offer most academic programs provided by state universities. However, recent reports indicate that some private institutions have not conformed to government regulations specifying that they should provide academic programs required by the Egyptian labor market. In addition, private institutions offer mostly undergraduate degrees, with the exception of the German University which offers doctoral studies in some fields of study. Students interested in pursuing post-graduate studies generally enroll in state universities.

The Regulatory Framework

State universities are under the authority of the Supreme Council of Universities, while private universities are under the authority of the Supreme Council of Private/Non-governmental Universities. Both councils are under the supervision and authority of the Ministry of Higher Education, which regulates public and private higher education institutions with the same minister presiding over both councils.

Both public and private universities have full academic and administrative autonomy. Private universities are entitled to implement their own criteria of admission, but within a stated quota or number of students set by the Ministry of Higher Education for each private university. Moreover, they are allowed to set fees without intervention from the Ministry of Higher Education.

A recent legislative amendment supports the full autonomy of private universities, especially with regard to generating and administering their own financial resources. The new law also supports establishing private/non-governmental universities in partnership with state universities and it seeks to enhance private higher education's role in scientific research and community development. In addition, the law requires new academic specializations and studies that are market-driven. Other important aspects of the recent law allow private institutions to accept endowments, donations and grants from third parties, and private institutions are fully exempted from taxes, subject to the approval of the Ministers of Higher Education and Finance. In addition, government supports public-private/non-governmental educational institutions with land and other infrastructure facilities for free or at significantly reduced prices.

Private Universities, Enrollment and Staff

Table 4.2 shows the number of private universities' (excluding the AUC) total enrollment and staff (both faculty or academic and administrative staff).

TABLE 4.2: PRIVATE UNIVERSITIES IN EGYPT – NUMBER, ENROLLMENT, STAFF (2007)

	Enrollment	Faculty			Admin.
	(thousands)	Full	Visit	Total	
6th of October Univ.	15,746	65	165	230	285
Univ. for Modern Sciences & Arts	3,893	56	31	87	222
Misr Univ. for Science & Technol.	20,552	124	82	206	362
Misr Int'l	4,262	31	39	70	183
French Univ.	93	16	0	16	33
German Univ.	3,326	74	32	106	209
Al-Ahram Canadian	155	5	9	14	11
British Univ.	224	21	11	32	19
Modern for Technology & Infom.	123	27	3	30	31
Farous Univ.	2,000	–	–	–	–
Sinai Univ.	1,000	–	–	–	–
Future Univ.	900	–	---	–	–
Russian Univ.	250	–	–	–	–
Total	52,524*	419	372	791	1,355

Source: Supreme Council of Egyptian Universities, the Ministry of Higher Education
This number has reached 70,383 students in 2010

There are currently 20 private universities (including AUC) with total enrollment of 70,383 students. While private university enrollment is significant and increasing, it is still small relative to the more than 1.4 million students enrolled in public universities.

Conclusion

Clearly private higher education plays an increasingly important role in providing access in Egypt. However, the growth of the sector raises at least three critical issues: 1) the extent to which private universities are equitable and accessible to students from low-income households; 2) the extent to which private universities contribute to national goals of higher education; and 3) the extent to which private higher education should feature in national higher education strategic planning and regulatory frameworks.

To address these issues, policy makers should rethink and redefine the main objectives and functions of the private provision of higher education. In particular, they should decide which regulations and financial mechanisms are most suitable to enable both public and private higher education to function more effectively in terms of access and equity. Further, a link in educational policies should be established for both types of educational provisions within a national comprehensive plan. In addition, this plan needs to be implemented along with the development of financial mechanisms that can guarantee the necessary support to deserving low-income or disadvantaged students unable to meet the cost of private education.

Kenya

Kenya has established private universities in recent decades as the demand for higher education has outstripped the supply by public universities. By 1984, ten privately funded institutions offering university-level education had been established (Mugenda, 2009). Currently, Kenya has 23 private universities, 11 of which are "private chartered universities" or fully recognized institutions, eight with "interim letters of authority" and four with "certificates of registration."

Private universities are concentrated in major towns and cities, particularly in the capital city of Nairobi, where 90 percent of them are found. This causes accessibility problems for students in rural areas, as well as increasing the cost of private university education for rural households. Moreover, recent studies (e.g., Odebero, 2008) indicate that the cost of education in universities located in urban areas is much higher than in rural areas, especially with respect to meals, accommodation and medical care. This poses further challenges to students from poor families.

Equity and Quality in Private Higher Education

Kenya, like most developing countries, relies on public funding for higher education. Therefore, those who seek private higher education have to rely on private funding.

In Kenya, private university education historically has been misconstrued as being only for the academically inferior or those who fail to gain admission to public universities through the rigorous Joint Admission Board (JAB). However, an increasing number of students are turning down JAB admissions, choosing instead admission into private universities which generally offer them their preferred courses and programs.

Higher quality students are also moving to private universities because of the inefficiency in public universities. Public universities often take one to two years to admit eligible students, while students applying to private institutions are admitted immediately upon graduation with a diploma. Students in public institutions have also complained of congestion in residence halls and a general lack of instructional facilities. While the Commission for Higher Education (CHE) has been firm on quality in private universities, its mandate in public universities has been severely compromised because several heads of the Commission are former chief executives in public universities.

Even with this plethora of problems bedeviling public higher education, people still regard graduates from private universities as inferior and believe that private higher education institutions are for the rich. Perceptions likely will change, as public universities introduce parallel programs, admit private, fee paying students and admit students beyond those deemed eligible by the JAB. Studying access to public and private universities in Kenya by socio-economic status, Odebero (2008: 69) found that in private, rural universities, 75 percent of those enrolled came from medium and high income groups (Table 4.3).

TABLE 4.3: Access to Private and Public Universities in Kenya by Socio-economic Status

Type of University	Socio-economic status						
	LSES		MSES		HSES		Total
	No.	%	No.	%	No.	%	%
PR (284)	91	32.04	105	36.97	88	30.98	100
PU (310)	100	32.26	160	51.6	50	16.13	100
PVR (94)	24	25.53	36	38.3	34	36.2	100
PVU (75)	2	2.8	26	34.7	47	62.7	100

Note: PR =Public rural; PU=Public urban; PVR=Private rural; PVU=Private urban.
LSES=Low socio-economic status; MSES=Medium socio-economic status;
HSES= High socio-economic status
Source: Odebero, 2008

Table 4.3 shows that in private, urban universities, more than 97 percent of the students enrolled came from medium and high income classes. This means that a paltry 3 percent of the students enrolled in urban private universities hailed from low-income classes. Since most of the private universities are located in urban areas, it implies that students from low-income families are grossly under-represented in private higher education in Kenya.

Access to Private Higher Education

Student enrollment in private universities has grown from around 9,500 in 2003 to 21,132 in 2008. If current growth rates continue, it is projected that enrollment in Kenya's private universities will reach approximately 33,000 by 2012-13. Notwithstanding this expansion in the past several years, the capacity of private university education sector in Kenya is still limited, accommodating only 17.8 percent of the total student population in universities (Odebero).

Higher education enrollment in Kenya historically has been dominated by men; women constitute only one-third of the total student enrollment. However, private universities seem to attract more women students compared to men, as shown in Table 4.4.

TABLE 4.4: ENROLLMENT BY GENDER, PRIVATE UNIVERSITIES IN KENYA, 2003 – 2008

Years	2003		2004		2005		2006		2007	
Type of Institution	M	F	M	F	M	F	M	F	M	F
Private Accredited	3,650	4,371	3,796	4,546	4,215	4,624	8,975	6,973	9,688	10,469
Non-accredited	763	757	801	907	853	947	2853	2091	583	392
Total	4,413	5,128	4,597	5,453	5,068	5,571	11,828	9,064	10,271	10,861

Source: Economic Survey, 2008

In 2003-2004, female enrollment was higher than male enrollment in private universities, standing at about 54 percent of the total enrollment. The gains were not long lasting as the gap narrowed to 51 percent and 47 percent, respectively, by 2008. What should be appreciated is the effort by private universities to create equitable opportunities for women in higher education—a goal that has eluded public universities over the years.

Despite the expansion in access to higher education over the years, the capacity of higher education in Kenya is still limited and accommodates only 7.5 percent of students graduating from secondary schools, and 2 percent of the expected age cohort (Weidman, 1995, cited in Mugenda, 2009). Between 1990 and 2000, it was reported that 180,000 of the students who attained the minimum university entry requirements of grade C+ failed to gain admission to public universities (Kigotho, 2000, cited in Mugenda, 2009). This clearly demonstrates how competitive it is to gain access to higher education in Kenya; students must earn a grade point average on the Kenya Certificate of Secondary Education significantly over and beyond the minimum eligibility requirement to ensure their chances of admission.

Modes of Financing Private Higher Education

Private university education in Kenya is self-financing and draws its revenue from several sources which have their limitations. As private higher education in Kenya has grown, so have the costs. One reason for the rapid increase in costs has been the massification of higher education, increasing the demand of higher education. Similarly, the expenditure per student has increased to cater for inputs that go with expectations of quality higher education. The most challenging issue has been how to fund it. Overall, private higher education in Kenya has been funded as follows:

- **Tuition fees**—This main source of revenue varies according to different programs. On average, the charges are about kshs. 100,000 per semester (US$1,300) for most programs. Although the stated motive of most private universities, especially those sponsored by churches, is not-for-profit, their behavior has been for all purposes quite the reverse. The tuition charges are high and this has limited access to students from high- and middle-income families. This has ultimately defeated the goals and mandates of private universities, which is to open access to higher education in the country (Nwamuo, 2000). Table 4.5 shows tuition charges for one of the private universities.

TABLE 4.5: TUITION CHARGES IN A PRIVATE UNIVERSITY IN KENYA (AMOUNT IN US$)

Program	1st year		2nd year		3rd year		4th year	
	1st sem	2nd sem	1st sem	2nd sem	1st sem	2nd sem	1st sem	2nd sem
Law	1,716	1,496	1,616	1,429	1,439	1,519	1,493	1,319
Education	1,533	1,313	1,433	1,246	1,433	1,336	1,256	947
Commerce	1,436	1,136	1,256	1,070	1,433	1,246	1,433	1,313
Arts	1,533	1,313	1,433	1,246	1,256	1,070	1,256	1,136

- **Grants from churches and philanthropic organizations**—Church-sponsored private universities get grants and donations from their mother churches outside the country mainly for capital development. Local grants and donations target support to students under the sponsorship of local churches and organizations.

- **Funding from alumni; local and foreign donor agencies**—Although not fully exploited, this type of funding is foundational to private universities. Local and foreign donations from banks, corporate companies, NGOs and other private organizations have been in the form of grants and scholarships for talented, but needy students. Many private universities now have operational offices for alumni, but their funding ability has been hampered by lack of clear policy on endowments and donations in the country. For example, whereas taxation remains very high, there is no policy for favorable tax regimes to those who offer donations and endowments. The general view in the country is that private universities are for the rich and that they do not need individual support and donations.

- **Scholarships and Loans**—The Higher Education Loans Board (HELB) initially denied private university students from accessing loans and scholarships, which strengthened the argument that private universities were for the rich, but this policy changed in 2002. Students now enrolled in private universities can apply for HELB loans provided they score grade B+ and above in KCSE examinations. Public universities have raised objections, arguing that HELB loans are a government subsidy that can only be used to finance public universities. As the controversy rages on, HELB loans and scholarships are accessed by bright, but needy students in private universities. Those enrolled in post-graduate programs also access HELB loans and scholarships on condition that the programs fall within HELB priority areas. Some banks have also collaborated with HELB to offer education loans to students. Other sources of scholarships include trust funds, such as Rattanssi Education Trust fund and DAAD scholarships, which target specific disciplines especially at the post-graduate level.

- **Constituency Development Fund (CDF)**—In setting up the CDF fund, the government stipulated that 4.5 percent must go toward education development in each local constituency. Consequently, CDF committees at the constituency level have allocated bursaries to needy students to pursue private higher education. As with HELB loans, although the CDF is a government fund financed from public funds, the argument for private financing has been that it should be used to directly finance education of students. Complaints abound about the constitution of CDF committees, nepotism and political patronage. There have also been complaints that the amount allocated is too small, given the high tuition fees charged by private universities.

- **Income-generating activities**—Private higher education institutions have pursued income-generating activities such as short courses, contractual research and consultancy services. Other income-generating activities include shops, hotels and restaurants and accommodation/residential charges, which offer a substantial amount of revenue to private institutions. The controversy has been that research funds financed from the public purse have ended up in private institutions mainly because those who make policy decisions have connections with private university proprietors and thus harbor interests in policy formulations.

Conclusion: Policy Issues and Challenges

Equity in access. Although private higher education has enhanced access to university education, there is growing fear that their higher tuition fees may be pricing out prospective students from lower-income backgrounds (Kim, et al., 2007). A recent study in Kenya on equity in access to university education (Odebero, 2008) confirms that more than 90 percent of students in private universities come from high- and middle-income families. An attempt to use HELB loans and other funds from the exchequer to finance private higher education has proved to be regressive. There is need for more ingenuity on the part of policymakers in confronting the issue of access and equity in access to private higher education. At the policy level, the government could explore means tested, loans, a voucher system and a possibility of a certain percentage of scholarships in every private university in key disciplines to be set aside for students from low socio-economic backgrounds. This could be extended to parallel degree programs in public universities.

Financing. As the cost of private higher education rises unabated, one of the major challenges relates to financing. Although private institutions are not supposed to be publicly funded, some argue that private students should be entitled to government funding (Kim, et al., 2009). Proponents of this school of thought argue that higher education produces both social and private benefits through research activities. By extension, therefore, private higher education produces public goods. Some scholars have dismissed this argument on the grounds that it does not encourage equity, arguing that we cannot transfer income from the poor to the rich echelons of the society. Clearly, therefore, further research is required in this area that will guide a fair policy decision.

Quality and Relevance. In the face of the high demand for private higher education, and inadequate physical infrastructure, questions have been raised about the quality of education provided. More questions have risen about the inability of private institutions to attract high quality staff and their over-dependence on temporary staff, especially in urban areas. The spotlight is now on the Commission for Higher Education. As more and more institutions seek accreditation, the Commission must step up its efforts to guarantee quality in private higher education.

Higher education results in external benefits important for economic development. However, Kenya needs to make greater efforts to enhance quality and equitable access to private higher education. Market imperfections persist to curtail in particular the participations of deserving, but economically disadvantaged groups. Private higher education requires a coherent and well-defined legal framework and policies to enhance its growth and development. In addition, the Commission on Higher Education needs to guide the public by publicizing institutions' performances for the benefit of prospective students.

Nigeria

The priority of the Nigerian government in recent years has shifted toward increased private participation in education. Beginning in 1999, the number of licensed private universities in Nigeria had increased to 34 (NUC, 2007). One of the factors responsible for their rapid growth is the pervasive inadequacy of the public higher education system.

Public higher education in Nigeria is presently facing several challenges: rising costs, coupled with constraints on public revenues, declining quality and increasing irrelevance of university education. Moreover, the public higher education system has been criticized for being inefficient and ineffective, raising an increasing number of questions about its relevance to the needs of a new democratic environment. Other major issues mentioned in literature are limited access, infrastructural decay, incessant strikes by the members of the academic and the non-academic staff unions, poor funding, bad management and governance (Longe, 1999; Adedeji & Bamidele, 2003).

Accordingly, government has found it appropriate to encourage privatization of the higher education system to allow the market to reward or penalize institutions that can or cannot measure up. The rationale for this policy is that in the long run, quality will pay off, substandard practices in the education system will disappear of their own accord, and private sector efficiency will be entrenched. Nigerian government's approval for the establishment of more privately owned higher education is in line with the expectation that this will serve to increase access, improve opportunities and raise standards.

This section first offers a brief review of private higher education; second, it assesses household expenditure on higher education; and third, it looks at an important non-governmental source of funding for universities, namely endowments.

An Increasing Shift Toward Private Universities

For the new academic session (2009-10), the National Universities Commission (NUC) allowed public universities to admit around 138,000 new students and private universities to admit 32,000 students—numbers based on the carrying capacity of institutions, including their infrastructure and staff strength. Despite the limited carrying capacity of private universities, there has been an unprecedented increase in the number of would-be students applying for admittance.

The increase was due to an eight-week trade union strike among public universities, which compromised entrance examinations for the next academic session and greatly discouraged parents from sending their children to these institutions. Private universities, which do not allow trade unionism, therefore experienced a dramatic increase in the number of candidates applying for admission. However, only students from middle- and upper-class families who can afford the high fees apply, including the children of staff in strike-crippled public universities (University World News, 2009).

Other factors have also impacted the increased enrollment at private universities. Parents have voiced fears that industrial action and occasional student unrest affected teaching and research and made the public university calendar unstable and unpredictable. Also, the introduction of IT professional certifications and entrepreneurial skills into the curriculum of private universities has attracted parents who can afford the fees. These skills are now key requirements for job seekers in both the public and private sectors of Nigeria's economy, but are not readily available in public universities.

Recently, in Lagos, consultancy firms recruiting graduates for petroleum, banking and telecommunications companies conducted a series of interviews in which graduates from foreign and private universities performed very well, but those from public universities performed poorly. Successful foreign and private university graduates were placed in managerial jobs and those from public universities in less senior jobs (University World News, 2009).

Additionally, *The Guardian*, one of Nigeria's leading newspapers, investigated the views of parents regarding private and public universities. A mere 20 percent said they wanted to send their children to public universities, partly because only these institutions offer professional courses in medicine, pharmacy and to some extent engineering, which are capital-intensive and demand highly skilled and scarce personnel. According to the newspaper, the great majority of parents, nearly 70 percent, said that if cost were not the issue, they would want their children to obtain degrees from private universities (University World News, 2009).

Household Expenditure on Education

While national statistics, which give the relative shares of the households on public and private expenditure on higher education, are unavailable, primary data collected shows that household expenditure per student varies across disciplines and programs in both public and private institutions. For instance, the average household spending per student attending public higher institution is ₦201,000 for girls and ₦150,000 for boys in the 2008-2009 session. The corresponding expenditures for students attending private higher institutions are between ₦495,500 and ₦504,800 depending on the programs and institutions attended. The mean household expenditures for educating a child in private tertiary school were ₦428,000 for girls in the arts discipline and ₦440,000 for boys.

In some private institutions, tuition and accommodation are tied together, accounting for more than 85 percent of total household spending, while expenditures on books, transport and other living expenses account for only 15 percent. Average expenditure on a child attending a private university is two to three times higher than for a child studying at a public university.

On the decision of sending a child to private rather than public institutions, it was found (Okuwa, 2007) that problems of frequent strikes, limited access and declining quality in public institutions combine to influence parental decisions. Moreover, considering the willingness to pay for higher education, it was revealed that for all income groups and at any percentage increase in school fees, parents are more willing to pay for their male children than female (Okuwa, 2007). This finding reveals that apart from the institutional factors, which wield significant influence on household's decision, gender discrimination is also an important determinant of parental decisions.

Endowments

An *endowment* is a property, fund or revenue that provides support on a permanent basis. It is typically set aside for investments; accruing interest is divested to meet ongoing expenses, cover capital expenditures or fund special projects and programs (Poderis, 2005). These can be singular or numerous in one institution. Donors may determine the form and shape of endowment by restricting the use of revenue to particular causes such as a professorial chair or scholarship/fellowship in a specified discipline. Donors may also dictate use of the principal.

Universities require continual financial support and endowments are suitably preferred. Some Nigerian universities do not have any endowments, others are seeking to establish endowments and still others operate with existing endowments.

- **Non-Existent Endowments**—For various reasons, more than half of Nigeria's universities do not have any form of endowment. First, many private universities started as extensions of business establishments or religious groups, possessing a perception of ownership that makes it difficult to attract endowment support.

  Second, private universities are relatively young (first established in 1999), and many of their alumni are still job hunting. Consequently, the universities are in the process of cultivating alumni for endowments, which includes integrating alumni into convocation activities, like the graduation ceremony for Covenant University owned by the Living Faith Church.

  Many regionally, state-owned universities lack endowments for similar reasons. They, too, are relatively young; the oldest was established in 1979 and the youngest in 2009. Also, they possess a perception of ownership, because the

State Governors over these institutions maintain a vice-like grip. In some cases, the universities have been named after such Governors, as was the case of Prince Abubakar Audu University before it was reclaimed as Kogi State University after he left office, or named after the Governors' own benefactor, as is the case of Ibrahim Badamasi Babangida University, Lapai.

- **Endowment Start-ups**—Some universities engage in ad hoc "endowment fund launchings," which indicate the beginnings of endowment programs. Popular particularly during graduation or convocation events, these Kenyan "Harambee"-type gatherings encourage wealthy individuals and corporate organizations to make donations to the institutions. Certain universities have been criticized for inducing such patronage with questionable honorary doctorate degrees. And, indeed, some of the inducements have failed to generate the expected financial proceeds, so the strategy isn't foolproof.

Two patterns emerge from these endowments. First, universities will solicit funds to support specific short-term objectives, like provision of a water system or lecture hall. However, when management becomes engrossed in micro-managing such daily operations, the leaders' ability and capacity to focus on long-term vision is limited. "The question of what kind of students, and what kind of society, university funds should be used to advance, tends to get lost in the immediate and short term focus of crisis management (Pereira, 2007)." Second, the meager amounts raised at such launches mean that the university is forced to hold such events more often than should be necessary.

The issue of investments is also endemic to universities in this category; however, little information is available on how received sums have been invested to grow the capital and secure profits. Where investment occurs, it is too meagre to count. What is lacking is the vision needed to optimize on the "endowment fund" concept to leverage the universities in this category. The blame for lack of dynamic funding policies has been laid on both federal and state governments (Munzali and Obaje, 2008), but this blame must be enlarged to accommodate university leadership.

- **Existing Endowments**—Only two universities in Nigeria boast vibrant endowments: the University of Lagos and the University of Ibadan. The University of Lagos offers multiple endowments, which are identified on its website: general; specific professorial chair; buildings; funding research journals and publications; research, scholarship, fellowship awards, seminars and conferences; academic programs; university services and staff/students welfare projects; and student scholarships.

Endowments at the University of Lagos may not be a programmatic success yet, but they have been used to mobilize its alumni to massively support the university. A case in point is the construction of a multipurpose auditorium by one of its alums, Afe Babalola, who is a one-time chair of the University's Governing Council.

Because information is sparse on the structure and operation of the Lagos endowment, and the public cannot access yearly financial accounts, the University of Lagos cannot be considered a model for other universities. What is evident is that the University has taken advantage of its location in Nigeria's commercial capital to create strings of income-generating programs to sustain its activities. Perhaps this has become the albatross of the University, shielding it from the reality of a properly planned and managed endowment.

In contrast, the University of Ibadan presents the only classic case of endowment in a Nigerian university. Perhaps, this is because it began as a college of the University of London and had the advantage of inheriting a structure that recognized endowment. The University's campaign to raise endowment funds dates as far back as the 1950s; however, it wasn't until 1973 that the University formally launched an endowment as part of its twenty-fifth anniversary celebration. An initial sum of ₦670,156.02 (US$4460) was raised during the celebrations and managed by a team comprising prominent alumni in the business world and representatives of the University. The endowment was later registered and incorporated in 1999. All the while, its managers invested in stocks and shares of more than 80 quoted companies. From 1988 to 1994, the University of Ibadan generated approximately ₦22.02 million from endowments and grants (Dawodu, 1999). By 2007, the University estimated the value of its endowment at ₦1 billion (US$6.6 million).

As an independently managed fund, the endowment makes annual appropriations to the University for its services. In 2000, the endowment fund made a profit of ₦20,659,563 and appropriated ₦5,000,000 to the University. In 2001, the fund made gains of ₦24,858,916 and appropriated ₦7,500,000 to the University (University of Ibadan Endowment Fund, 2001). In 2002, the fund made gains of ₦13,235,489 and appropriated ₦10,000,000 to the University targeted at the commencement of the Institution's ICT building (University of Ibadan Endowment Fund, 2002). The appropriations were modest, but the success of the endowment is that the fund is being sustained and profitably managed and its capital has been steadily growing.

Endowment of Professorial Chairs

The Petroleum Trust Development Fund (PTDF) was created to fund the training and education of Nigerians in the oil and gas industry. Its relevance is to serve as the vehicle for the development of critical indigenous human resource and technology to operate the petroleum and mining sector. It is funded from oil proceeds received by the Ministry of Energy. Its role is best appreciated against the backdrop of the petroleum sector being the backbone of the Nigerian economy, contributing over 90 percent of the country's foreign exchange earnings and over 80 percent of its Gross Domestic Product (GDP). The PTDF Universities' Endowment program is one of the measures devised to counter the petroleum industry's dependence on foreign technology and expertise for its operation. The PTDF also accommodates other educational intervention programs including Overseas and Local Scholarship Schemes and upgrade of ICT and other facilities in universities.

Eight universities have so far received the endowed professorial chairs: Ahmadu Bello University, Zaria; University of Nigeria, Nsukka; Usman Danfodio University, Sokoto; and the Universities of Benin, Ibadan, Jos, Port Harcourt and Maiduguri. The endowment provided each university with seed money in the sum of ₦60,000,000 (US$400,000). The total sum due to all the institutions was then invested with a professional fund manager, First Trustees Nigeria Limited (a subsidiary of one of Nigeria's foremost banks), and the annual yield from the investment has been used to support the chairs.

In 2006, the National Board of Trustees for the endowment approved an annual working budget of ₦15m for each university. In addition, the endowment comes with the condition of having an Endowment Management Committee in each institution. PTDF management has now increased the total endowed sum from the initial ₦360,000,000 for the first six institutions to one billion naira (US$6,666,000), an average of ₦125,000,000 (US$833,000) per chair (PTDF, 2007). After four years of operation, the management of PTDF asked for a program review team comprising resource persons from the oil and gas industry, government agencies and academics. One of the recommendations from the review is to further increase in the endowed sum.

Conclusion

Setting properly functional endowment funds appears to be a long way off in Nigerian universities, primarily because they have no lump sums to invest. Most importantly, there is a lack of vision on the part of leadership to begin the process of instituting the globally tested concept of endowment. Most university strategic plans do not envision this happening in the next few years. Until 2005, the criteria for the appointment of vice-chancellors did not include the ability to generate funds for institutional advancement. The implication is that for several years, vice chancellors were not required to have any skills in fundraising as this was not a key component of the vice chancellor's job. This accounted for the ad hoc or non-existing endowment culture.

Perhaps more serious is the poor understanding of the concept and operation of endowment. Key to the concept of endowment is the attention to growing the university's resources through economic investments while using part of the accruing profits to fund capital or recurrent projects and research. It is important to note that the principal of the endowment is not used for any purpose by the university, thereby allowing for the growth of funds for investment and ensuring a higher return on investment. Some of these investments may span real estate to capital market, depending on the volume of cash available for investment and the business proclivity of the university.

The PTDF model should be used by benefitting universities to kick-start their institutional endowments, but this is presently not the case. Whether the PTDF endowment is designed to deliberately stimulate creative funds management is uncertain. If and when the endowments emerge, competent personnel would be required to resource the operations of endowment offices or foundations. Time to begin preparing for staffing requirements within the context of global higher education framework is now. Alongside this would be the development of vibrant alumni groups to break the historically contrived systems of lost alumni where the universities were detached from their graduates in ways that are detrimental to the institutions. The few that have kept the relationships with their alumni have relied mostly on prominent alumni to the detriment of the larger group upon which endowment is grown. As the experience of the top leading universities in the world has shown, the future of higher education funding is endowment. If Nigerian universities hope to compete globally, they might as well start with the establishment of endowments, for the stability and autonomy it offers.

This chapter described aspects of private higher education in three African countries. In all three countries, it is evident that private higher education is expanding dramatically largely because of limited access in the public sector. However, there are differences in the institutional model across the three countries and important questions relating to equity of access, quality and government regulation.

REFERENCES

Adedeji, S.O. and R.O. Bamidele (2003). Economic Impact of Tertiary Education on Human Capital Development in Nigeria in Human Resource Development in Africa. Selected papers for the 2002 Annual Conference. Published by the Nigeria Economic Society (NES). Pp. 499-522.

Adedeji, S. O. (2007). Private Participation in the Provision of Basic Education in Nigeria: Options and Strategies. *African Journal of Historical Sciences in Education*. Vol. 3 No.1. Pp. 71–86.

Altbach, P.G (2005). Universities: Family Style, *International Higher Education*, 39 (Spring), pp. 10-12.

Baraka, Pakinaz (2007). "The Role of School Curricula in Citizenship Education for Sustainable Development in Egypt: Challenges and Key Strategies." *The Journal of Sociology and Education in Africa (JOSEA)*, Vol. 8, No. 2.

Baraka, Pakinaz. (2007). "Citizenship Education in Egyptian Public Schools: What values to Teach and in which Administrative and Political Contexts?" *Journal of Education for International Development* (JEID), Vol. 3, No.1.

Baraka, Pakinaz. (2007). "Policies of Public Participation in the Cost of Higher Education and Challenges of Implementation in Egypt (2007)." *Journal of Administrative Research*, Sadat Academy for Administrative Sciences, Vol. 4, No. 25.

Dawodu, Segun Toyin (1999). *Financing Higher Education in the Federal Republic of Nigeria: Developments and Trends.*

Interview with Professor Hatem El Bollock, the Head of the Supreme Council of Private Universities (SCU) in Egypt on 7/8/2009.

Jibril, Munzali and Obaje, Abdulkarim (2008). 'Nigeria', Higher Education in Africa: *The International Dimension,* ed. Teferra, Damtew and Knight, Jane. Centre for International Higher Education, Boston College & AAU, Ghana, 341.

Johnstone, D. Bruce (2009). Higher Education Finance and Cost-Sharing in Egypt. http://www.gse.buffalo.edu/org/IntHigherEdFinance/files/Country_Profiles/Africa/Egypt.pdf, p.11.

Kim, S. Gilani, Z., Landoni, P., Musisi, N. and Teixeira, P. (2007). 'Rethinking the Public- Private Mix in Higher Education: Global Trends and National Policy Challenges,' in Altabach P.G. and Peterson M.P. (Eds.) *Higher Education in the New Century: Global Challenges and Innovative Ideas.* Netherlands: UNESCO.

Levy, Daniel C. (2006).How Private Higher Education's Growth Challenges the New Institutionalism. Heinz-Dieter Meyer and Brian Rowan (Eds). The New Institutionalism in Education, Albany, State University of New York Press, pp. 143-61.

Mabizela, Mahlubi, Levy, Daniel C. and Otieno, Wycliffe (Eds.) 2007. Private Surge amid Public Dominance: Dynamics in the Private Provision of Higher Education in Africa (Special Issue). *Journal of Higher Education in Africa.* Vol. 5, Nos. 2, 3.

Ministry of Higher Education/Information and Documentation Centre. Egypt Information Portal Retrieved July 15, 2009 from http://www.eip.gov.eg/default.aspx.

Mugenda, O. (2009). Higher Education in Kenya Challenges and Opportunities. A Paper prepared for AHEC Scholars Meeting at the Serena Hotel, Nairobi, 30 March, 2009.

National Universities Commission (2007). *Presentation of Licences to New Private Universities in Nigeria.* December, Abuja.

Nwamuo, C. (2000). *Report of Study of Private Universities in Africa. Ghana.* Association of African Universities.

Odebero, O.S (2008). Equity in Access to University Education in Kenya through HELB Loans in Relation to Demand Supply and Effectiveness in Loan Recovery. Unpublished Ph.D. Thesis. Submitted to Egerton University, Njoro, Kenya.

Odebero, O.S. (forthcoming). An Introduction to Planning and Economics of Education: Challenges in Developing Countries and Innovative Ideas. Kakamega: Masinde Muliro University of Science and Technology.

Okuwa, B. O. (2007). Analysis of Households Willingness to Pay for Higher Education in Oyo Sate, Nigeria. An unpublished Ph.D. Thesis in the Department of Economics, University of Ibadan.

Pereira, Charmaine. (2007). *Gender in the Making of the Nigerian University System.* Oxford, James Currey, 110.

Petroleum Technology Development Fund (PTDF): The Journey So Far – Successes and Achievements (2007), Yaliam Press.

Poderis, Tony (2005). http://members4.boardhost.com/PNDtalk/msg/archive/38515.html. Reforms and Revitalization in Nigerian Universities: An Empirical Study of the South East Zone. http://www.herp-net.org/REVITALIZATION_OF_AFRICAN_HIGHER_ EDUCATION/Chapter%209.pdf.

UNESCO (2009). A New Dynamic: Private Higher Education, Svava Bjarnason, Kai-Ming Cheng, John, Fielden & others, UNESCO, World Conference on Higher Education, available on http://www.unesdoc.unesco.org/images/0018/001831/183174e.pdf, p.13.

University of Ibadan Endowment Fund Annual Reports and Accounts for the year ended 30th June 2002. http://www.uiadvancement.org/endowment/arac_2002.pdf.

University World News (2009), Nigeria: *Shift towards private universities,* 27 September.

World Bank (2008), Accelerating Catch-Up: Tertiary Education for Growth in Sub-Saharan Africa, Synopsis, Washington, D.C.

Chapter Five

Addressing Gender Inequality in Higher Education Through Targeted Institutional Responses: Field Evidence from Kenya and Nigeria

BY IBRAHIM OANDA, KENYATTA UNIVERSITY, AND
LILIAN-RITA AKUDOLU, NNAMDI AZIKIWE UNIVERSITY

Introduction

Over the last two decades, studies have documented the glaring gender inequalities that characterize access and participation in African higher education. Most of these studies show that globally, though enrollments in higher education institutions have increased, average rates of participation for those of the typical entrance age still remains low at 25 percent (UNESCO, 2009). For Sub-Saharan Africa, the participation rates in higher education remain among the lowest in the world, averaging less than six percent for most countries, although the region has experienced the highest rates of growth in terms of student enrollments (Morley, Leach and Lugg, 2008).

This growth in enrollments has, however, been accompanied by gender disparities in access and participation. Female enrollments and participation in higher education in most countries of Sub-Saharan Africa range between 34 and 38 percent for most countries. These disparities reflect the lower participation and transition rates of female students from secondary to higher education. Available data shows that though expansion in secondary enrollment has led to reductions in gender disparities in most regions, the disparities remain larger in secondary than in primary education (UNESCO, 2009).

Analysis of gender patterns of access to degree programs, retention and completion rates in most African countries reveal that institutions are admitting slightly more female students through affirmative programs or qualifying examinations. However, a higher percentage of this cohort are either placed in disciplines that have a lower premium in the labor market, are likely to drop out or take longer to complete their studies due to various gendered factors. Policy efforts to increase the percentage of female students in higher education and address gender-based barriers have so far focused on selective demand and supply factors. The increase in the number of higher education institutions has also increased places for female students, though this has not been the target. In fact, studies show that affirmative action policies and the increase in the number of higher education institutions have not comprehensively addressed the gender barriers that characterize access and participation in higher education.

Of greater concern is emerging evidence that despite the nominal increase in the number of female students accessing the institutions, the social class composition from where such female students are drawn has largely remained the same and restricted to those who can afford the rising costs of higher education (Morley, Leach and Lugg, 2008). This means that existing affirmative action policies as designed and implemented by the institutions have not addressed other intersecting barriers that limit the possibilities for many women to access and participate in higher education. The needed institutional responses and initiatives are those that go beyond access and address the gendered cultures of higher education institutions, provide practical support mechanisms that enhance chances of retention and completion, and contribute to deepening gender responsive policies in higher education institutions. This chapter provides a comparative review of gender patterns of participation in higher education in Africa, with emphasis on Kenya and Nigeria, discusses the 'new gendered zones' of exclusion in African higher education and documents some on-going, institutional-level interventions to address the challenges.

Transition of Female Students from Secondary to Higher Education in Africa

Throughout Sub-Saharan Africa, the percentage of female students accessing and participating in all levels of education is increasing. Successful international campaigns for gender equity in education and social development coupled with adoption of gender responsive policies at national levels have contributed to this increasing trend in enrollments. Progress achieved in primary and secondary education influence access and participation patterns in higher education. Data from current surveys show that whereas most countries in Sub-Saharan Africa registered primary school net enrollment rates (NERs) of more than 70 percent, half of the countries have not achieved gender parity in enrollments, with fewer females enrolling and completing the primary school cycle (UNESCO, 2009). About 58 percent of countries in Sub-Saharan Africa have differences in primary school participation between males and females that are smaller than six percent (Lewin, 2007). Of concern, however, is that increased access and participation of female students at the primary school level is not necessarily translating to higher enrollments at secondary and higher education levels. Overall, the transition rate from primary to secondary schools in Sub-Saharan Africa was 62 percent in 2006, while that of female students was 57 percent (UNESCO, 2009). Lewin (2007) shows that in most countries of the region, gender equity measured by the Gender Parity Index (GPI) at primary and secondary levels varies considerably. The GPI is more favorable to girls at primary than at secondary levels in almost all the countries of the region except six (Lewin, 2007).

Generally, most of the countries in Sub-Saharan Africa have female transition rates to secondary education of less than 50 percent. Exceptions include Kenya and Nigeria, which record high female enrollment and participation rates in primary and lower secondary education, but high attrition rates in upper secondary education and transition to university. Available statistics show that by 2008, Kenya had achieved a transition rate from primary to secondary of 58.5 percent for males and 61.1 percent for females (Kenya, Ministry of Education, 2009). This indicates higher participation rates for females at the primary level. However, the GER for females at the secondary level stood at 38.8 percent compared to 46.3 percent for males, while the NER was 27.9 percent for females compared to 38.8 percent for males within the same period (Kenya Ministry of Education, 2009). These show the high rates of attrition for female students in secondary schooling and indicate an even lower transition rate to higher education. For Nigeria, UNESCO statistics indicate that the country had primary school completion rates of 81 percent for males and 66 percent for females by 2006 (UNESCO Statistics, 2006). However, GER for secondary schools stood at 38 percent for males and 32 percent for females within the same period (UNESCO, 2006).

In addition, the transition rate of female students from secondary to university-level education is much lower than the transition rates from primary to secondary in most countries of Sub-Saharan Africa. In Kenya, for example, in 2005 female enrollment in public universities stood at an average of 35.3 percent of total enrollment compared to 46 percent at the secondary school level in 2005 (Republic of Kenya, 2006). Female students constituted an average of 32.9 percent of total enrollment in the seven universities studied in the Pathways research project in East Africa (Griffin, 2007). In Nigeria, female students comprised 31.2 percent of the students enrolled in 23 federal universities (Pereira, 2007), and in Rwanda, from 2001 to 2005, they constituted an average of only 26.8 percent of students enrolled in public universities (Huggins and Randell, 2007). Data for the overall tertiary education sector for Kenya and Nigeria show that Kenya had a gross female enrollment of 38 percent and Nigeria had 41 percent by 2006 (UNESCO, 2006). Hence, female enrollments in the public university sector for Kenya and Nigeria were much lower compared with the overall data for the tertiary sector as a whole.

The trends observed in most Sub-Saharan African countries require that interventions to expand access of female students to higher education should address factors that contribute to higher rates of female attrition in secondary schools. Indeed, attrition rates remain a critical problem despite increasing gross enrollment rates. In addition, primary/secondary transition is a striking problem. In the case of Kenya and Nigeria, data show that trends toward exclusion of female students from accessing higher education or channelling them to gendered disciplines in higher education begins at the upper secondary level. It is here that the majority of students either drop out or underperform due to socio-economic factors.

Comparative studies and data have documented gendered patterns of access and participation by female students in Sub-Saharan Africa. However, comparative data on transition and participation in higher education is not as comprehensive. A study by Morley, et al. (2006) on gender equity in selected commonwealth universities shows that the culture of higher education institutions deepens gender inequities. The study documents four themes that have dominated literature within the commonwealth on this matter. These are 1) descriptive accounts of the underrepresentation of women in higher education, where recent literature has examined the access and participation patterns of female students in science and technology programs in higher education institutions; 2) the socio-economic and material conditions that characterize and limit female access to higher education; 3) strategies for inclusion; and 4) the relationship between access and wider socio-economic transformations. The study points out that while government-initiated policies within most commonwealth countries have led to an increase in the number of women accessing higher education institutions, the manner by which the institutions have introduced and implemented the policies has not redistributed access opportunities equitably among all the social groups. As evidenced in Table 5.1, there is a common trend in the percentage of women accessing educational opportunities within the various levels of the education ladder.

TABLE 5.1: PROPORTION OF WOMEN ENROLLED IN PRIMARY, SECONDARY AND TERTIARY EDUCATION, 2000 – 2001

	Nigeria	South Africa	Tanzania	Uganda*
Primary	42.9	49	50	48
Secondary	47	52	45	39
Tertiary	39.9	53	24	34

Source: UNESCO, Institute of Statistics Global Education Digest 2003, as quoted in Morley, et al., 2006, p. 2

Access, Participation and Completion Patterns for Female Students to Higher Education

The key determinant of access patterns for female students to higher education institutions are performance and transition rates from primary and secondary schools respectively. In Nigeria, access to higher education depends on a candidate's performance in the competitive examinations organized by the Joint Admissions and Matriculation Board (JAMB). Female enrollments in Nigeria universities for 2000-2001, 2001-2002, 2002-2003, 2003-2004 and 2004-2005 academic sessions stood at 35 percent, 38 percent, 38 percent, 32 percent and 36 percent, respectively (Federal Office of Statistics, Nigeria, 2007). In the same vein, female enrollments in Kenya

Public Universities stood at 54 percent, 53 percent, 54 percent, 52 percent and 60 percent for 2003-2004, 2004-2005, 2005-2006, 2006-2007 and 2007-2008 academic sessions respectively.

In the case of Nigeria, the percentage of female enrollment is often higher in states from the Southern zone than in states from the Northern zone. A study by Omoike (2009) involving universities in the south shows that most of the universities have female enrollments above 40 percent. In fact, in the 2002 admissions, Akwa-Ibom State recorded 50.1 percent for females compared to 49.8 percent for males (Omoike, 2009).

Though no similar study is available for university admission in the north, the rate of female university admission is much lower in the Northern zone than in the Southern zone. For instance, the summary of higher education enrollments in Jigawa State (a Northern state) shows 89 percent male and 11 percent female for 2005-2006, 88 percent male and 12 percent female for 2006-2007, as well as 88 percent male and 12 percent female for 2007-2008 (Federal Republic of Nigeria, Jigawa, State Education Strategic Plan, 2008). The data on Nigeria indicates that the rates of female participation in higher education differ according to states and regions with the Northern states having lower rates than the Southern states. Consequently, policy interventions to promote female access to education are more pronounced in the Northern states than in the Southern states. For instance, all six target states under UNICEF Africa Females' Education Initiative (AGEI) are from the Northern zone.

The Nigeria Federal Ministry of Education (FME) notes that one of the challenges to access to tertiary education in Nigeria is inability of prospective entrants to possess the basic admission requirements of having credit in five subjects including English and mathematics in the Senior Secondary Certificate Examination (SSCE) or its equivalent. The FME maintains, "Only 23.7 percent of candidates passed SSCE with credit in Mathematics and English between 2000 -2004 (Federal Ministry of Education, 2009, 56)."

In Kenya, the performance of females in the secondary school, Kenya Certificate of Secondary Education (KCSE), form four examination is a key factor to their access to university education and admission to professional degree courses. Data collected show how performance in the KCSE examination continues to adversely impact the number of females joining universities and their admission into various degree programs. The insistence of universities in using KCSE performance as the singular indicator/determinant for admission accentuates disparities in access between male and female students. Table 5.2 below summarizes trends from Kenya related to female performance in the qualifying examination within a four-year period (2004-2008). Analysis of the data corroborates that of Morley, et al. (2006) with regard to the percentage of female students who attain qualifying grades for admission to the universities.

Year	Candidature	A	A-	B+	B	B-	C+
2004	Total No of Candidates Scoring Grade	544	3,025	6,660	10,764	15,859	21,369
	% of Female	34.5	29.65	32.0	35.62	38.9	42.3
2005	Total No of Candidates Scoring Grade	611	3,947	7,923	12,475	17,712	25,362
	% of Female	29.29	28.63	29.72	34.81	39.06	42.6
2006	Total No of Candidates Scoring Grade	1165	4280	7369	11,217	16,102	22,971
	% of Female	33.9	32.1	34.2	37.1	40.0	43.3
2007	Total No of Candidates Scoring Grade	1157	5094	9129	14,363	21,875	30,516
		1157	5094	9129	14,363	21,875	30,516
	% of Female	30.3	24.1	28.0	33.5	39.5	43.4
2008	Total No of Candidates Scoring Grade	817	5161	9365	13,369	18,423	25,514
	% of Female	40.1	33.8	34.4	35.8	40.1	42.5

Source: Kenya National Examinations Council, performance statistics for various years.

In Kenya, candidates qualifying to study science, mathematics and technology-based courses have to score between grade A and A- in the form four qualifying examination. The examination does not, however, provide for compensatory mechanisms for disadvantaged students such as females. Consequently, as shown in Table 5.2, the cumulative percentages of female students who score above grade B+ is more than that of those who score within the A and A-, which means that chances of a majority of women joining the professional courses are limited.

The data from Kenya and Nigeria mirror participation trends in other Sub-Saharan countries indicating a consistent stagnation of female access to universities fluctuating between 35 and 40 percent, with the average mean being 35 percent. There is also another dimension of access, though, that characterizes inequities in access to higher education by female students in Sub-Saharan Africa, i.e., access to science and technology and other professional programs in the universities. Transition of female students from secondary level to science, mathematics and technology-based academic programs in higher education institutions is particularly lower than transition for males. Low transition for female students is pronounced in engineering and other technical courses.

In Nigeria, for example, in the 1999-2000 session, there were zero enrollments for females in technical courses such as mechanical engineering, plumbing, fabrication and welding (Federal Ministry of Education, Nigeria, 2005). Similarly, in Nigeria in 1999-2000, female students constituted only 27 percent of those in science and technology programs in the universities. Moreover, while lack of role models for secondary school female students is cited in the literature as part of the reasons contributing to low achievement in science and mathematics courses at secondary schools, science education programs at the universities do not seem to attract high number of female students. In Kenya, data from 2002-2003 to 2004-2005 show that out of the 1,815 bachelor of education students who specialized in science, mathematics and technology-related subjects, only 470 or 25.9 percent were female, representing only 17.5 percent of the female students enrolled in education (Bunyi, 2006).

Female students from marginalized backgrounds are even more disadvantaged particularly in the critical fields of science and technology. Female disadvantage is more apparent at the post-graduate level. In the case of Kenya, data tracking access, participation and completion of female students in science and mathematics programs in higher education is not comprehensively up-to-date. Institutions usually capture student profiles based on gender, but not by area of study. However, studies on these themes reveal that female students are not only the minority in terms of access to education (see Table 5.3 below), but fewer enter science and mathematics-based programs and an even higher percentage of them fail to complete these programs compared to their male counterparts (Griffin, 2007). This is because children from poor/marginalized backgrounds (most of whom are female) generally attend poorly resourced schools; they do not perform as well as the others even when they meet the university admission criteria and for those who access universities in different academic programs, university environments and academic programs have not been made gender responsive. To the contrary, female students often encounter gender-biased environments and course content that results in drop out or underachievement (Griffin 2007). Since admission into professional courses is also competitive and dependent on performance in specific cluster subjects, most female students end up being placed in general Arts and Humanities courses.

Table 5.3 shows enrollment trends by gender and course at the University of Nairobi for the academic years 1996-97 to 2004-05. Though this data is not up-to-date, it serves to illustrate the pattern of female students' restricted access to science and mathematics-based academic programs.

TABLE 5.3: ENROLLMENT TRENDS BY GENDER AND COURSE AT THE UNIVERSITY OF NAIROBI

Course/ Degree	1996/97		1998/99		2000/01		2002/03		2004/05		Total %	
	M	F	M	F	M	F	M	F	M	F	M	F
Architecture & Engineering	201	1,478	229	1,333	219	1,404	235	1,498	277	1,546	14.4	85.6
Agric/ food technology	144	695	190	660	143	455	156	491	197	570	22.6	77.4
Veterinary medicine	43	201	30	177	45	188	54	233	88	323	18.4	81.6
Biological/ physical sciences	299	1187	244	989	292	977	381	1,106	492	1,313	23.2	76.8
Education	515	1064	587	947	591	900	527	836	651	947	41.2	58.8
Health Sciences	275	771	322	724	398	717	368	748	393	716	32.2	67.8
Humanities	1,444	3,271	1,338	2,689	1,486	2,858	1,692	2,563	2,504	3,201	36.4	63.6
Computer science	16	87	16	112	15	122	13	144	19	121	12.4	87.6
Total	2,937	8,754	2,956	7,631	3,189	7,621	3,426	7,619	4,621	8,737	29.8	70.2
Percentages	11.691		10,587		10,810		11,045		13,358		23.6	76.4
Average Female %	27	73	24	76	26	74	26	74	29	71	26.4	73.6

Source: Griffin, 2007

As indicated by statistics from Table 5.3, female composition as a total of the students admitted to the institution and as a percentage of the students in key science and mathematics-based courses remained low within the period. The highest total of female composition was in the 2004-05 academic year when they constituted 29 percent of the students enrolled. In terms of courses enrolled, cumulatively females were concentrated in education (41.2 percent) and humanities (36.4 percent). Their enrollment in science and mathematics courses remained low, averaging below 20 percent, other than in health sciences, which recorded 32.2 percent.

However, since these statistics are not aggregated by socio-economic and regional considerations, one is not able to comment conclusively on the equity implications. Besides, the slightly higher enrollment of females in health and sciences may be attributed to their high enrollment in nursing sciences. However, data in Table 5.4 capture information up to the 2004-05 academic year. It serves to indicate trends in female enrollment in science and mathematics courses. A similar trend exists in Nigeria, as can be seen from data on student enrollment by discipline presented in Table 4 below for the University of Ibadan.

TABLE 5.4: STUDENT ENROLLMENTS BY DISCIPLINE AND GENDER AT THE UNIVERSITY OF IBADAN, NIGERIA 2004 – 2005

Faculty	Female	Percentages	Male	Percentages	Total
Arts	656	51.7	614	48.3	1,270
Social Sciences	477	36.6	828	63.4	1,305
Law	208	38.7	329	61.3	557
Science	248	36.3	1138	63.7	1,786
Technology	120	11.5	923	88.5	1,043
Agriculture and Forestry	473	42.6	637	57.4	1,110
Basic Medical Sciences	129	40.8	187	59.2	316
Clinical Sciences	464	41.5	655	58.5	1,119
Dentistry	59	44.0	75	56.0	134
Pharmacy	120	56.6	92	43.4	212
Vet Medicine	210	38.7	332	61.3	542
Education	682	50.8	658	49.1	1,340
Public Health	67	55.4	54	44.6	121
Total	4,313	39.8	6,522	60.2	10,835

Source: Odejide, *Feminist Africa*, 2007: 46

Table 5.4 illustrates trends in the limited access of female students to professional degree courses in Nigeria. From this example, the percentage of female admission is highest in pharmacy (56.6 percent) and lowest in science (36.3 percent) and technology (11.5 percent).

A related issue is the percentage of female students who enroll and successfully complete science and mathematics-based courses. Again, comprehensive statistics for all the public universities in Kenya, showing rates of retention by gender in science and mathematics academic programs, are not available. Overall, there are studies pointing to a higher rate of female dropout from universities compared to male students. At Moi University, one of the public universities, 4.6 percent of female students dropped out compared to 0.3 percent male students between the 1999-2000 and 2003-04 academic years. In the school of medicine, the male dropout rate was 13 percent compared to 21.3 percent for females within the same period (Griffin, 2007). This shows that female students are not only fewer in terms of enrollment in science and math courses, but their completion rates are also lower compared to those of male students. Again, if this data is aggregated by socio-economic profiles, then a clear picture emerges of how expanding higher education institutions in Africa are creating new zones of exclusion for female students.

Data from Kenya showing the percentage of females working in key research institutes can be used as a proxy indicator of the nature and percentage of female students successfully completing post-graduate programs within time. The data, compiled by African Women in Agricultural Research and Development (AWARD), reveal that in 2008 five of Kenya's largest agricultural research agencies together employed 967 professional staff, of which 25 or 26 percent were female. The share of female professional staff increased from 21 percent in 2000 to 26 percent in 2008 (ASTI/AWARD, 2008). This increase is largely due to an increase in the share of professional women employed at the Kenyan Agricultural Research Institute (KARI) during the eight-year period. In contrast, the share of female professional staff decreased from 33 to 25 percent at the University of Nairobi's Faculty of Agriculture, and remained low and constant, at about 15 percent, at the Faculty of Veterinary Sciences (ASTI/AWARD, 2008). Furthermore, of the professional staff at the agricultural research and higher education agencies, 22 percent of those with Ph.D. degrees, 28 percent of those with M.S. degrees and 38 percent of those with B.S. degrees were female (ASTI/AWARD, 2008).

The data further reveal that in 2007, female students accounted for about 32 percent of the total student population in agriculture and veterinary sciences at the University of Nairobi and Jomo Kenyatta University of Agriculture and Technology (JKUAT) (ASTI/AWARD, 2008). Notably, there was a relatively higher proportion of women among the total number of students undertaking Ph.D. degrees, but a relatively low proportion of female students actually graduated. In total, 39 women and 55 men were enrolled in Ph.D. degree training in 2007, while two female and 15 male students graduated that year (ASTI/AWARD, 2008). This data shows three trends related to female students participating in and completing science and technology courses. First, the number of female students decreases as they proceed into higher academic levels. Second, completion and transition rates for female students are lower compared to male students. Third, female students take longer to complete their graduate programs compared to male students. More importantly, there is no indication that female students perform differently compared to males. This is perhaps a strong reason to advocate for institutional interventions to enable female students to complete their programs on time.

In a study examining democratic access to higher education in Ghana and Tanzania, Morley, Leach and Rosemary Lugg (2008) contend that policy interventions aimed at widening access to higher education should show that increased participation rates in public and private higher education reflect greater social inclusion. They argue that students in higher education in Sub-Saharan Africa are predominantly male, with female students represented in much smaller numbers and concentrated in low status, non-science subjects. Both female and male students are also largely from socio-economically advantaged backgrounds and from elite secondary schools. Students' retention, performance and completion rates reflect this unequal access, which relates directly to access to social and economic positions of influence in society. In the case of female students, considering all these factors is important when designing alternative affirmative policies for widening access.

Interventions to Address and Enhance Female Access and Participation

Students who qualify can access higher education opportunities in Kenya through two avenues. The first is through regular admissions where students qualify for government loans, scholarships and bursaries. The majority of students who qualify through this mode, however, are those from high cost public schools and private academies, which indicates that regular admissions are skewed toward students from higher socio-economic income groups. The second avenue is through private sponsorship. These students pay tuition fees and associated higher education costs at market rates as a requirement for admission. The implication here is that both access avenues work to the advantage of students from high socio-economic income groups. If gender and socio-economic factors are correlated with these trends, then gender bias in favor of male students is evident.

Affirmative action has been the policy most used to increase female access to higher education in Kenya. This is also true of most countries in Sub-Saharan Africa. However, as evidence from Kenya shows, affirmative action has certain limitations. Affirmative action policy benefits qualified female students who cannot get admission to the institutions due to competitive access requirements. While this slightly increases female enrollments in the institutions, it does not ensure their entry into professional science and math-based courses. The policy also does not require higher education institutions to initiate linkages with secondary schools in order to address the low transition rates of female students from secondary schools to higher education institutions. Developing such links will be critical to address the low transition rates and enrollment of female students in science and math-related courses. As UNESCO (2009) documents, much of the gender disparities evident in higher education in Africa stem from access and participation dynamics in primary and secondary schools. Affirmative policy again needs to go beyond just increasing the number of female students to understanding other socio-economic factors that limit female student participation in higher education. Only then can the institutions develop equity-based affirmative interventions for female students.

The current affirmative policy not only disregards the socio-economic status of students, but also does not have the mechanisms of getting students into professional programs. As studies have shown, various factors besides gender determine access to higher education in most African countries. These other factors are place of residence, parents' level of education, family income and ethnicity or religion. Both female and male students are also largely from socio-economically advantaged backgrounds and from elite secondary schools. Student retention, performance and completion rates reflect unequal access (Morley, et al., 2008). Holistic affirmative programs should therefore address all these bases of gender inequities in higher education.

It is evident from Table 5.2 that affirmative action benefited approximately four percent of the eligible female cohort. Since the socio-economic status of those who benefited is disregarded, it is possible that affirmative action in Kenya is not a measure for equitable distribution of access opportunities for women in Kenya's higher education system. The intervention merely allows female access, and students are placed mostly into general degree programs. The universities have not developed any institutional interventions to enhance the students' academic qualifications to access professional degree programs. In Nigeria, current admission status is "between 33-39 percent in favour of females" (Federal Ministry of Education, 2009:58).

Nigeria has no concessional admission for any category of students and relies completely on the JAMB-controlled admissions. The federal and state governments in Nigeria, with the assistance of some international agencies like UNICEF, have been initiating actions to close gender gaps and increase female access to education. Most of these externally assisted policy interventions are geared toward promoting female access to primary and secondary school education. In 2001, Nigeria joined the UNICEF Africa Females' Education Initiative (AGEI), which aims among other things at using the avenues of public awareness campaign, rallies and seminars to raise national awareness of female education. To demonstrate the commitment of UNICEF to the acceleration of female education in Nigeria, the organization made female education a priority in its 2005-2007 strategic plan. The Nigeria Country Office (NCO, 2007) reports that in July 2003, the Federal Government of Nigeria (FGN) and UNICEF launched the Strategy for Acceleration of Females' Education in Nigeria (SAGEN); this project resulted in the launching of Females' Education Project (GEP), a joint initiative between FGN, DFID and UNICEF aimed at eliminating gender disparity in all levels of education no later than 2015. Evaluation of the GEP program in 2006 revealed improvement in the percentage of females attending school. According to the NCO report, female enrollment increased by 15 percent with more than 25 percent actual attendance, indicating that the GEP resulted in about 12,000 females attending schools more regularly than before. The report affirms that gender gaps were reduced to about two-thirds of what they used to be. While acknowledging that the gender gap has narrowed from 12 to ten points, the NCO affirms the existence of wide variations of gender gap in female access to education across the states in Nigeria with the worst situations existing in states in the North Central and North West geo-political zones.

In an effort to achieve the goals of Education for All (EFA), most of the Northern state governments have instituted a free lunch policy, which involves not only giving pupils' free lunch in schools, but also the provision of free writing and reading materials, uniforms and textbooks. However, these initiatives are increasing female access to education at the primary and secondary school levels. They have not remarkably increased female access to higher education in these states. The percentage of females gaining admission into higher institutions is still low. For instance, in Niger State which is one of the states in the North Central geo-political zone of Nigeria where the free lunch policy is being implemented, the state government recognizes "gender imbalance at all levels of education" as a challenge (Niger State of Nigeria, 2007:42). The document reveals that to face this challenge, the state government not only supports the UNICEF GEP project, but also offers free education to females at all levels of education. In addition, to ensure that lack of financial resources does not prevent any qualified student from taking external examinations at the end of senior secondary education, the government pays their examination fees directly to the relevant examination bodies such as the West African Examinations Council (WAEC) and the National Examinations Council (NECO). Despite these institutional interventions, the overall data on enrollment patterns in Nigeria public universities show that in higher education, female enrollment in science and mathematics-based programs is still low.

The Need for Widening Access Coupled with Redistribution of Opportunity

The number of female students entering universities as private students has actually increased. This increase has not, however, been based on broad social access criteria. Rather, it represents an increasing number of female workers and females from wealthy families who are now accessing university education locally (Oanda, Fatuma and Wesonga, 2008) and has masked the plight of poor female students and female high school graduates who cannot access university education. Even when women and other disadvantaged students from poor backgrounds access universities, either through the regular or parallel programs, there are no institutional programs to support the academic progress of these students.

Second, affirmative policies implemented from the 1990s for females and students from disadvantaged backgrounds are not being enhanced because of the false picture created by the above growth in enrollments. Third, institutions have not put in place mechanisms to help them cope with the stress of academic life and complete their studies. Emerging evidence shows that more of these students fail their examinations and some drop out before they complete their courses or take longer to complete them. Data collected for this study in Kenyan public universities showed that Kenyan female students enjoy little support to complete their academic programs. Female students from poor backgrounds in need of financial help drop out of university after being involved in relationships that end in motherhood. Many female students under such circumstances find it expensive and time-consuming minding their babies while attending classes. The introduction of cost-sharing has left young women from poor socio-economic backgrounds disadvantaged. In Kenya, the public universities have included in their strategic plans and mission statements a reaffirmed a commitment to improving student welfare services as a benchmark to improving the quality of the learning environment.

One of the consequences of not coupling widening access policies with other support mechanisms is that implementation of the policies does not conclusively address gender inequality in terms of access and participation in higher education. Affirmative policies, such as those implemented in Kenya, do not critically consider the underlying constraints. Hence, rather than address inequities in access and participation in higher education, they introduce an alternative form of disparity. This creates new bottlenecks for the targeted students in regards to their participation and completion of academic programs. Thus, institutional interventions need to focus beyond numbers and target initiatives that not only increase female student participation, but also enroll them into science, mathematics and technology academic programs. Some institutions have introduced such interventions, but they need to complement them by other support services. For example, Nigeria allocates 60 percent of admissions to higher education for science, technology and mathematics disciplines (Morley et al., 2006: 82). At Kenyatta University, a donor-funded research project has been running in the last five years targeted at enhancing access for females in secondary schools to science and mathematics-based courses in the universities.

In Kenya, current policies in the education sector tend to acknowledge the need for a broad based affirmative policy, linking admission of students to skills needed for socio-economic development. The 2005 session paper for the education sector notes that there still exists inadequate capacity for access to universities, that there is a mismatch between skills taught at universities and demands of industry, a continuing imbalance between students studying science and arts-based courses and persisting regional and gender disparities in access to the institutions (Republic of Kenya, 2005). The public universities have also reaffirmed a commitment to improving student welfare services as a benchmark to improving the quality of the learning environment in their strategic plans and mission statements. Kenyatta University has, for instance, emphasized that student welfare services play a critical part in ensuring student completion rates and strengthens the quality of counselling and pastoral care (Kenyatta University, 2005:56). The Nigerian Federal Ministry of Education has reaffirmed commitments to eliminate or reduce disparities in gender participation in tertiary education (FME, 2009). In this regard, one of the turnaround strategies to be adopted by the Nigerian government is to "ensure continuous gender-focused education programmes by considering policies such as quota-based admission, fees reduction, scholarships and other incentives based on gender (FME, 2009:58)."

In the public universities in Kenya and Nigeria, some level of institutionalization of academic and social mentorship programs for students is taking place. The public universities also have the traditional guidance and counseling units, but student numbers have overstretched the services and do not focus on gender-specific concerns. Since universities do not profile students and lectures, it is difficult to develop services geared toward individual student needs. Besides, the guidance and counseling services do not have an academic component, but gear more toward addressing disciplinary problems among students. It is imperative institutions adopt holistic approaches when designing interventions to increase female access to higher education. This will require that higher education institutions forge linkages with secondary schools, develop programs for enhancing female participation in science and mathematics and enhance mentoring and academic advising to increase the rates of female participation and completion, especially in science and mathematics-based programs.

In the long-term, universities need to establish linkages with secondary schools, especially those for female students, as a strategy to strengthen the teaching of mathematics and sciences. As a short-term measure, universities can replicate the interventions of the University of Dar es Salaam that have increased female access into the university and entry into science and technology-based courses. The University has operated a Pre-entry Programme (PEP) in science and mathematics for female students since 1997, first as a pilot scheme under a Teacher Education Assistance in Mathematics and Science (TEAMS) project managed collaboratively by the Faculty of Education and the Faculty of Science. The emphasis of the program is to provide bridging courses for female students who do not qualify to enter university, enabling them to qualify and join science and mathematics-oriented courses. The Ministry of Education and the University have created a dedicated budget to ensure long-term sustainability of the program. The program is sustained through advocacy for third-party sponsorship by local and external organizations. In this regard, positive response has been received from Sida/SAREC (Sweden), NORAD (Norway) and Carnegie Corporation of New York (USA). Since 2001-02, the annual female student intake has been boosted by guaranteed sponsorship to 50 eligible female applicants by the University's Female Undergraduate Scholarship Programme (FUSP), created in partnership with the Carnegie Corporation and guaranteed for a period of nine years to 2009-10 (Luhanga and Mashalla, 2005).

Nevertheless, interventions to increase access and participation must be accompanied by other welfare support services for female students to ensure their persistence and completion. Since poverty and other socio-economic factors determine female participation in higher education, increased access and financial aid policies should complement each other. Institutions such as Kenyatta University have a student aid office that assists students from less privileged backgrounds to get through college. However, identifying needy students readily is hindered by the fact that most higher education institutions in Africa do not have in place policies profiling students in terms of socio-economic background. Again, the fact that government budgets for higher education do not force institutions to commercialize their activities limits the financial outlays they have to redress the situation of female students who are needy.

More importantly, it is imperative that institutions inculcate a culture of academic mentoring and advising as part of their academic programs. Currently, most institutions do not consider the services as core to the academic culture and offer them on a voluntary basis. In others, what exists are the traditional guidance and counseling services, which sometimes only reach a few students, often when it is too late to positively intervene in a student's academic progress. Consequently, given the rapid institutional expansion in enrollments that has taken place, the number of academic staff trained to act as academic mentors and advisors is inadequate. The institutions should explore strategies to address such gaps, including the use of ICT for virtual mentoring and advising.

Conclusion

Higher education is critical to development and poverty alleviation. However, in most of Africa, equity considerations have not accompanied expansion of higher education institutions. Female students from poor backgrounds are not only accessing the institutions in fewer numbers, but they are also finding it difficult to enroll in science and mathematics-based courses. National and institutional policies articulated to increase access have most often not considered the gendered dynamics involved in accessing and participating in higher education by female students.

The discussion here shows that equity interventions have not accompanied policies for expanding access to the institutions. Instead, such interventions have had three limitations. First, interventions have not been comprehensive and holistic enough to enhance participation and transition from basic education to higher education in a manner that the two levels can synergize each other. Higher education policies for widening participation of female students target only those who have finished secondary schooling and have no linkages to basic and higher education institutions. Second, policy interventions have targeted quantitative increases in female enrollment in higher education rarely addressing some of the qualitative gendered contexts in higher education institutions that circumvent female retention and completion. Policies have inadvertently created gendered higher education contexts resulting in 'new frontiers of exclusion.' Third, there has been limited theorization of access, not only in Nigeria and in Kenya, but also generally in Sub-Saharan Africa. Treating women as a seamless category ends up giving women from higher socio-economic backgrounds enhanced chances of accessing higher education while widening the gap for women from poor socio-economic backgrounds who cannot even complete secondary education, let alone access higher education. It is therefore critically important that policies targeting widening participation for female students also ensure that disadvantaged female students access such opportunities.

REFERENCES

Abiola, Odejide (2007). 'What can a Woman Do', Being a Woman in a Nigerian University.' Feminist Africa, Issue 8, pp. 42-89.

ASTI/AWARD (2008). Women's Participation in Agricultural Research and Higher Education: Kenya Fact Sheet, *International Food Policy Research Institute*, Washington, USA/ Viale delle Terme di. Caracalla, Italy

Bunyi, G. W. (2006*). Gender Equity in Higher Education in Kenya.* A background paper prepared for the Public Universities Inspection Board, Nairobi, Kenya.

Federal Ministry of Education (2009). Roadmap for the Nigerian Education Sector: Consultative Draft, Abuja, Federal Republic of Nigeria.

Federal Ministry of Education (2007). Statistics of Education in Nigeria: 1999-2005. Abuja, Statistics and NEMIS Branch, Federal Ministry of Education Nigeria.

Federal Republic of Nigeria (2008.) Jigawa State Education Strategic Plan (SESP) 2009- 2018, Draft.

Griffin, Anne-Marie (2007). Education Pathways in East Africa: Scaling a Difficult Terrain, Kampala, Association for the Advancement of Higher Education and Development (AHEAD), Kampala, Uganda.

Huggins, A. & Randell, S. (2007). 'Gender Equality in Education in Rwanda: What is Happening to Our Girls?' Paper presented at the South African Association of Women Graduates Conference on "Drop-outs from School and Tertiary Studies: What is Happening to our Girls?" Cape Town, May 2007.

Ibrahim, Oanda, Chege, Fatuma & Wesonga, Daniel (2008). Privatization and Private Higher Education in Kenya: Implications for Access, Equity and Knowledge Production. CODESRIA, Dakar Senegal.

Kenya, Ministry of Education (2009). Ministry of Education, EMIS Statistics.

Kenyatta University, (2005). Strategic and Vision Plan, 2005-2015.

Lewin, Keith (2007). Improving Access, Equity and Transition in Education: Creating a Research Agenda. CREATE, Research Monograph No. 1.

Luhanga, M.L. and Mashalla, Y.J.S. (2005). Reforms and Innovations in Higher Education: A Reflection on the Initiatives and Lessons at the University of Dar es Salaam in Tanzania, 1994-2004. Paper prepared for the Nuffic Conference 'A Changing Landscape', The Hague, 23-25 Ma.

Morley, L., Leach, F. and Lugg, R. (2008). 'Democratizing Higher Education in Ghana and Tanzania: Opportunity Structures and Social Inequalities.' International Journal of Educational Development 29(1): 56–64.

Morley, L., Gunawardena, C., Kwesiga, J., Lihamba, A., Odejide, A., Shackleton, L. and Sorhaindo, A. (2006). *Gender Equity in Selected Commonwealth Universities.* Research Report No. 65, London, Department of International Development (DFID).

Nigeria Country Office (2007). Information Sheet: Girls' Education. Accessed 2nd March 2009 at http://www.unicef.org/wcaro/WCARO-Nigeria-FactSheets-Girls Education.

Omoike, Don (2009). Sensitizing the Female in University Admission in South-South Geo-Political Zone for Assurance of Sustainable Development in Nigeria. Accessed 11th October, 2009 at http://ozelacademy.com/EJES-v1n2-Omoike.pdf.

Pereira, C. (2007). *Gender in the Making of the Nigerian University System.* Ibadan: Heinemann Educational Books.

Republic of Kenya (2006). *Transformation of Higher Education and Training in Kenya to Secure Kenya's Development in the Knowledge Economy. Report of the Public Universities Inspection Board.*

UNESCO (2009). *EPA Monitoring Report: Overcoming Inequality: Why Governance Matters.* UNESCO Publishing/Oxford University Press.

UNESCO (2006). *EFA Global Monitoring Report 2007: Strong foundations; Early childhood care and education*, Paris, UNESCO.

UNICEF (2009). Girls Education in Nigeria. Accessed May 20th http://bellecollege.edu/ liberlarts/sir/images/ Nigeriafinal.pdf.

Chapter Six

ADDRESSING ACCESS AND SUCCESS ISSUES IN HIGHER EDUCATION WITH A SPECIAL FOCUS ON TEACHERS IN SOUTH AFRICA

BY MICHAEL CROSS, UNIVERSITY OF THE WITWATERSRAND, AND
HAROON MAHOMED, NATIONAL DEPARTMENT OF EDUCATION
IN SOUTH AFRICA

Introduction

Higher education worldwide has changed extensively in the last few decades due to considerable increases in access and the impact of globalization. In Africa, the sector is comparatively smaller than almost all other parts of the world, but the major features of change, massification and globalization affect its institutions similarly. This chapter presents a particular aspect of the international change process in South Africa. In worldwide research, equity and access receive attention, but a crucial dimension that has not received sufficient attention is the experience of most "non-traditional" students and staff as they transition to higher education.

International Context

Progress in access and success in higher education worldwide in recent years is notable and significant. The 2008 EFA Global Monitoring Report shows that 138 million students were enrolled in tertiary education worldwide, an increase of about 45 million from 1999. The vast majority of these new admissions were found in large developing countries. In Brazil, China, India and Nigeria, the total combined tertiary students rose from 47 million in 1999 to 80 million in 2005.

China, with the largest higher education system in the world, has 17 million students enrolled in post-secondary education following 20 years of expansion. India, with the third highest enrollment at 10 million students, has plans to increase by 15 percent.

Despite these impressive statistics, access relative to the size of the age group is small. The EFA report concludes that "a relatively small share of the relevant age group has access to this level. The world tertiary Gross Enrollment Ratio (GER) was around

24 percent in 2005, but participation rates vary substantially by region, from 5 percent in Sub-Saharan Africa to 70 percent in North America and Western Europe (p. 59)."

Overall, research on higher education shows trends such as worldwide massification of higher education (as illustrated above), the transformation of higher education from a public good to a private one, a stronger service orientation, post-industrial economics and the impact of information technologies on higher education and society. The massification drive has resulted in differentiated higher education systems. Diverse populations have to be served, which has led to diversified forms of provision, varying quality, purposes and resources. In Africa, despite comparatively low enrollment rates, the patterns are similar with added challenges of strong outward mobility, lack of adequate funding, overcrowding, low quality and poor conditions.

South African Context

South Africa's reform agenda in higher education flows from the national socio-economic and political context of a highly unequal, complex, stratified and polarized social structure. Its massive program of change for higher education was undertaken following the first-ever democratic elections in 1994 and a broad policy pathway set up in 1998. Subotzky (2003) contends that "the scale and scope of this transformation is unrivalled on the African continent and, arguably, in the world." He states further that this was necessary, because "enrollments are distorted, and the system fails to provide the required range, number and quality of graduates to drive national development, and that the system is characterized by severe race, gender and institutional inequalities inherited from the apartheid era."

The change process has resulted in dramatic increases in access to higher education for historically disadvantaged students, but graduation rates for these students are still very far behind the access rates.

Recent research in this field indicates that the transition from school to university is associated with stress, anxiety and tension, and in the case of students who come from socio-economic and cultural backgrounds radically different from the academic culture of the university, the transition leads to students failing, withdrawing from their studies, taking longer than required to complete, rote learning and inadequate acquisition of the required competences (Thomas, Bol and Warkentin, 1991; Darlington-Jones, Cohen, Haunold, Pike and Young, 2003). Actual student experiences range from pride in being part of the university to desperation, alienation and marginalization, depending on their perceptions about the university, their expectations and the individual resources they carry with them or use on campus. Research has also been done on the question of the kind of transition assistance and academic support required to enable an enculturation process for students from historically disadvantaged backgrounds (Tinto 1987, 1993, 1995a, 1995b, 2000; Tinto and Goodsell-Love 1993; Tinto and Russo 1993; Tinto, Goodsell-Love and Russo 1993; McInnis, James, and Hartley, 2000).

This chapter discusses the practices, norms and values that constrain or enable successful participation of undergraduate students at South African universities. It looks at how students and their lecturers negotiate their needs and aspirations, and it reflects on their expectations from the university and from themselves. Further, the chapter examines several constructs, which together cover the social and academic resources that university students draw on when they seek to integrate into a culture of academic practice. Discussion will show how students and lecturers draw on these conditions to reflect on the question of institutional and epistemic access and success. The chapter considers these primarily at two main levels of university experience, namely pedagogic and social and what can be done to improve institutional and epistemic access, contributing to academic success.

The pedagogic level considers the following elements: 1) internal regulation, which refers to the ways in which students experience the difference in relation to authority when compared to their school experiences and how their lecturers manage this experience; 2) individual responsibility, which is the distribution of responsibilities between 'the student' and 'the institution' in relation to the process of learning and teaching (Cross et al, 2009); 3) distantiation and/or pedagogic distance, which refers to the ways in which lecturers establish cognitive distance from the students' own established knowledge and taken-for-granted assumptions in relation to academic practice when compared to school teaching and learning experiences (Slominsky & Shalem, 2004: 91); 4) facilitating appropriation, i.e., working with knowledge which is outside the students' current understanding and making it familiar to them; 5) explicit and implicit rules, connected to the ways in which students understand how the university learning environment works; 6) research, which requires both distantiation and appropriation and thus some level of cognitive distance from one's established knowledge of the object of study through established and rigorous modes of inquiry; 7) articulation, or being able to articulate or communicate findings verbally or in writing, so that the lecturer's knowledge becomes the object and means of reflection and learning for students (Cross et al, 2009a); and 8) revisiting the familiar, i.e., how students reconceptualize and engage with their common sense understandings.

The social level considers two main elements: 1) institutional affiliation or institutional membership, the process through which one gains affiliation to a group, an institution in this case, which requires progressive mastery of the common institutional language, norms and values, a process which depends largely "on each one's particularity, the individual manner each one encounters the world" (Coulon, 1993: 44-45) and 2) institutional responsibility or mediation, or facilitating dialogue and negotiation of shared spaces and construction of shared meaning about academic practice and experiences (Cross, 2008), depending on the institutional identity and cultural identity of the university. The social level encompasses students' experiences of failure and alienation and how these experiences elicit past experiences of racial and economic oppression.

Consequently, two important issues arise. The first is if access to the university by "new students" is accompanied by difficulties of adaptation which principally, but not exclusively, manifest themselves through a higher rate of failure and dropping out, it becomes important to inquire about the process of becoming successful students. Similarly, in a crisis situation, when the lecturers express their certainties and their uncertainties concerning their profession, their status and their role, how can they become and remain effective teachers/educators (Cross & Carpentier, 2009)?

What follows is a multi-dimensional discussion. The first part reviews patterns of student enrollment in higher education to contextualize the research problem. The second part deals with the biography of access in South African scholarship to frame the argument epistemologically and theoretically, and determine the social conditions that have been shown to have an impact on students' academic performance. The third part examines constructs outlined above, which together cover the social and academic resources that students draw upon when they seek to integrate into the university culture of academic practice. The fourth part analyzes the main characteristics of the learning environments in South African universities and highlights prevailing modes of academic and pedagogic practice with reference to the patterns of student enrollment. The last part looks at student life on university campuses and highlights prevailing patterns of student social integration, concluding with some of the institutional dilemmas universities in South Africa face at the policy level regarding epistemic access.

Growth in Intake and the Re-composition of the Student Population: The Phenomenon of "Non-Traditionality" and the Discourses of "Under-preparedness"

A university campus represents an important space in social life where individuals experience ideological upheavals regarding place, location, identity and desire. For academics, this experience is articulated through debates on academic freedom, individual autonomy, collegial governance and truth seeking. Students too negotiate their needs and aspirations; they interpret policies, rules and guidelines, and they respond to institutional administrative and academic provision. In South Africa, the university campus has been characterized by rapid and complex change linked to an unprecedented increase and diversification of the student population.

In 1980, there were 159,756 students enrolled in South African universities. By 1990 this number increased to 304,625 and close to 490,000 by 2003. What's most significant is not the overall increase in enrollment, but the racial re-composition of the student body. An increase in the number of black students was accompanied by a corresponding decline in the number of white students (220,000 in 1993 to 164,000 in 1999). This decline has been linked to 1) the movement of white students to private higher education or to institutions outside of South Africa and to 2) problems in accessing funds for students who did not qualify for funding through the National

Student Financial Aid Services (NSFAS) (Bundy, 2006: p. 12). In addition, the number of international students increased from 30,943 in 2000 to 52,453 in 2004 (DOE/HEMIS data) with respectively 47.2 and 68 percent of these from the SADC region. The most significant increase began in 2000 and reached a total 761,087 in 2007. However, in terms of access, the proportion of African students enrolling in universities jumped from 40 percent in 1993 to 65 percent in 2002.[1] The increase has been particularly significant at institutions which had been exclusively white.

While many of the black students enrolling at historically white universities came from the ranks of the middle class, the number of students from working class and rural backgrounds also increased. While students were expected to adapt to campuses largely dominated by a European academic culture, this change in the demographic profile of the campuses had a wide ranging impact in changing campus cultures. Students from a wide range of school and life experiences came with different expectations of their role and the role of the lecturer in teaching, and they questioned the established institutional cultures. More languages were spoken on campuses where previously English or Afrikaans had dominated, and so campuses had to adapt to an increasingly multi-lingual social and learning environment. Questions of race and difference, which had been largely invisible when campuses were socially homogeneous, became visible and had to be addressed. These factors were instrumental in the emergence of discourses of under-preparedness that have dominated academic practices recently. Originally these emphasized the alleged academic deficit that characterized the so-called 'non-traditional' students or students from historically disadvantaged backgrounds. Currently, they are also linked to staff who, due to increasing pressure to perform across different contexts and teach increasingly diverse students, feel under-prepared for the tasks they are expected to undertake in dealing with 'under-prepared' students.

TABLE 6.1: PROPORTION OF HIGHER EDUCATION HEADCOUNT ENROLLMENTS IN SOUTH AFRICA BY RACE, 1993-2006

Race	1993	1995	1997	1999	2001	2002	2005	2006
African	40	50	58	59	60	60	60	61
Coloured	5	6	5	5	5	5	6.3	6.6
Indian	7	7	7	7	7	7	7.4	7.4
White	47	37	31	29	27	27	25.3	25
TOTAL	**100**	**100**	**100**	**100**	**100**	**100**	**100**	**100**

Source: Council on Higher Education (2004), South African Higher Education in the First Decade of Democracy, The Council on Higher Education (CHE), Pretoria.

Retention and Graduation Rates

Key indicators of equity and redress are retention and graduation rates of enrolled students. Throughput and retention rates in South African universities are generally low, particularly among mainly black, educationally disadvantaged and under-prepared students. The absolute number of black graduates has increased, but the overall proportion of the total remains low (Subotsky, 2003).

According to the *Review of National Policies for Education Report—South Africa* (OECD, 2008), retention rates declined after 1997 except in historically white, English institutions. It reports that in 1993, 17 percent of new university students completed their qualifications, whereas in 2000 there were 16 percent. The technikons showed similar declines from ten percent to nine percent over the two years. In 2005, of 120,063 South African graduates, the average success rate of black students in contact undergraduate programs was 69.8 percent in comparison with 84.7 percent completion rates for white students.

In addition, the low throughput rate and limited access of male African students and women to high-status study fields are cause for concern. Subotsky contends that the focus on improving equity has tended to be on access rather than success and this creates a revolving door syndrome. Details of graduate rates for historically disadvantaged students (Black, Coloured, Indian) in the "high status" fields show an even bleaker picture, as illustrated in the table below:

TABLE 6.2: RETENTION AND GRADUATION RATES BY FIELD OF STUDY

Field	% Graduates
Medicine and Engineering	9
Natural Sciences	12
Law	13
Social Sciences	20
Humanities and Arts	28
Education	32
Literature and languages	39
Business and Commerce	11
Accounting	2

Source: Subotksy 2004.

Explaining Student Academic and Social Experience: Theory and Conceptual Framework

The question of successful participation in formal institutions of learning is not new in South African research. It has undergone different metamorphoses in its discourse, in the concerns it has raised and how it has been approached as the context of higher education changed. (For a comprehensive review, see Cross, 2009b.) One can identify three periods. The first period consisted of studies of contestation or resistance to the apartheid barriers to formal access to higher education in the late 1970s and early 1980s, particularly the role of youth and student movements in the contestation of apartheid education (e.g. The Open Universities in South Africa, 1957; Molobi, 1987; Nkomo 1984; Solomons, 1989; Nkomo 1990; Webster E. et al. 1986; Brooks, Brickhill, 1980; Molteno 1979; Molteno 1987; Molteno 1983; Bundy 1986; Bandy, 1987; Gwala, 1988).

The second period responded to the re-composition of the student body in terms of race, gender and other forms of identity throughout the late 1980s and the early 1990s, which resulted in the increase of non-traditional students, or students from historically disadvantaged groups, and increasing concerns with the question of academic disadvantage and epistemic access (Badat, et al., 1994; Craig A, 1989; Morrow, 1992; Jansen, 2001:2-3; see also Ensor, 1998). The third period is bound up with the massive expansion of the student population throughout the late 1990s into the present millennium, which shifted the debate from "educational disadvantage" to the question of "throughput and retention" determined by both accountability and cost factors. These included national and institutional surveys on throughput issues and institutional culture and nuanced approaches to epistemic access and the nature of the university teaching and learning spaces. (See Cloete et al., 2002; Nkoli, 2003; Nolutshungu, 1999; Kotta, 2006; Rollnick & Tresman, 2004; Coughlan, 2006; Paola, Lemmer & Van Wyk, 2004; Howell & Lazarus, 2003; Van den Berg, 2006; De Beer, 2006; Cele, 2005; Cele, Koen and Mabizela, 2002; King, 2001; Koen and Roux, 1995; Sakarai, 1997; Badat, 1999; Maseko, 1994; Jansen, 2004; Cross et al, 2009a).

The literature points to complex combinations of variables that affect student academic achievement. These include: 1) student age, maturity and life experience (Clark and Ramsey, 1990; Long, Carpenter and Hayden, 1995; Shah and Burke, 1996; West, Hore, Bennie, Browne, and Kermond, 1986); 2) institutional cultural differences between the school and the university (Abbott-Chapman, Hughes, and Wyld, 1992; Bourke, Burdon and Moore, 1996; Dobson and Sharma, 1995; McClelland and Kruger, 1989); 3) gender differences (Scott et al., 1996); 4) socio-economic status (Western, et al., 1998); and 5) previous school performance (McClelland and Kruger, 1998; Coulon, 1993; McInnis, et al., 2000). We consider three sets of social conditions that have been shown to impact students' academic performance: student biography (socio-economic, cultural and linguistic backgrounds), institutional mediation (the nature of the social and learning environment presented by the institution) and student agency (negotiating powers in the teaching and learning processes).

Student biography or background consists of "skills, abilities, pre-intentional assumptions, attitudes, practices, capacities, stances, perceptions and actions" (Broekman & Pendlebury, 2002: 291; see also Searle, 1995) that students carry from one milieu to another. It facilitates certain kinds of readiness and disposes them to certain sorts of behavior (Searle, 1995: 136). In this sense, background enables and constrains what they intend, how they interpret their actions and the world around them, and how they are interpreted or socially constructed by and within their interactions with other people. It may be an asset or resource that is individually and socially produced or owned, but it may also be a liability. Our contention is that students from different social backgrounds (race, gender, ethnicity, nationality, etc.) experience and negotiate affiliation to and membership of campus life and their student identities differently. The needs of specific students and the difficulties they might encounter as a result of their academic, social, cultural and linguistic backgrounds, their individual personalities and financial difficulties, have received wide attention (McJamerson, 1992; Terenzini, Rendon, Upcraft, Millar, Allison, Gregg and Jalomo, 1994; Lewis, 1994; Long, 1994; Shields, 1995; Scott, Burns and Cooney, 1996; Western, McMillan and Durrington, 1998; Dobson, 1999; Strage, 2000; McInnis, et al., 2000).

Institutional mediation refers to the idea of social and academic responsiveness, which focuses on social accommodation mechanisms, instructional strategies and learning pathways which a university employs while socializing students into a form of academic inquiry that is aligned with their academic disciplines. *Social responsiveness* is concerned with the role of the institution in constructing everyday campus life, including leisure time and recreation activities, cultural and religious rituals and the constitutive rules (how to live on campus) and institutional facts (what is reasonably accepted). The root of this analysis is on how to enable "epistemological access" (Morrow, 1992) to students of different social and cultural backgrounds. Social studies on campus diversity that gained prominence in India and the USA are still to be embraced in the South African debate. A recent case study of pedagogical responsiveness (Griesel, 2004) provides useful examples of pedagogical forms of engagement with learners' thinking and systematic socialization of under-prepared students.

In terms of student-lecturer interaction, international research provides important notions such as "pedagogic distance" and "social presence" (Richardson and Swan, 2003), which reveal the complexity and multi-dimensionality that characterize such interaction. This work includes Gunawardena's analysis (1995: 151) of "the degree to which a person is perceived as a 'real person' in mediated communication;" Moore's (1997) claim that by narrowing the pedagogic distance between lecturers and students, learning mediation is enhanced in its different domains—emotional, political, pedagogical, linguistic and physical; and Witt, et al.'s (2004) description of "teacher immediacy" or "the act of reducing the physical and/or psychological distance between lecturers and students through touch, direct body orientation, eye contact, gestures and positive head nods and related body language." In one way or another, these studies aim to find ways to enhance student perceptions and feelings of connectedness to the academic expectations transmitted by their lecturers (Hostetter and Busch, 2006).

These studies must be seen alongside those that examine the notion of epistemological access from the viewpoint of curriculum design, which emphasizes the importance of sequence and progression (Muller, 2006), and academic practice, which examines such pedagogical forms such as lectures that can socialize under-prepared students into specific forms of text-based practices (Slonimsky and Shalem, 2004).

The concept of *student agency* or *positionality* maps the dialectic that occurs as students negotiate campus membership—dialectic between individual agencies on the one hand, and institutional and external pressures (e.g., local and global cultures) on the other. Student agency in this context refers to openness to being challenged or to having enough self-confidence to challenge or defend one's view. The positionality of students has some bearing on the possibilities of success or failure. Studies on student agency examine the difficulties of adaptation of "non-traditional" or "under-prepared" students due to their disadvantaged background. Coulon (1993:165) looks at affiliation or the passage or effort by which a pupil becomes a student. He shows that to become a student requires "a progressive mastery of common institutional language" of the learning space through which a student emerges as "a person endowed with a pool of procedures, methods, activities, know-how, which make him/her able to invent mechanisms of adaptation to give a meaningful sense to the world which surrounds him/her (Ibid: 183)." For Coulon (1993:165), the problem today is not "to enter the university but to remain there;" for this purpose students must discover "*that it is necessary to learn to become so*, otherwise one is eliminated or eliminates him/herself because they remain foreign in this new world."

School and University as Binary Teaching, Learning and Social Spaces

As already indicated, the transition between school and university is not an easy one for any learner (Thomas, Bol and Warkentin, 1991) and is often associated with stress, anxiety and tension which, in many cases, lead to student failure or withdrawal from the university regardless of race, gender, background or class (Darlinton-Jones et al., 2003). Transition assistance and support is required to assist in an enculturation process for students entering a system of higher education for the first time, particularly for those whose previous school performance was poor (McInnis et al., 2000). Tinto proposes a combined approach to transition or orientation programs that introduces students to university life in an atmosphere of fun and support, which does not cause stress and anxiety, and which recognizes the role of high schools, family and peers, as well as the university (Tinto 1987, 1993, 1995a, b, 2000; Tinto & Goodsell-Love 1993; Tinto & Russo, 1993; Tinto, Goodsell-Love & Russo, 1993).

Students encounter in South African elite campuses vastly different learning environments than their earlier schooling. Ironically, as learning environments, these appear to be open, in contrast to the rules and regulations of regimented school environments. As an urban planning student at Wits University said, "In school… you're constantly being watched, you're being monitored, kind of so you don't break the rules." In contrast to this, the academic environment is attractive because of its freedom:

"I did come around once when I was in school and I saw people having like freedom, you know the freedom, which you do have in university and it was kind of attractive, I thought, from a young age." In the learning space of the university, no one "nags" you to do things or to do them on time. Socially, they appear to be flexible and accommodating.

We characterize the context of the university as appearing to be open, because underpinning the apparent openness, a particular relation of authority marks the social space of learning and teaching – the lecturer authorizes knowledge. Students describe what procedures they follow when they seek advice or help. What comes out of these descriptions is their sense of educational hierarchy: first lecturers at the top, then senior students (tutors) and finally peers. At times, the view of authority is mediated through perspectives that emanate from outside the academic culture from a perceived African culture. In this regard, some students claim that they find it difficult to consult their lecturers because, in their view, it is difficult in an African culture to interact closely with people who are older than oneself. The challenge for them is to develop the necessary confidence to communicate with elders and lecturers. We characterize this as appearing to be flexible and accommodating because, in this respect, many students, particularly those from disadvantaged backgrounds (township schools, rural background and poor socio-economic families, etc.) express feelings of cultural displacement: "You are either in or out, but to be in you have to be like them."

In the pedagogical encounter in elite universities, students are expected to engage knowledge by marshalling evidence rather than by deferring to teacher authority. This encounter brings to mind the famous distinction made by Peters (1966) between demanding consent in lieu of being "in authority" and dealing with knowledge from a position of "an authority." The former uses formal authority to demand consent, whereas the latter requires analysis and explanation as a mode of justification of an idea. The rules of the former are far more explicit because they relate to specific roles, e.g., a school teacher or university lecturer. The rules of the latter are implicit and debated because they are drawn from the field epistemology and refer to the form in which ideas are produced academically. They may appear to allow freedom, but the criteria for justification are formal. Therefore, what appears to be free and open by contrast to the learning and teaching spaces at school is, in fact, structured around the authority of the lecturer and those who are close to the lecturer in the hierarchy (senior students, tutors and so on) with tight constitutive rules on how to behave and what to do to demonstrate competence. The challenge facing students on these campuses is how to reconstitute and position themselves productively in relation to the educative authority. This depends largely on how they understand or interpret the nature of this authority or how they learn the rules of the university academic and social space, as well as their own responsibility toward it.

Varied Learning Goals and Identities

Contributing to the complex picture is how individual students approach their studies. When students speak about their study choices, three different kinds of goals and experiences or social identities emerge. First, there are those who have an instrumental goal and see a degree as useful to secure a job. They have what might be called a *market-related identity*. The market-related identity feeds off the globalization discourse where the usefulness of knowledge is defined with reference to the economic advantage that a degree can purchase.

Second, there are those who are more inwardly oriented and focus on building themselves through the expressive aspects of the field. They may express, "I like our department because we get to think and create our own ideas, make them come to life and watch what we really want... the whole issue of being able to express myself as a student – I think that is really wonderful." Being recognized as central to the production of new knowledge rather than as responding to external needs or criteria is primary in this identification, which may be named *knowledge for the sake of knowledge identity* and is grounded in the classic liberal view of education. This includes those who see the value of what they study in understanding themselves or others better, e.g., a student of media and international politics who enjoys what she is doing because she loves meeting people from other countries and learning about new cultures and how things are done in other countries.

Third, there are those who attach to their degree altruistic concerns and seek some form of improvement or change to society through their study. These students embody a social justice or *socially responsive identity*. Examples include an international relations student who better understands the conflict and the turmoil that is going on in the world, particularly in the Middle East; a student of industrial psychology who seeks to understand work in terms of unions and what drives people to excel or what behaviour leads them to strikes; and a student in surveying who saw a need in the construction industry for people who develop infrastructure.

These different identities need to be matched to the kinds of courses students are studying. Where student aspirations complement their studies, this can be beneficial, but where there is a mismatch, it can affect student success.

Learning the Rules for the Social Space of Learning and Teaching

How do students understand how the university learning environment works? What are the rules for the social space of learning? Rules of communication are important for expectations and central to creating a social order in which there is consistency and predictability. Rules provide structure and habituation (Bernstein, 1975). From contrasting comments that students give from different institutions, it is clear that these rules are not transmitted or monitored the same way at university as they were at school. At the university, student interviewees do not mention being monitored or watched, but they do speak of rules of behavior that are inscribed in the university academic culture and to which they need to adjust. The rules are not always explicit. As such, students clearly require a degree of social and intellectual adjustment, a process of affiliation or in Coloun's words, a mastery of institutional language and an understanding of guiding *institutional facts* (university gowns and hymns) and *constitutive rules* (e.g., acceptable dress code, acceptable English accent, etc.).[2] Rules are inscribed in academic expectations (e.g., the ways the educative authority transmits criteria) and in social practices and they require some form of adaptation, which is not always conscious. Students might express, "It's not like you know that you're changing; it's just that you adapt" or "It was a completely different environment, and I had to start from scratch in terms of adjusting."

The social sphere of learning and teaching consists of layers of criteria and assumptions. Whether and how students interpret or attach meaning to these depends on their capacities, their know-how and dispositions—in other words, a sort of pre-intentional knowledge about how the institution works and a set of abilities for coping in and with the institution (Cross, 2008: 267). Very often students can only access the explicit practice of learning, such as time frames, course outlines, etc. These are important, but they do not disclose the evaluation criteria of the knowledge base itself or the kind of text that the student is expected to produce. Students have to come to grips with less explicit principles that underlie the specialization or the discipline. Making the underlying criteria explicit is important in a culture of performance, where the idea of standards to be achieved is paramount. When the rules and expectations are not clearly communicated, students feel overwhelmed or frightened. When this happens, some withdraw, while others rely on their own personal discipline. Where and when to consult with lecturers, the pacing of the work, timetabling of exams, when to expect test results to be published and more seem to be some of the ways the social environment of learning and teaching is marked with institutional rules on how to behave.

Consequently, students need clear expectations laid down in a course outline, which is followed consistently by the lecturer, and a good explanation of how to prepare for an exam. Learning can be difficult when expectations are not communicated, when the rules and principles are not clearly spelled out, and when students face problems and do not know what support options are available.

The sphere of social life is much more complex; there are no clear rules or criteria on what constitutes standard behavior, except for the normative framework that regulates issues of alcohol or drug abuse, sexual harassment, etc. Many students, for example, do recognize the value of student academic, religious and political associations out of their previous experiences, but they are unable to discern their significance for their academic development to be able to make informed choices. This is certainly an area where stronger institutional mediation is required. Overall, it appears that making the underlying criteria explicit is important in a culture which emphasizes individual regulation and self-responsibility, and where the idea of standards to be achieved is paramount. Indeed, Broekman and Pendlebury (2002: 293) were correct that "impossible though it seems to make the rules explicit, it may be worth the attempt because the very exercise of trying to specify institutional facts and their constitutive rules . . ." may help the institution reflect on and refine its own institutional rules and procedures. Institutional reinvention is a fact in the same sense that students reinvent themselves, whether through negotiation or contestation.

Individual Responsibility: Positioning Oneself as Student Within Assumed Social Relations of Authority

So far we have dealt with how students relate to the educative authority of lecturers. How do students see *their* role in this relationship? Many of the students convey a clear sense that it is up individual students to get the most out of what the university offers. This includes a form of individualism which encourages "a sense of expressing your own opinion and thinking for yourself so that you can draw your own conclusions," a social space of being yourself or "basically, this is where you get to establish yourself as an individual." This is not to say that students lack expectations of the institution, but they talk more clearly (and more repeatedly) about the need for understanding their role vis-à-vis learning and performing than they do about the responsibilities of their lecturers. Lecturers are described as 'interesting,' 'boring,' 'resourceful,' 'passionate' or 'racist.' Students, on the other hand, are tasked with the responsibility to work hard and get the results; they need initiative. They need to approach the specialist, the lecturer, and confirm that they have understood: "I'm one of those people that you'll find following the lecturer after lectures, to go and confirm, 'yes.'" Emerging from this account is the *expansion of self as the center of power, action, change and responsibility.*

Lecturers, too, reinforce the idea that students have to be resourceful, independent and work hard:

> "My very first lecture is one of establishing the contract between my student and myself. What is my duty and what is their duty? We look at what we are supposed to get out of the time that we spend together. So that's the one thing that I would establish. The second question is always, always the same. Are there any disadvantaged students in this class? And it is interesting to see who puts up their hands. And I always look right through and never find any disadvantaged students – simply because we are all at Wits University. Do you understand? So I already set the course straight. I don't believe in hard luck stories; I believe in effort."

These comments show a different dimension to the idea of individual responsibility, because they convey a sense that institutional responsibility, which has characterized South African elite universities, has been reduced. Rather than focus here, however, it's important to consider the ways students negotiate their power in relation to educative authority. Students speak about being vulnerable and shy in the public space of learning. They deal with that by deciding where to sit, and when and if at all to participate actively in public discourse. Lecturers may mediate this process minimally, if at all. For some students, active participation is associated with embarrassment or even sheer fear.

What emerges here is a picture of students who acknowledge that they need to try and take responsibility for knowing the work that is required, seek the initiative to make a mark, address the lecturer when needed and, when they feel vulnerable, keep a low profile. There are two important markers in the social space of learning: lecturers have a clear sense of authority over knowledge and students are the primary locus of responsibility. The constitutive rules for effective student engagement in these processes tend to be assumed; they are not always made explicit. Reduced institutional responsibility emerges clearly when students speak about 'personal problems.' Despite the existence of official support structures in some departments of these universities, students feel that depression, family problems and financial problems have to be faced alone.

Distantiation and Pedagogic Distance: Race and English Language in the Learning and Social Space

Some students express feelings of not belonging to the same tradition of knowledge as their lecturers (and some of their peers in the courses) and they were being prevented from entering it. Instead of being brought into the tradition by inter-subjective means of dialogue, these students experienced alienation. They were prevented from asking questions or from saying that they did not understand, which kept them from testing their own ideas in public: "Even though I could be having an idea, I could not say it because I would think that it is wrong. So I would just let the other people talk, including the black people who grew up around Gauteng because they had the privilege of going to multiracial schools." In their attempts to make sense of such alienating experiences, these students tend to resort to explanations from everyday experience as victims of the apartheid legacy, an experience largely defined by racism. Their claims are revealing. Some explain their experiences with reference to the color of their skin: "White students are offered academic support that is not offered to black students" or "Black students are undermined from an academic perspective and deliberately prevented from succeeding." Unfortunately, this is a reality that many lecturers, who are predominantly white, are unable to understand given their social space and identities.

English as the medium of instruction is widely accepted as an institutional fact; it is an aspect of institutional life according to which they conduct their daily lives on campus, and whose use, function, status and meaning they collectively agree on, even if they do not think about it (Broekman and Pendlebury, 2002: 289). Most students who attended private or 'Model C' schools have no difficulty with English. However, the English language is a major constraining factor for students who come from black and rural schools, where the mother tongue is predominant. In fact, for some, the use of English represents a barrier to conceptual access: "Here you are struggling to conceptualize what is being delivered in the lecture and catch each and every English word, that itself is a challenge to you." Some feel de-motivated, given the difficulties they experience in expressing themselves: "I'm a hard worker, but I was de-motivated because I would work hard and because of the language problem, my results would come out as average, although I never had that thought of dropping out of school." Nonetheless, students do not always get much sympathy from staff members regarding their language difficulties. A humanities lecturer might say, "Look, I got to France without speaking a word of French and I wrote a Ph.D. in French, so I don't see why you can't make an effort to write English properly."

Becoming a University Student: Challenges and Pathways to Campus Membership

Students come to the elite universities with their own constructs embedded in their expectations about what is like to live there. Such constructs have some bearing on the ease or difficulty with which they experience initiation and integration into campus life. This maybe facilitated or complicated by initial student orientation. Once on campus, these constructs become an object of fierce contestation centered on meaning and difference. These include constructs about the nature of the institution (e.g., "top research institution in South Africa," "center of excellence," "top university in Africa" or "high standing institution," etc.), constructs about the perceived path to success and coping strategies, and constructs about what is expected from them on campus. The difference in how students rate the three institutions is mainly a matter of terminology; they are all highly regarded institutions. Related to these constructs is the expectation of a profound acculturation and assimilation into an established institutional culture, which can be individually taxing. This process may require a radical change in language, values, attitude and behavior, depending on one's background. Constructs about expectations are generally geared at aligning ambitions; that is, setting goals and devising strategies for meeting them. More specifically, these constructs are about recognizing and interpreting the specific constitutive rules, adjusting to established living standards, and coping with the challenges of campus life. In this respect, many students, particularly those from a disadvantaged background, express feelings of cultural displacement.

Surprisingly, once on campus and familiar with its institutional rules, many students tend to interpret the tension between their own identities and the institutional environment as a battle between student subcultures. They do not make the connection between these battles and the displacement they feel due to the nature of the institutional cultures. This tends to be perceived as an institutional fact and, as such, an object of little contestation. The most cited example is the presence of "the model C school phenomenon" on campus, expressed in language, group identities, materialistic values and lifestyles.

To emphasize English as *lingua franca* provides important cultural capital and creates a contradiction that Lodge (1997) has labeled 'the access paradox.' If you provide students with access to the dominant language, you contribute to perpetuating and increasing its dominance. If instead, you deny students access, "You perpetuate their marginalization in a society that continues to recognize this language as a mark of distinction . . . [and] you also deny them access to the extensive resources available in that language; resources which have developed as a consequence of the language's dominance (Janks, 2004: 33)."

The boundaries of race and ethnicity are certainly thinning and becoming more porous. As a result, many students interviewed do not see manifestations of racism in their interaction with peers, but rather in relation to the University administration and some staff. However, in real life, group identities on campus still reflect the apartheid legacy, which constitutes a surprising puzzle for many South African and foreign students. They attach a different meaning to race and ethnic grouping, which is justified through affinity arguments.

Because group identities often follow ethnic lines, xenophobia is an issue that has had significant repercussions. According to one international student, xenophobia is something that makes South Africa a very intimidating society. Overall, student accounts point to a multilayered and hierarchical structure of institutional membership among students. Apart from race, three main groups can be identified. The first group involves those who are open to the rules, codes, norms and standards, including rituals that characterize elite institutional life. They have adapted to them, have the resources to negotiate their social and learning spaces and have developed a sense of identity with the campus community. This sense of identity sets boundaries very often expressed with some pride: "This is how we do things at UCT." Generally, they have easily adapted to campus life, and they can say with certainty, "I feel like I belong here." By virtue of their previous socialization, the environment matches their habits, their intuition, their dispositions and pre-dispositions, i.e., their *habitus* (Grenfell and James, 1998: 14). Students encounter the university as a meaningful world, a world endowed with sense and value, in which it is worth investing one's practice (Bourdieu 1989: 44). In this case, habitus minimizes social displacement. This is not to deny however the choices and consequent actions made by some students as active agents of their own lives; in other words, the role of agency. In contrast, when graduates from rural and township schools come to campus, their habitus encounters a social world which does not match and has little to contribute to it. As a result, they encounter an environment that has little meaning and value to them.

The second group – the survivors – includes those who have found the institutional facts or constitutive rules of the university community alienating or a threat to their identities. As such, these rules are contestable, and they have opted to negotiate membership in their own terms through struggles of different sorts. They associate themselves with campus life, but they resist any form of assimilation and fundamental change in identity and personality. They are unwilling to undergo a metamorphosis; they stress the value of difference and diversity. They struggle for asserting or re-negotiating their identities in their own terms or within a framework of mutual compromises.

The third group comprises those who lack the resources to negotiate their identities in either way, either in their own terms or in terms already established on campus. They may develop feelings of cultural displacement, alienation, withdrawal, isolation or marginalization. Within this category, besides those who feel excluded, there are also those who choose to remain on the margins. They concentrate on their studies and very often have their social life off campus. We should not, however, underestimate the radical possibilities of the discourse of marginality articulated by this group. As Hooks has indicated (1990: 147), sometimes there is a need "to create spaces where one is able to redeem and reclaim the past, legacies of pain, suffering and triumph in ways that transform present reality." The margins very often offer the conditions that make such action possible. This is, in our view, the rationale behind the establishment of gender-specific or race-specific student associations, which is a declining phenomenon on campus.

Pertinent questions to ask are: What happens to students in the last group? Are their chances of academic success compromised or diminished? There is certainly a perception among students that participation in the university community and in the varied campus activities enhances the chances of epistemic success, though it is not essential to one's success. According to student accounts, full participation in campus life and initiatives provides opportunities for leadership development, social and cultural awareness and replacement of family or institutional support by providing common spaces or resource networks and channels for reaching out to communities. There are instances where students resort to resources off campus. Overall, given their diversity and the legacies they carry, at a subjective level, students have different expectations about campus life and attach different meanings to the different aspects of campus life. The limited presence – or complete absence – of shared meanings within common or wider shared spaces creates a sense of displacement as illustrated in their accounts.

Coming to Grips with Difference and Meaning: The Role of Student Activism, Religious, Academic and Social Engagement

Tierney's (1993) notion of *communities of difference* refers to the range of campus organizations, forums and social groups through which students find spaces for mutual engagement, joint enterprise, construction and expression of group identity. They affirm differences and develop awareness and learning. Students also use these groups to negotiate meaning over social issues of interest to them. Such communities represent constellations of competing and, in some cases, conflicting interests and values. The communities of difference include social, academic and religious organizations. In this regard, the survey points to a highly fragmented and diverse student body, constituting different interests and socio-cultural activities, leisure and recreation activities and sports. The survey highlights three patterns in student behavior. The first pattern concerns changes in form and content of student politics. There has been a shift from traditional predominance of student affiliation to political organizations to a preference for social, cultural, academic and religious organizations. These student organizations do operate as, or have the potential to become, effective 'communities of practice (Wenger, 1999; Tierney 1993; Bellah, et al, 1991).' This is particularly true for those groups focusing on intellectual and academic engagement. As a locus of engagement in action, interpersonal relations, shared knowledge, and negotiation of enterprises, "such communities hold the key to real transformation – the kind that has real effects on people's lives (Wenger, 1999: 85)."

The second important pattern in student behavior concerns the incubating and nurturing role of student organizations. Student organizations form a parameter for understanding others in the midst of and across multiple socially constructed realities (Rowe, 2003). Most students see student organizations as providing common spaces and resource networks within a community at loggerheads or in confrontation with itself on racial, religious, ethnic and cultural issues and in confrontation with a some-what strange or unfriendly institutional environment. They provide spaces where once-isolated individuals may now live in communities or, as some have indicated, in adopted 'families.' The impersonal and carefree environment on campus, combined with the intimate and relatively closed communities of these organizations, forces stu-dents "to live with one another and to come to terms with the meaning of citizenship, social responsibility, conflict and how to resolve it, and intellectual freedom" (Tierney, 1993: 43), very often constrained by the codes and norms of academia.

The third important pattern in student behavior, which remains largely unex-plored by both the institution and the students, is about the interface and interplay between student activities and institutional life or culture. There seems to be a degree of institutional uncertainty about what strategies should be put in place to facilitate constructive engagement between current student organizations and the university, a task that cannot be played effectively by the SRC under the circumstances. If stu-dent engagement in institutional life is understood as being mediated by the com-munities in which meanings are negotiated in practice, then student organizations – as critical nodal points in the creation and recreation of institutional culture – should be taken very seriously. Such organizations can form part of the social fabric of learning and enrichment.

Student academic associations, for example, have an important role to play as agencies for learning, skills development and academic citizenship. Briefly, student organizations as *communities of difference* serve different purposes; they are spaces for identity formation, intellectual engagement, imagination, spiritual healing and affir-mation of power. As networks of civic engagement, student organizations serve sev-eral useful purposes: 1) to foster sturdy norms of mutual trust and generalized reciprocity within the group or organization; 2) to facilitate coordination and com-munication; 3) to amplify information about the trustworthiness of individual mem-bers; and 4) to lower transaction costs and speed up information transfer and innovation. They embody past success at collaboration, which can serve as a cultural template for future collaboration. As such, student organizations can promote the development and sharing of social capital as a vital ingredient in meeting the challenges of campus life.

One matter of concern is that these fragmented communities seem to demonstrate little effort toward promoting politics of articulation, beyond individual or group boundaries. Students tend to accept dispersion and fragmentation as part of the construction of a new social order that reveals fully where they are and what they can become, and which does not demand that they forget (Hooks 1990: 148) or consciously unlearn certain forms of behavior.

Negotiating a Shared Space and Meaning and Strengthening Institutional Mediation: The Need for Institutional and Social Reinvention

Socially, the challenge facing elite universities in South Africa on their campuses is about how to find and foster a sense of community among diverse individuals, and how to offer integrity in a highly disintegrated society and in an environment with strong centrifugal tendencies. Within a university campus, where students from different backgrounds are brought together with an assumed common purpose, the challenge is to recognize differences and consider the consequences in accomplishing that common purpose. This task may require recognizing "the educative value of understanding different constructions of social reality and the possibilities of establishing new, shared meanings and practices (Broekman and Pendlebury, 2002: 291)." It may also require identifying the problematic nature of the university's expectations for the students and the institution's approach to its own institutional facts and constitutive rules, which it often takes for granted.

Institutional facts and constitutive rules of the university are dynamic aspects of institutional life. However, collective agreement about their function, status and meaning may be disrupted, contested and changed as the university community adjusts to new currents of people and ideas. As Durkheim has indicated, social order could deteriorate into a fragmented anomic culture if moral 'glue' does not arise spontaneously for persons when they realize their fundamental interdependence with one another (Durkheim 1984: 85). The university is undoubtedly an institution *par excellence* where people intelligently become individuals as they realize this interdependence, and thus it is "an indispensable source from which character is formed (Bellah et al. 1991: 6)." From this point of view, universities are not instruments of repression and social control, or simply loci of power that reproduce culture. They are agents of social change that empower individuals to open up to new possibilities of citizenship and interrelatedness. Such processes should certainly provide leverage for tackling the taken-for-granted elements of institutional life and for negotiating and building a dynamic institutional "culture that is more dependent on process than stasis and an understanding of education oriented toward social change rather than social reproduction (Rowe, 2003: 3)."

Some of the tensions that persist on campus result from the fact that students from different backgrounds experience campus life differently. Against this background, the challenge is to enable students to live on campus guided by the rules of a dynamic academic environment by establishing a space of dialogue and possibilities that allows for regeneration, innovation and enrichment. The notion of mediation is essential. Establishing a space of dialogue and possibilities necessitates facilitation of meaning construction around the experiences that students have of campus life, regardless of their diverse backgrounds. In our view, Woolcock and Narayan's (2000: 230) concepts of *bonding, linking* and *bridging* provide insights that could prove useful in devising mediation strategies. Bonding means building connections to people who are like you or who are 'getting by,' which is mostly a survival strategy. Bonding explains how students with similar backgrounds build connections among themselves that can culminate in student organizations around politics (e.g., Independent Students' Association), religion (e.g., Muslim Students' Association) or music and dance (e.g., Ballroom Dancing Club) and other forms of recreation. Bridging refers to building connections to people *not* like you. It provides a channel for mobility or 'getting ahead.' Linking is about building connections to people in positions of power, which can provide access to new and ample resources. This could be translated into vertical links or tying students from historically disadvantaged to people with historically advantaged backgrounds. With few exceptions, strategies that reflect this dynamic seem to be lacking in student organizational life and in campus life in general. A widespread pattern is that students are open to and cooperate with those who have something in common; who share similar biographies or backgrounds; who share the goals of the organization, its norms, values and principles; and who share its traditions.

Competing Discourses: Performance-Driven vis-à-vis Competence-Driven Pedagogic Practices

Overall, the learning environment in elite institutions is dominated by *performance-driven pedagogic practices*.[3] These are linked to a low-participation model, the defining aspects of which include a particular conception of specialization of knowledge and modes of transmission and evaluation based on a particular relationship between students and lecturers. On the one side of this relationship are the students who focus on individual academic achievement or success (high performance) in a competitive environment with limited peer collaboration or faculty support. They focus more on meeting the requirements defined by the lecturer and less on being recognized as different and particular individuals with specific experiences, needs, problems or aspirations. Their major resource for success is the accumulated social and cultural capital they carry with them, their ability to work independently and their individual autonomy. On the other side is the lecturer, who has the power to define what constitutes academic knowledge, what constitutes a good academic text, what knowledge is relevant and how it should be assessed, and when a student has attained the required performance level.[4]

Performance-driven approaches to learning in the universities considered in this study have their roots in the liberal-meritocratic discourse that dominated academic practices throughout the 1970s and 1980s and are now supported by the globalization discourse of competition and use value for the economy. They are essentially economic; they do not allow students extra time, too much individual attention or different evaluation criteria because of personal circumstances or need. Students have to be self-reliant, resourceful and motivated. Minimal support is made available and students are expected to take the initiative in finding any extra support they need. Academic selection replaces academic support, and relations between students and lecturers are sporadic and formal. In Schneider's words, students are expected to have "aligned ambitions" (Schneider & Stevenson, 1999) and to set goals and devise strategies to achieve them on their own. The fittest students will survive in a kind of educational or intellectual *laissez passer*. For such an approach to work, the institution needs to be highly selective and exclusionary; the performance-driven approach does not cater to the complex learning needs of non-traditional students.

Alternative Pedagogic Approaches

While performance-driven approaches form part of the dominant discourses in elite universities, there are meaningful pockets of innovative pedagogy grounded in principles of social justice and perceived as more effective for addressing the needs of non-traditional students. Besides examples given by academic staff, these are implicit in the ways students describe their lecturers as 'authorities (Peters, 1966).' Student descriptors may also indicate the lecturers are teachers, whose knowledge base enables them to work with ideas and develop them for the student: 'intelligent,' 'interesting,' 'challenging,' 'informative,' 'firm,' 'dedicated,' 'eye-opening,' 'absolutely brilliant' and 'motivating.' Students express their belief in the authority of some of their lecturers; they trust what these lecturers transmit. This is what Peters (1966) sees as the challenge for educative authority; it needs to continually prove and justify itself. The process of justification is rational as the lecturer, who claims an authority over knowledge, communicates his or her knowledge in an intelligible way. Authority is educative when it appeals to reason, when its pronouncements can be challenged and when its incumbent understands that his or her authority is provisional (Peters, 1966: 240). Educative authority will not seek consent to a view through fear, command, indoctrination, hypnosis or appeal to a particular person. This means that the student's trust is gained because the lecturer follows a process that is trustworthy. According to student accounts, the defining features of this process include inter alia: 1) recognition of individual potential; 2) teaching with passion; 3) motivating students; 4) validating different points of view; 5) encouraging interaction; and 6) building a relationship.

Students also articulate the benefits of a supportive rather than competitive relationship with their peers. These comments were offered when students were asked to think of happy experiences on campus or about lecturers who had made an exceptional impression on them. In other words, the ideas about community and care come when students think about the ideal. Ideal lecturers break the formal boundaries between the lecturer and the student. They are those who take the trouble to know their problems (their private and vulnerable self) and to support them when they need it. These lecturers are mentioned for the time they devote to guiding and motivating students.

Further, students emphasize the benefits of community (e.g., small classes), equality, counseling (e.g., advice on how to become a good person or achiever), interaction, attunement (listening) and intimacy (e.g., knowing what's going on in another's life). These are emerging practices are called *competence-driven* practices.

Competence-Driven Pedagogic Approaches

Generally, competence-driven practices focus on the 'person' over the 'student' and emphasize the potential of the wholistic self rather than just one's performance; such practices consider 'inclusion' and 'integration.' Success is not predicated only on personal effort and hard work, but also on help from others who care. Formal roles and boundaries are secondary, and students are given the opportunity for self-affirmation and self-definition and to make a mark. Economically, it is a more expensive model, which requires small classes for its interactive aspect, academic support, and mentoring and academic enrichment initiatives. Psychologically, it stands for an approach to learning that emphasizes empowerment and emancipation over and above acquisition of skill for an instrumental purpose (e.g., a career) (Bernstein, 2000: 50–56). Learning and teaching are construed as a space of possibilities and choice, where the primary goal is self-development. In curriculum terms, this approach allows for loose boundaries between academic knowledge and everyday life. While pockets of this practice exist in all elite institutions, more systematic aspects of this model in the academic support program are being developed at the University of KwaZulu-Natal.

Each of these two sets of practices – performance-driven and competence-driven – assumes more specific modes. Their construction in specific historical circumstances "may give rise to what could be called a pedagogic palette where mixes can take place (Bernstein, 2000: 56)." The data is not quantitative; it does not tell us how many lecturers are perceived to offer advice and guidance and to empower students and how many lecturers are perceived to position themselves primarily as knowledge specialists. This could be an interesting study, but it is not the point of this analysis. Also, more of these practices do not suggest throughput and retention will improve and debate about this is beyond the scope of this study. The tentative conjecture that can be made is that, in the absence of guidance, academic support, advice and personal care and in view of language difficulties, students who are able to 'crack the code', understand the modality of knowledge and work hard, will thrive. Other students manage unevenly, or drop out, depending on the availability of personal empowerment.

Some Implications: Policy Institutional Dilemmas

Performance-driven strategies are dominant in South African elite institutions, which emphasize high student performance and low participation. These practices recall a time when these institutions catered to a predominantly white and carefully selected student population, and emphasized merit and equal opportunity, competition among students, and the survival of the fittest. Indeed, students had to adapt or perish. This model concerns has limited concerns with social justice or access beyond a meritocracy framework. Institutionally, it is an inexpensive model demanding very little from the lecturers, but it is very taxing and demanding on students.

Pockets of competence-driven strategies have emerged, promoted by individual staff members and informed by concerns with institutional social responsiveness around equity, higher student participation and epistemic access. This is a response to the challenges posed by the increasing numbers of non-traditional or under-prepared students. In these strategies, a learning contract goes hand in hand with a moral contract. In some cases, current academic practices in some departments can be described as hybrid, embracing mixed approaches.

This legacy leaves the institution with three options: 1) to stick to traditional, performance-oriented approaches and align its selection and admission policies accordingly; 2) to emphasize competence-driven approaches; or 3) to adopt a hybrid model that retains the performance focus but offers greater support to students in need.

Emphasize high performance. This would require an admissions policy that carefully selects candidates who can make it, predominantly on their own, and a policy based on the assumption that the fittest will survive and succeed in a very selective and high-standard teaching and learning context. This option would align with the elite university's strategic orientation toward research because it would lessen the burden of undergraduate teaching and allow more time for research. It would also be relatively inexpensive, making it a pragmatic choice. It would not, however, address the broader transformation concerns, particularly in the short term, and there is a risk that the best students coming from inadequate schooling would be missed in the selection process. The selection would filter out students likely to fail. There is enough evidence to speculate that Wits, UCT and Rhodes University have already opted for this model, while the University of Kwazulu-Natal seems to favor a hybrid model.

Emphasize competence. Economically, this is the most expensive option. It requires considerable investment in staff time and resources because it demands small classes for its interactive aspects, academic support, pastoral care, and mentoring and academic enrichment initiatives. At present, the academic staff who promote competence-based pedagogies in elite universities often do so at the expense of their personal time and research, and they sacrifice their careers in the process. If an institution were to commit to this option, it would be critical to address staff development issues more comprehensively to maximize preparation and to put in place appropriate recognition mechanisms for their efforts. The clear message from staff interviews is that staff members are worked to the limit. Providing more support for students with the same level of resources is not practical. Generally, this approach requires considerable trade-offs between research and teaching, which would be likely to compromise the research orientation of the university. Further, the institution's best students might feel neglected, as most efforts would concentrate on historically disadvantaged students.

Go hybrid. A hybrid model would retain the best aspects of high performance and contextualize them within a framework of social justice. If throughput and retention are to be improved with the current student diversity, the best elements of performance must be retained and enhanced through more open social relations that emphasize the person over the student and through pastoral care and personal and collective forms of recognition. This does not mean compromising standards, but rather making them explicit, actively and collaboratively to students by providing enabling socialization and learning opportunities especially for those who are unable to crack the code. This approach could work with all three categories of students mentioned above, enhancing top students' capacity to navigate through the system while catering for the needs of those students who do not share the academic code and who experience knowledge gaps and by specifying criteria, norms and standards through suitable support strategies. This model would require the good efforts of academic staff operating within a competence model to be expanded systematically and made mainstream.

In this view, the choice is not between high participation and high performance, but rather about confident participation for high performance. Economically, the third choice is relatively expensive. It requires, at a minimum, investment in staff time and resources similar to those given to postgraduate students: small classes for interactive aspects, academic support and mentoring and academic enrichment initiatives. Institutional differentiation would certainly provide suitable spaces for such an option.

The Overall View

The picture that emerges in the context of social and pedagogical practices in elite universities is varied, multidimensional and not without paradoxes. On the positive side, both the staff and students, in their different and diverging understandings and interpretations, have embraced the idea that academic achievement within a logic of performance requires a great deal of individual discipline, independence, hard work and an appropriate work ethic. On the negative side, the university has not yet clearly found a pedagogical formula that matches the profile of its complex student population. While there are considerable efforts and well-targeted accomplishments in some institutions and underexploited potential and delivery practices in some of their faculties, no comprehensive strategies exist to meet the diverse needs of the undergraduate students they attract, with the relative exception of UKZN.

Against this background, this chapter argues that comprehensive *institutional, academic and social support and mediation* should complement the emphasis placed on individual effort, which are rooted in performance strategies in an almost unproblematic way. Better communication and more visible application of policy, as well as clearly articulated academic expectations at the university, faculty and course levels would benefit all students, while specific support should be provided to new students, particularly second-language students, those who have graduated from disadvantaged schools and those who come from communities with limited resources and social capital. These students are increasingly mainstreamed in the student body. This challenge cannot be effectively addressed through the current scattered, fragmented and uncoordinated initiatives championed by dedicated faculty members.

The challenge begs for an integrated, broader programmatic and institution-wide support strategy, which requires the allocation of resources, leadership and institutional pragmatism tied to institution missions. In this regard, one cannot overemphasize the need for synergy among support strategies, communication strategies and initiatives to mediate student experience and the mission of the institution and its strategic planning instruments.

NOTES

[1] These figures include both universities and technikons.

[2] By *institutional facts,* we refer to those aspects of institutional life against which we conduct our daily lives on campus, and whose use we collectively agree on – even if we do not think about them (e.g., wearing a gown for graduation). As Broekman and Pendlebury (2002: 289) put it, 'institutional facts assume collective agreement on function, status and meaning.' *Constitutive rules* refer to the normative framework, not always explicit, that creates the very possibility of a particular form of practice (what students at university should do, how they should behave or spend their leisure time, etc.). The concepts originate from Searle's work (Searle, J. 1995. *The construction of social reality*. Harmondsworth: Penguin.).

[3] We borrow some of the characteristics of these practices from Bernstein (2000), as described earlier.

[4] This is similar to what Sfard (1998) refers to as the 'acquisition metaphor.'

REFERENCES

Abbott-Chapman, J., Hughes, P. and Wyld, C. (1992). *Monitoring Student Progress: A Framework for Improving Student Performance and Reducing Attrition in Higher Education*. Youth Education Studies Centre, University of Tasmania.

Badat, S., Barron, F., Fisher, G., Pillay, P. & Wolpe, H. (1994) *Differentiation and Disadvantage: The Historically Black Universities in South Africa*. A Research Report to the Desmond Tutu Educational Trust.

Bellah, R, Madsen, R, Sullivan, W, Swidler, A. & Tipton, S. (1991). *The Good Society* New York, Alfred A Knopf Press.

Bernstein, B. (1975). *Class, Codes and Control (Vol.3): Towards a Theory of Educational Transmission*. London: Routledge and Kegan Paul.

Bernstein, B. (2000). *Pedagogy, Symbolic Control and Identity: Theory, Research, Critique*, revised edition. Lanham, Rowman and Littlefield Publishers, London.

Bourdieu, P. (1989). Towards a Reflexive Sociology: A workshop with Pierre Bordieu. In Wacquant, L. (Ed.) *Sociological Theory*, 7: 26-63.

Broekmann, I. & Pendlebury, S. (2002). Diversity, Background and the Quest for Home in Postgraduate Education. Studies in Higher Education, 27(3) 287-295.

Bourke, C. J., Burdon, J. K. and Moore, S. (1996). Factors Affecting Performance of Aboriginal and Torres Strait Islander Students at Australian Universities: A Case Study. DETYA. http://www.dest.gov.au/archive/highered/eippubs/eip9618/front.htm.

Brooks, A. and Brickhill, J. (1980). *Whirlwind Before the Storm: The Origins and Development of the Uprising in Soweto and the Rest of South Africa from June to December 1976*. London: International Defence and Aid Fund.

Cele, G., Koen, C. and Mabizela, M. (2002), "Post-apartheid Higher Education Emerging Trends in Student Politics, Education Policy Unit." University of Western Cape, Bellville.

Cele, Mlungisi Gabriel (2005) Opinion Piece: Student Funding Crisis. *Cape Times*. 28 February 2005. Available.

Clark, E. and Ramsey, W. (1990). Problems of Retention in Tertiary Education. *Education Research and Perspectives*. 17(2): 47-59.

Cloete, N., Fehel, R., Maassen, P., Moja, T,, Perold, H. & Gibbon, T. (Eds.) (2002). *Transformation in Higher Education: Global Pressures and Local Realities in South Africa*. Lansdowne, South Africa. Juta.

Coughlan, F. (2006). Access for success. *South African Journal of Higher Education*, Vol. 20, Issue 2, p.209-218.

Coulon, A. (1993). *Ethnométhodologie*. Collection Encyclopédique *Que Sais-je?* Presses Universitaires de France, Paris.

Craig, A. P. (2001). Education for All. *South African Journal of Higher Education* 10(2): 47-55.

Cross, M. & Johnson, B. (2008). Establishing a Space of Dialogue and Possibilities: Student Experience and Meaning at the University of the Witwatersrand. *South African Journal of Higher Education* 22(2)

Cross, M., Shalem, Y., Backhouse, J. and Adam, F. "Wits Gives You the Edge:" How Students Negotiate the Pressures and Pleasures of Undergraduate Study at Wits University. CHE: 2008, forthcoming.

Cross M. and Carpentier, C. "New Students" in South African Higher Education: Institutional Culture, Student Performance and the Challenge of Democratization. *Perspectives in Education*, Volume 27(1), March 2009, pp.6-18.

Cross, M., Shalem, Y., Backhouse, J. and Adam, F., "How Undergraduate Students 'Negotiate' Academic Performance within a Diverse University Environment." *South African Journal of Higher Education*. Vol. 23, No 1 (2009a), pp. 21-42.

Cross, M. (2009b). "Explaining student access and academic performance in South African higher education: a theoretical review". CHE Book, forthcoming.

Darlington-Jones, D., Cohen, L., Haunold, S., Pike, L. and Young, A. (2003). The Retention and Persistence Support (RAPS) Project: A Transition Initiative. *Issues in Higher Education Research* 13.

De Beer, K.J. (2006). Open Access, Retention and Throughput at the Central University of Technology. *South African Journal of Higher Education*, Vol. 20, Issue 1, p.31-45.

Dobson, I. (1999). Performance Indicators in the Measurement of Institutional Success in Transition from Secondary to Tertiary: A Performance Study. Department for Education, Training and Youth Affairs, Canberra. Retrieved 18 January 2007 from http://www.dest.gov.au/archive/highered/hes/hes36.htm.

Dobson, I. and Sharma, R. (1995). Student Performance and the Diversification of Modes of University Study and Bases of Admission. DEETYA. Durkheim, E. 1984. *The Diision of Labor in Society*. New York: The Free Press.

EFA Global Monitoring Report. (2008). *Education for All by 2015. Will we make it?* Paris. UNESCO/OXFORD.

Ensor P. (1998). Access, Coherence and Relevance: Debating Curriculum in Higher Education. *Social Dynamics.* 24(2): 92-104.

Grenfell, M. & James, D. (1998). *Bourdieu and Education: Acts of Practical Theory* London, Falmer Press.

Griesel, H. (2004). *Curriculum Responsiveness: Case Studies in Higher Education.* South African Universities Vice Chancellors Association (SAUVCA), Pretoria.

Gunawardena, C. (1995). Social Presence Theory and Implications for Interaction and Collaborative Learning in Computer Conferencing. *International Journal of Educational Telecommunications,* 1(2-3): 147-166.

Hooks, B. (1990) *Yearning Race, Gender and Cultural Politics.* Cambridge, South End Press.

Howell, C. and Lazarus, S. (2003). Access and Participation for Students with Disabilities in South African Higher Education: Challenging Accepted Truths and Recognising New Possibilities. *Perspectives in Education.* 21(3): 59-74.

Hostetter, C. & Busch, M. (2006). Measuring Up Online: The Relationship between Social Presence and Student Learning Satisfaction *Journal of Scholarship of Teaching and Learning,* 6 (2): 1–12.

Janks, H. (2004). The Access Paradox. *English in Australia* 139: 33–42.

Jansen, J. D. (2004). "Race, Education and Democracy After Ten Years: How Far Have We Come?" Prepared for IDASA. Lessons from the field: A Decade of Democracy in South Africa.

King, K. L. (2001). "Stumbling Toward Racial Inclusion: The Story of Transformation at the University of the Witwatersrand," in Apartheid No More: Case Studies of South African Universities in the Process of Transformation. (Eds.) Reitumetse Obakeng Mabokela and Kimberly Lenease King. Westport, CT: Bergin and Garvey.

Koen, C. and Roux, M.C. (1995). The Vicissitudes of Non-racialism: A Case Study of Social Interaction Among UWC Students. Unpublished paper: Cape Town: UWC.

Kotta, L. T. F (2006). Affording or Constraining Epistemological Access: An Analysis of a Case-based Approach in a First Year Process and Materials Engineering Course. M.Ed. Research Report, Faculty of Humanities, University of the Witwatersrand 14-Nov-2006.

Lewis, D. E. (1994). The Performance at University of Equity Groups and Students Admitted via Alternative Modes of Entry. Australian Government Printing Service, Canberra.

Lodge, H. (1997). Providing Access to Academic Literacy in the Arts Foundation Programme at the University of the Witwatersrand in 1996 – The Theory Behind the Practice. Unpublished Masters Research Report. Johannesburg: University of the Witwatersrand.

Long, M. (1994). A Study of the Academic Results of On-campus and Off-campus Students: Comparative Performance within Four Australian Tertiary Institutions. Australian Government Printing Service, Canberra.

Long, M. Carpenter, P. and Hayden, M. (1995). Graduating from Higher Education. Australian Government Printing Service, Canberra.

Maseko, Sipho (1994). Student Power, Action and Problems: A Case Study of UWC SRC, 1981-1992. *Transformation.* Issue 24: 72-90.

McClelland, A. and Kruger, P. (1989). Performance in Tertiary Studies of Students Admitted through the Queensland Tertiary Admissions Centre in 1989-1990. Canberra: Australian Government Printing Service.

McInnis, C., James, R., and Hartley, R. (2000). Trends in the First-year Experience in Australian Universities. Department of Education, Training and Youth Affairs, Canberra. Retrieved 18 Jan 2007 from http://www.dest.gov.au/archive/highered/eippubs/eip00_6/fye.pdf.

McJamerson, E. (1992). 'Undergraduate Academic Major and Minority Student Persistence: Individual Choices, National Consequences.' *Equity and Excellence,* 25: 35-48.

Moll, I. (2004). 'Curriculum Responsiveness: The Anatomy of a Concept' in Griessel, H. (Ed. 2004). *Curriculum Responsiveness: Case Studies in Higher Education,* South African Universities Vice Chancellors Association, Pretoria.

Molobi, E. (1987). "The University as White Elephant." University of the Witwatersrand: Richard Feetham Memorial Lecture.

Molteno, F. (1987). 'Students Take Control: The 1980 Boycott of Coloured Education in the Cape Peninsula.' British Journal of Sociology of Education 8, No. 1.

Molteno, F. (1983). 'Reflections on Resistance: Aspects of the 1980 Students' Boycotts.' Kenton Conference Proceedings, 56.

Molteno, F. (1979). 'The Uprising of 16th June: A Review of the Literature in South Africa 1976.' Social Dynamics 5, No. 1.

Moore, M. (1997). "Theory of Transactional Distance." Keegan, D. (Ed.) *Theoretical Principles of Distance Education*. Routledge, pp. 22-38.

Morrow, W. 1992. Epistemological Access in University. *AD Issues* 1: 3-5.

Muller, J. 2000. *Reclaiming Knowledge: Social Theory Curriculum and Educational Policy*. Routledge Falmer, London.

Muller, J. (2006). 'On the Shoulders of Giants: Verticality of Knowledge and the School Curriculum,' in Moore, R., Arnot, M., Beck, J. and Daniels, H (Eds.). *Knowledge, Power and Educational Reform: Applying the Sociology of Basil Bernstein*, Routledge, London.

Nkoli, M. I. P. (2003). "A Sociological Analysis of Restructuring at the University of the Witwatersrand, 1999-2001." M.A. thesis (Johannesburg: University of the Witwatersrand.

Nkomo M. (1984). *Student Culture and Activism in Black South African Universities: The Roots of Resistance Contributions in Afro-American and African Studies*. Vol.78. Westport: Greenwood.

Nkomo M. (1990). *Pedagogy of Domination*. New Jersey: Africa World Press.

The Open Universities in South Africa. (1957). Johannesburg: University of the Witwatersrand.

Nolutshungu, S. C. (1999). "Beyond the gold standard? The Idea of a (Post-apartheid) University." *Journal of Modern African Studies 37*, No. 3 (1999): 373-87.

OECD. (2008). Reviews of National Policies for Education. South Africa.

Paola, R. J., Lemmer, E. M. and Van Wyk, N. (2004). Factors Influencing the Participation of Undergraduate Students from Sub-Saharan Africa in Higher Education in the United States of America. *Africa Education Review*, Vol. 1, Issue 1, p. 65-80.

Peters, R. S. (1966). "Authority and Education" in *Ethics & Education* (London: Unwin University Books).

Richardson, J. C. & Swan, K. S. (2003). Examining Social Presence in Online Courses in Relation to Students' Perceived Learning and Satisfaction. Journal of Asynchronous Learning Networks, 7(1): 68-88.

Rowe, D. (2003). *Fostering Community in an Increasingly Disintegrated World: A Discussion of William Tierney's "Building Communities of Difference" and Robert Bellah and Colleagues' "The Good Society."* LaGrange College.

Rollnick, M. and Tresman, S. (2004). Widening Participation in Science Education: The Potential for Distance Learning to Deliver Programmes of Study in Foundation Level Science: The Practice of Higher Education. *South African Journal of Higher Education*, Vol. 18, Issue 1, p.382-394.

Sakarai, L.J. (1997). The Political Marginalisation of the Coloured Student Community of the University of the Western Cape. *African Anthropology*. 4(1): 4-35.

Schneider, B. L. and Stevenson, D. (1999). The Ambitious Generation: America's Teenagers, Motivated But Directionless. Yale University Press, New Haven.

Scott, C., Burns, A. and Cooney, G. (1996). 'Reasons for Discontinuing Study: The Case of Mature Age Female Students with Children.' *Higher Education*. 31: 233-253.

Shah, C. and Burke, G. (1996). Student Flows in Australian Higher Education. Australian Government Publishing Service, Canberra.

Shields, N. (1995). 'The Link between Student Identity, Attributions, and Self-esteem among Adult, Returning Students.' *Sociological Perspective,* 38 (2): 261-273.

Slonimsky and Shalem (2004). Pedagogic Responsiveness for Academic Depth in H. Griessel (Ed.) *Curriculum Responsiveness: Case Studies in Higher Education.* 2004. Pretoria. South African Universities Vice-Chancellors Association.

Solomons, Collette (1989). *"Sexism at the University of the Western Cape: With Special Reference to Progressive Student Organizations."* Unpublished mini-thesis. University of the Western Cape.

Strage, A. (2000). 'Predictors of College Adjustment and Success: Similarities and Differences among Southeast-Asian-American, Hispanic, and White Students.' *Education* 120(4): 731-740.

Subotsky, G. (2003). 'South Africa' in Teffera, D. and Altbach, G. (Eds.) *Africa Higher Education: An International Reference Handbook.* Bloomington: Indiana University Press.

Terenzini, P., Rendon, L., Upcraft, L., Millar, S., Allison, K., Gregg, P. and Jalomo, R. (1994). 'The Transition to College: Diverse Students, Diverse Stories.' *Research in Higher Education* 35(1): 57-73.

Thomas, J. W., Bol, L. and Warkentin, R. W. (1991). 'Antecedents of College Studies Study Deficiencies: The Relationship between Course Features and Student Study Activities.' *Journal of Higher Education* 22: 275–296.

Tierney, W. (1993). *Building Communities of Difference: Higher Education in the Twenty First Century.* Westport, CT, Bergin and Garvey.

Tinto, V. (1987). *Leaving College: Rethinking the Causes and Cures of Student Attrition,* University of Chicago Press, Chicago.

Tinto, V. (1993). *Leaving University: Rethinking the Causes and Cures of Student Attrition* (2nd edition). University of Chicago Press, Chicago.

Tinto, V. (1995a). 'Educational Communities and Student Success in the First-year of University'. Retrieved 18 January 2007 from http://www.adm.monash.edu.au/transition/activities/tinto.html.

Tinto, V. (1995b). 'Learning Communities, Collaborative Learning, and the Pedagogy of Educational Citizenship.' AAHE Bulletin. 47: 11-13.

Tinto, V. (2000). 'Learning Better Together: The Impact of Learning Communities on Student Success in Higher Education.' *Journal of Institutional Research.* 9 (1): 48-53.

Tinto, V. Goodsell-Love, A. and Russo, P. (1993). 'Building Community among New College Students.' *Liberal Education.* 79: 16-21.

Tinto, V. and Goodsell-Love, A. (1993). A *Longitudinal Study of Freshman Interest Groups at the University of Washington.* Jossey-Bass, San Francisco.

Tinto, V. and Russo, P. (1993). A *Longitudinal Study of the Co-ordinated studies Programme at Seattle Central Community College.* Jossey-Bass, San Francisco.

Van den Berg, A. (2006). Alternative Academic Access - Analysing the Success (Part One). *Interdisciplinary Journal,* Vol. 5, Issue 1, p.62-68.

Wenger, E. (1999). *Communities of Practice: Learning, Meaning and Identity.* Cambridge, Cambridge University Press.

Webster E. et al. (1986). The Role of the University in a Changing South Africa: Perceptions of Wits. Johannesburg: University of the Witwatersrand.

West, L. (1985). 'Differential Prediction of First-year University Performance for Students from Different Social Backgrounds.' *Australian Journal of Education* 29: 175-187.

West, L., Hore, T., Bennie, C., Browne, P. and Kermond, B. (1986). *Students Wtdrawing from Full-time Higher Education.* HEARU, Monash University, Melbourne.

Western, J., McMillan, J. and Durrington, D. (1998). Differential Access to Higher Education: The Measurement of Socio-economic Status, Rurality, and Isolation. Department of Education, Training and Youth Affairs, Canberra. Retrieved 18 January 2007 from http://www.dest.gov.au/highered/eippubs/eip98-14/eip98-14.pdf.

Witt, P. L., Wheeless, L. R. & Allen, M. 2004. "A Meta-Analytical Review of the Relationship between Teacher Immediacy and Student Learning" in the journal *Communication Monographs* 71 (2): 184-207.

Woolcock, M. and Narayan, D. (2000). Social Capital: Implications for Development Theory, Research and Policy. *The World Bank Research Observer* 15(2): 225-249.

Woolcock, M. (2002). "Social Capital and Development: Concepts, Evidence and Applications. Workshop on Understanding and Building Social Capital in Croatia, Zagreb." World Bank.

Chapter Seven

HIGHER EDUCATION ACCESS AND RETENTION OPPORTUNITIES FOR STUDENTS WITH DISABILITIES: STRATEGIES AND EXPERIENCES FROM SELECTED PUBLIC UNIVERSITIES IN EGYPT AND KENYA

BY VIOLET WAWIRE, KENYATTA UNIVERSITY; NADIA ELARABI, AIN SHAMS UNIVERSITY; AND HELEN MWANZI, UNIVERSITY OF NAIROBI

Introduction

Access opportunities to higher education throughout the world have improved in terms of increased numbers of tertiary institutions and student enrollments. Enrollments in tertiary institutions had increased to 152.5 million in 2007, roughly 50 percent more than the number in the year 2000 (UNESCO, 2009). In Africa, growth in the university education sector has been influenced by political motivations, as well as the social demand for higher education, given expansions at the primary and secondary school levels (Mwiria, 2007). Within the period between 1985 and 2002, the number of students enrolled in tertiary institutions in Africa increased from 800,000 to 3 million, registering a 3.5 percent increase (UNESCO, 2009; Materu, 2007). While these enrollment statistics look impressive, African countries are yet to make meaningful gains made by developed countries in North America and Western Europe whose access rates stand at 71 percent in comparison to Africa's six percent (UNESCO, 2009). Further, within countries, national enrollment trends and graduation rates mask regional, ethnic, socio-economic differences, and continuing discrimination against students with special educational needs.[1]

This chapter offers a comparative study of provision of access for students with disabilities in Kenya and Egypt from the perspective of recognized international and country conventions for the provision of opportunities to such students, and actual conditions in the institutions surveyed. It concludes with recommendations for strategies to address the problems identified.

Access in Kenya and Egypt

Using the two countries of this study's focus as illustration points, it is noted that although Kenya's higher education has grown to seven public and 19 private universities with a total enrollment of 119,849 in 2000, this translates into only 7.5 percent of the students completing secondary education and 2 percent of the expected age cohort (Mugenda, 2009). Similarly, Egypt's egalitarian higher education system, where university education comprises 75 percent of the enrollments in this sector and comes with guaranteed government employment for graduates, attracts only 28 percent of the relevant age group (Cupito and Sanford, 2008). In both countries, economically endowed regions tend to send more students to universities, negating the assumption that increased enrollments translate into improved access for traditionally disadvantaged groups in society.

Access Issues for Students with Disabilities

Equity of access in higher education remains a major concern of African scholars and policy makers, particularly gender and socioeconomic disparities (Mwiria, 2007; Asiie-Lumumba, 1995; Ajayi, 1996; Saint, 1992). Consequently, while strategies have been implemented to ensure equity of access for non-traditional students, students with disabilities (SWD), who are equally marginalized in terms of access to higher education, have been ignored (Saint, 1992). Yet, because they account for to 10 percent of most populations, their plight needs to be brought to the center stage.

In Egypt and Kenya, this neglect is bound to persist, given the complete absence of SWD in higher education national statistics and in future government plans like economic surveys, national development plans and education policy reform guidelines (GOK 2007, 2006, 2005; HEEP, 2004). Yet, even if the policy framework existed, the two countries, and many others in Africa, would face difficulties in planning, implementing and monitoring it, given the lack of reliable and comprehensive data on the number of SWD in higher education and the number of institutions and support services available for them (GOK, 2007; GOK, 2006). Extensive research on the disability question in higher education in Africa is only available from South Africa, whose socio-political climate and its impact on educational provision may be dissimilar to the conditions in other countries in the region (Howell, 2005; CHE, 2005; UNESCO, 1999). However, the growing opportunities for SWD at the primary and secondary levels, following the inception of the inclusion policy of educational service, mandates that African governments and their higher education institutions anticipate and accommodate the needs of SWD (GOK, 2005; Cupito and Sanford, 2008). The limited opportunities in higher education indicate that when these students complete high school, they cannot advance to the tertiary level (GOK, 2006). Further, access to higher education for SWD must be seen not only as a human right but also as an obligation, because this group, as a collective or as individuals, may have both the experiences and talents to be of great value for the development of society (UNESCO, 1999). Impetus on this issue from the international circles is drawn from declarations made by the World International Conference on Higher Education (WCHE) held in Paris in October 1988, which reaffirmed that:

"….In keeping with the Article 26.1 of the Universal Declaration of Human Rights, admission to higher education should be based on merit, capacity, efforts, perseverance, and devotion, showed by those seeking access to it and can take place in a life-long scheme. No discrimination can be accepted in granting access to higher education on the grounds of race, gender, language, religion, economic, cultural or social discrimination or physical disability" (Article 3(a) World Declaration of Higher Education for the 21st Century, Vision and Action, Paris, 1988).

In highlighting the need to consider factors other than ability, the World Conference set the stage for revision of existing admission criteria to higher education, making them more flexible and sensitive to and widening access for the needs of special groups like SWD. Where available, research literature from African universities indicates low enrollments of SWD who are susceptible to droping out (Mwiria, 2007; UNESCO, 1999). Thus, an emerging argument is that equity of access and opportunity for SWD in higher education involves much more than gaining physical entry into the institutions.

Low enrollments and high dropout rates observed among SWD in Africa, specifically in Egypt and Kenya, point toward barriers both to access and retention that need further investigation if the chances of advancing education for this marginalized group would be maximized. Under the umbrella of the Africa Higher Education Collaborative (AHEC) program on access and equity to higher education, two studies were conducted, one on Kenya and the other on Egypt. They explored the opportunities available for SWD in terms of current enrollments and services in public universities where most of them were likely to be admitted. The goal of the studies was to provide information for planning, monitoring and evaluating programs that improve access and retention of SWD in higher education. The studies endeavored to answer such critical research questions as these:

- What was the nature of historical and present national and institutional policy environments that explained the absence of SWD from the higher education scene?

- What was the number of SWD enrolled in public universities as a percentage of the cohort that completed secondary education, and what were the indicators of poor retention?

- What were the characteristics of these students in terms of subjects they took, nature of disability and source of sponsorship and reasons behind the patterns exhibited?

- What opportunities, barriers and challenges existed for SWD in public universities that determined whether they accessed and completed university education?

- What lessons could be drawn from public universities in Egypt and Kenya in the form of strategies that could enhance the access and retention of SWD in higher education?

National and Institutional Policy Contexts: Egypt

Policies that favor the rights of people with disabilities in Egypt date as far back as 1975 in the form of law number 39, although the policies focus on their rehabilitation and the provision of job opportunities. It is not until 1996 with Childhood Law No. 12 of the Peoples' Assembly that rights of disabled people in relation to education are addressed, and at that time their participation rate in education was just 4 percent (JICA, 2002). Yet, even this policy did not account for people with disabilities in higher education. A recent development whose impact is yet to be determined is the ratification of the UN convention on the rights of persons with disabilities by Egypt in 2008. Article 24 declares that respective states should ensure an inclusive education system at all levels and lifelong learning (Kotb and Hak, 2008).

Similarly, there is hope for the implementation of the 2002 Higher Education Enhancement Project, which was part of the Ministry of Higher Education's strategic plan and was sponsored by the World Bank. The project responded to the deteriorating quality of higher education in the country and aimed at improving quality, efficiency, and relevance of the sector. However, going by the quality assurance and accreditation handbook for higher education that was released in 2004, the issues of SWD at this level are far from being addressed. The handbook, whose main focus is quality of curriculum aspects, does not in any way target the special needs of SWD who require an adjusted curriculum to succeed (MOHE, 2004).

National and Institutional Policy Contexts: Kenya

Few national policies in Kenya exist to promote education for SWD, mirroring the general neglect they have experienced in the country. The Sessional Paper No. 5 chaired by Mwendwa in 1968 broke new ground on educational provision for Persons with Disabilities (PWD) in Kenya. It provided space for the establishment of national special education infrastructure in the Ministry of Education through its recommendations on the care and rehabilitation of disabled people in Kenya (GOK, 1968). However, not until 1988 was a policy adopted to expand access for disabled people in education. Sessional paper No. 6, commonly known as the Kamunge Report, spearheaded the integration of children with disabilities into regular schools to supplement activities already underway in a few special schools (GOK, 1988). While two, rather old government policy documents have been used as reference points in the country's development of special education, their impact has been minimal because the broad policy statements they give have not influenced specific frameworks of action to guide sector activities. Consequently, they have not increased the participation of disabled people in higher education.

A general approach to special education is also reflected in government policy documents like development plans and economic surveys that do not respond to the specific education needs of disabled people (GOK, 2008; GOK, 2001). And given the growth and development of the special education sector, an updated policy framework is imperative. Specifically, a policy is needed that addresses access and participation in higher education given the increased number of disabled people with secondary school qualifications. While this was less important when policies were developed in the 1960s to the 1980s, it should be a priority now, given that disabled people have increased in number and acccess to primary and secondary education (GOK, 2005). In addition, Kenya has embraced democratic principles, which should be reflected in the practice of education where equal opportunity is provided for all, especially at the higher level where their skills can be used to contribute to national development.

The Persons with Disability Act of 2003 is the latest legislation in the support of SWD in Kenya. This is an Act of Parliament that provides for their rights and rehabilitation to achieve equalization of opportunities as well as establish the National Council for Persons with Disabilities (NCPD) through which they can express their needs to government (GOK, 2003). The Act is comprehensive, covering all areas which would present barriers to disability enablement, and it includes a clause that mandates accurate representation of disabled people in national figures, reversing actions like those that led to their omission in the 1999 National Household Census. In terms of education, the Act also mandates provision of special facilities and equipment, assistive devices, appropriate curriculum and examinations and scholarships for SWD. However, the contents of the Act have clearly not been implemented to date.

Regionally, policies meant to enhance the quality of education, especially for SWD, led to a quality assurance practice handbook for universities in East Africa. Developed by the Inter-University Council of East Africa (IUEA), institutions of higher education must adhere to it. The handbook is a product of a decision by three higher education regulating agencies: CHE for Kenya, National Commission for Higher Education of Uganda and Tanzania Commission for Universities. It harmonizes the quality assurance systems in the region in order to operate on international terms (IUEA, 2008; Buchare, 2009).While this document addresses the gender concerns in higher education, once again the SWD as a special group is omitted.

Institutional Policies

Regrettably, government policy pronouncements have not been reflected in relevant individual policy environments of higher education institutions, including intermediary bodies in Egypt and Kenya. For example, the Commission for Higher Education (CHE), which is responsible for the overall quality assurance in public and private universities in Kenya, ignored the provision of SWD in terms of facilities, curriculum and learning environment as evaluation criteria for new university accreditation or quality assurance for established universities. Similarly, while an affirmative action policy has existed for female students for several years, a policy for SWD has not yet been actualized. Further, the Higher Education Loans Board (HELB) and Joint Admissions Board (JAB) do not consider the special financial and social needs of SWD during the process of loan allocation and university admissions, respectively. However, JAB, which is responsible for selecting and admitting government-sponsored students to university courses, is developing affirmative action admission criteria in favor of SWD to allow them to join universities at lower cut off points, given the challenges they face in school in comparison to able-bodied students. However, this is subject to approval by the Ministry of Education and HELB, given that government-sponsored JAB students receive government-subsidized loan allocations unlike their privately sponsored counterparts.

In Egypt, the Supreme Council of Universities (SCU), the body responsible for administering higher education in the country, has two entry criteria that deter the access of SWD to public universities. While SWD can only enroll in some colleges like the women's, art, law and commerce colleges, their numbers cannot exceed 5 percent of the total opportunities in each.

While some of the universities had mission statements and visions ascribing to equal opportunity provision, only one had plans of developing a SWD policy to guide its activities. In half, or three, of the universities in Kenya, the focus on SWD needs was totally absent in their strategic plans, which are instruments used to improve the performance of organizations.

Access and Participation of SWD in University Programs

Enrollment trends from six public universities each in Kenya and Egypt were not easily available because of poor record keeping of disability data by the universities. In some cases, the data had to be computed manually from the overall student records. Table 7.1 below provides enrollments from the institutions where data was available.

TABLE 7.1: ENROLLMENTS OF STUDENTS WITH DISABILITIES (SWD) IN KENYAN AND EGYPTIAN PUBLIC UNIVERSITIES, 2008

Kenya	SWD	Total Enrollment	Egypt	SWD	Total Enrollment
Kenyatta	64	18,597	Alexandria	579	114,000
University of Nairobi	16	36,343	Aim Shams	645	180,000
Jomo Kenyatta University of Science and Technology	9	7,963	Zagazig	474	107,908
Moi	41	14,832	Helwan	91	100,000
Egerton	9	12,467	Assiut University	133	68,841
Maseno	30	5,586	Almenia	90	50,000
Total	169 (0.18%)	95,788	Total	2,012 (0.324%)	620,749

Source: Kenyan and Egyptian Universities, 2008, Economic Survey, 2008

The enrollments shown here do not account for students who resist registering their disabilities with the universities' Students Affairs Office, due to the stigma attached or because they do not require special mobility or audio-visual learning assistive services. The quote below by one student elaborates:

"...Being disabled is an embarrassment especially when you need help. So we avoid being seen as a bother by people so we try doing things by ourselves" (Kenyan, male, physically disabled student, 2008).

Nevertheless, the numbers obtained present a general picture of SWD studying at public universities in Kenya and Egypt. Although Egyptian public universities have slightly better access opportunities for SWD than those in Kenya, the overall participation of SWD in university education in the two countries is poor, translating to below 0.4 percent of the total number of students enrolled. In both countries, SWD seemed to be attracted to disability-friendly universities in terms of policy and/or courses offered. Kenyatta University, which attracts the majority (38 percent) of the Kenyan SWD, had the historical advantage of catering for SWD and, therefore, relatively developed infrastructure and courses to cater for their special needs. In Egypt, Ain Shams University hosted a majority of the courses that SWD were officially allowed to take.

In terms of SWD by gender, only the Kenyan study was able to obtain data. The access of female SWD to university education mirrors the picture observed in Kenyan universities where the gender gap favors male students. The female population, which was only 32 percent (54 out of the total 169) of the total SWD, fell within the same range as the overall Kenyan university female statistical trend of 38 percent.Table 7.2, on the other hand, provides a breakdown of SWD in the two countries by disability. Data for Kenya is derived from Kenyatta, Moi, Nairobi, JKUAT and Egerton universities; for Egypt, Alexandria, Ains Shams, Helwan, Assiut, and Zagazig universities.

TABLE 7.2: ENROLLMENTS OF STUDENTS WITH DISABILITIES (SWD) IN KENYAN AND EGYPTIAN PUBLIC UNIVERSITIES BY TYPE OF DISABILITY, 2008

Disability Type	Egyptian Universities	%	Kenyan Universities	%
Visual	629	32.8	59	42.4
Physical	1270	66.2	68	49.0
Hearing	20	1.0	6	4.4
Other	-	-	6	4.3
Totals	1,919	100	139	100

Source: Kenyan and Egyptian Universities, 2008

The results from both countries indicate that hearing impairments are the least represented disability in public universities. Historically, students with visual and physical impairments have had more advantages at the primary and secondary level. Those with physical impairments are more likely to register with the university because of the visible nature of their impairment. Further, they are likely to be integrated within regular schools and universities, even when facilities like ramps may be minimal.

An important observation to note from the data is the absence of students with mental disabilities, indicating that such students do not register with the university, are not acknowledged and, therefore, do not have their needs met. The high percentage shown of students with visual disabilities may be attributed to the historically developed opportunities available at Kenyatta University, which caters to the needs of students with visual impairments through its basic learning infrastructure. This university has been attracting visually impaired students since the early 1980s. The study went further to analyze the courses SWD take at the various universities. Table 7.3 gives this breakdown.

Courses	Egyptian Universities				Kenyan Universities			
	Visual	Physical	Hearing	Totals	Visual	Physical	Hearing	Totals
Arts/ Humanities	639	811	2	1,452	3	8		11
Law	13	57		70		1		1
Education	2	1	-	3	64	42	6	112
Architecture						1		1
Agriculture						3		3
Pharmacy/ Science		3		3		1		1
Information Studies						1		1
Chemical Engineering						1		1
Commerce		1,012		1,012		4		4
Totals	654	1,884	2	2,540	62	67	6	135

Source: Kenyan and Egyptian Universities, 2008

In both counties, SWD were observed to be undertaking theoretically-based courses that included arts and humanities, education and law—subjects that do not involve field and laboratory work or manipulation of figures that are found in science subjects like mathematics, chemistry and physics. However, structural and policy contexts provide an explanation of this pattern. SWD often face discrimination when they apply for jobs even when they have the qualifications; yet in Kenya the field of education attracts SWD because of the available job opportunities in the profession. The Teachers Service Commission (TSC) had for a long time guaranteed SWD employment after completion of their training. The following quote from an interview with one student further elaborates the dynamics behind the choice of subjects to study at the university that include a background in arts. Again, Kenyatta University attracts the most number of SWD taking education courses because it is the pioneer education offering institution in the country.

"…Education is better because you can't cope with the practicals in science. There is an issue of the foundation that we had all the way in high school. The focus was not on other science-based courses. It was only arts-based courses, and we just opted for that. I also like teaching so I think I am on the right path" (Kenyan, male, visually disabled student, 2008).

In Egypt, SWD are attracted to arts, humanities, law and commerce courses because of the university admission policy that restricts SWD to theoretically- based colleges that offer these courses. The few SWD that have ventured in science-based disciplines have defied the policy. Similarly, it is students with physical challenges who are observed to venture into areas of study other than the traditional theoretically-based disciplines. The reason behind this pattern is the fact that students with mild physical challenges do not necessarily need specialized learning facilities like their counterparts with visual and hearing impairments.

Also, in Egypt the education colleges refuse to admit students with any kind of disability. One student affairs director said, "How can they can be teachers? How will the students respect them? They are people with disabilities."

Completion Trends of SWD

It was not enough that SWD were joining universities, but it was equally important to establish whether they were completing their courses within the stipulated four years and, if not, why not. The study found no significant programs targeting SWD to enhance their retention chances. No mentoring, peer counselling or orientation programs that specifically target SWD were in place in all the universities in Egypt and Kenya to ensure the perseverance of SWD. The programs available to the general student population were irrelevant to the needs of this group either because the staff concerned were not trained to handle them or the stigma attached to disability hindered SWD from visiting them. While statistics to support this observation were only available from Kenya, the quote below from a director of student affairs from a public university in Egypt confirms a similar practice:

"These disabled students are absent all the time and they can't pass every year" (Director of student affairs, public university, Egypt, 2008).

This statement implies rampant absenteeism among students with disabilities, which may result in prolonged time in college, poor performance or even dropping out. Table 7.4 provides completion trends of SWD attending public universities enrolled between 2002 and 2005.This data should be considered with the understanding that it was not possible to follow cohorts through the four-year cycle from the information universities made available. Thus, the graduating students may not necessarily be those from the same enrollment cohort.

Enrollment year	2002	2003	2004
Number of students	43	38	40
Clearance year	2006	2007	2008
Number of students	37	27	25
Deficit	6	11	15
Completion rate	86%	69%	52%

Source: Kenyan Universities, 2008

The table indicates low completion rates of up to 52 percent. Interviews revealed that delayed graduation trends among SWD was mainly due to college tuition problems that were occasioned by their low socio-economic backgrounds.

The Provision of Infrastructure and Learning Facilities

The needs of SWD consist of mobility assistive services and equipment, like ramps, wheelchair slides, wheelchairs and lifts for students with physical disabilities; Braille transcribers, readers and audio reading equipment for those with visual impairments; and sign language interpreters and hearing aids for students with hearing impairments. In addition, all categories of SWD require appropriate accommodation services situated on the ground floor for easy accessibility and custom-designed toilets with large doors to accommodate wheelchairs. Transport services are also needed for SWD given the long distances between the hostels and where classrooms are allocated, found in most of the spacious public universities. Further, the learning environment should be one that provides special allowances in terms of extra time and assistance to SWD given their special needs. The curriculum should be adjusted in terms of course content where appropriate activities and materials are used in place of the regular ones. All these services should be managed and coordinated by a center of SWD, possibly under the Dean of Students that has trained technical staff to handle these students. Table 7.5 indicates the levels of infrastructure and learning services available for SWD in the five public universities sampled by the studies in each country.

TABLE 7.5: PROVISION OF SPECIAL INFRASTRUCTURE AND LEARNING SERVICES FOR STUDENTS WITH DISABILITIES (SWD) IN KENYAN AND EGYPTIAN PUBLIC UNIVERSITIES, 2008

Type of Service	Egyptian Universities					Kenyan Universities				
	Ax	An	Zz	H	As	Ku	N	M	E	JK
Ramps/Lifts/Wheel chair slides	••	•	•	•	•	••	•	•	•	•
Accommodation	•			•		•		•		
Sign language interpreters										
Hearing devices										
Braille transcribers	•••	•••	••	•••	••	••		•		
Wheelchairs	••	••		••	•				•	•
Audiovisual machines/room		•••	•••	••	•••	••	••			
Sensitive lecturer/ learning practices						•	•	•	•	•
Officer for SWD (For visual only)						••				
Trained technical personnel (for visual only)	•	•	•	•		•	•	•	•	•
Adapted texts										
Examination allowances	•	•				•				
Flexible content										
Transport	•	•		•						

Ax-Alexandria, An-Ain Shams, Zz-Zagazig, H-Helwan, As-Assiut, Ku-Kenyatta, N-Nairobi, M-Moi, E-Egerton, JK-Jomo Kenyatta

Key
• Low levels of services
•• Medium levels of services
••• Adequate level of services

The table indicates low levels of special infrastructure for SWD, with visually disabled students benefiting the most. Although Egyptian universities seem to have slightly better services than Kenyan, especially in the areas of audio equipment and Braille transcribers, these services target students with visual disabilities, and when one considers the comparatively large number of students they serve with disabilities, the difference in benefits appears minimal. In addition, students with hearing disabilities were observed to be the most under-serviced group, mirroring the trend at the national level where schools for hearing-impaired students number the least. Similarly, while Kenyatta University offers most services, they are inadequate given that they again focus primarily on students with visual impairments. The picture from the two countries reveals that SWD enrolled in public universities face some serious challenges that impact effective learning. University administrators justify this state of affairs in terms of the low numbers of students enrolled who do not warrant investment of scarce university resources. The quote from one student exemplifies the disabling physical environment that students face at the university.

> "I have a car. I can go everywhere, but once I come to my college and get down from my car, I feel that I am disabled; I can't move—steps everywhere" (Egyptian physically disabled student, 2008).

Similarly, with reference to pedagogical applications, university lecturers admitted to having been ignorant to the special needs of SWD in their classes, pointing toward the need for sensitization and training as a stop gap measure. The following segment from an interview with one Kenyan lecturer indicates the inappropriate use of pedagogical practices observed by the way lecturers moved too fast during lectures, wrote on the board when they had students with visual impairments in their classes and did not provide allowances and assistance during examinations.

> "…Normally, we have large classes, and at times the only thing that makes you notice that you have some students who are visually impaired is the sound of the Braille machine when they are typing the notes. In most cases they go unnoticed" (Kenyan, female lecturer, 2008).

In one university in Egypt, some lecturers were unwilling to accommodate SWD in specific courses claiming their disabilities would hinder effective participation at college and performance in the respective careers after graduation. The extract below illustrates this:

> "For the last two years we stopped accepting special needs' students because the teacher must have the ability to do everything without the students in the schools laughing at the teacher" (Egyptian, male lecturer, 2008).

Social Experience of SWD

Most students generally attested to having fruitful social lives on campus with several admitting to having friends of the opposite sex. However, an analysis of the challenges faced due to limiting physical environments brought to surface negative social experiences of SWD which centered around the discrimination and stigma they faced from their peers and care-givers, limiting their participation in social activities around campus. For example, interviews revealed that other students view SWD as incapable of doing simple tasks and treat them with sympathy, rather than on equal terms.

Consequently, most SWD avoid social events like watching movies and doing sports. In actual fact, the majority of the SWD interviewed from Kenya were members of the Christian Union where they say they are treated on equal terms with everybody else. In addition, they participated in indoor games like table tennis and the gym, which draw less attention to their disability. The following statement from one Kenyan student sums up their view on the matter.

> "…We interact very well with other students of any sex, only we don't engage in sports apart from the mild sports like shooting pool. As for any other entertainment, we rely on ones provided by the university. But when it comes to going outside the university, we don't" (Kenyan, female student with physical disability, 2008).

Regrettably, this practice extended to the academic circles where lecturers reported that SWD participated less in class and group discussions and rarely offered to present in class. Survey results from lecturers in Egypt indicated that in addition to not adjusting their lessons to accommodate the needs of SWD, they were unaware of issues surrounding the welfare of SWD that included social activities, numbers and the subjects they were taking. The quote from a Kenyan lecturer below illustrates the similarity in the experiences in the two countries.

> "…Come to think of it, I am realizing now that I have never seen a SWD presenting in class. I don't know why, but it is something I may want to find out" (Kenyan, male lecturer, 2008).

In contrast, one university through two initiatives encouraged the participation of SWD in social activities with the intention that this might favorably impact academic experiences. Kenyatta University held a sports day for the physically challenged in 2008, organized by the games department in conjunction with the students association. Its success was so remarkable that it is to become an event on the university calendar. The university also has a peer counseling program which involves SWD as peer counselors on social issues, like HIV/Aids.

Conclusions

Our comparative study findings indicate very limited access and retention opportunities for SWD at the university level in Kenya and Egypt. Enrollment and completion patterns are low, coupled with disabling policy, social and physical environments. While this is the general trend globally and in South Africa where similar studies have been conducted, Kenya and Egypt are distinctive in their complete disregard of the needs of students with hearing and mental disabilities, respectively. Such observations indicate that there may be socio-cultural and historical issues that surround educational provision for specific impairments in the two countries that require further probing to establish underlying factors (Nichols & Quaye, 2009; Paul, 2000; Stage & Milne, 1996; UNESCO, 1999). This finding also points to the need for reconstructing the definition of disability in Kenya and Egypt that currently favors visual impairments in order to achieve practical provisions and relevant policies.

Further, the lack of reliable data on SWD in higher education in the two countries obfuscates study of higher education opportunities either for planning purposes or for prospective students who seek opportunities. Researchers from Kenya and Egypt faced enormous difficulties in accessing data on SWD due to the fact that records were not well kept or were unavailable. This finding was congruent with other empirical findings in the area (UNESCO, 1999; CHE, 2005). While unfortunate, most countries on the continent similarly lack data, because higher education institutions are not required to provide returns desegregated by disability as part of their periodical submissions to Commissions of Higher Education. However, the fact that regional quality assurance guidelines (in the Kenyan case) and a national quality reform program (in the case of Egypt) had overlooked SWD needs indicates a serious omission in the definition of equity of access to higher education. One way of overcoming this gap is to encourage more quantitative and qualitative analysis of variables surrounding SWD experiences in higher education, to bring the issue to the forefront in academic, as well as policy settings (CHE, 2005).

In addition, similar to the trends observed in other countries, access opportunities for SWD in Kenya and Egypt were available only in the theoretically based subjects of the humanities, education, law, and arts courses, with implications on the types of careers SWD acquire (UNESCO, 1999; CHE, 2005). The study identified a major barrier to academic and social engagement to be lack of an adapted curriculum for SWD in almost all courses. This practice limits the courses that SWD take to those that do not need scientific manipulations or field or laboratory work, and it confines them to specific careers which may not be their choice. Given that academic support is one of the major prerequisites for a successful experience for SWD in higher education, research should be devoted to revising the curriculum in all subject areas to adapt them to the special needs of SWD.

Access for and retention of SWD in higher education should be enhanced to ensure that not only do more students enroll and complete their courses on time, but they are also supported in undertaking the courses they desire. The studies identified strategies from similar work that can be used to attract, maintain and ensure the graduation of SWD in higher education programs in Egyptian and Kenyan universities.

Mentoring Programs

Institutions should adopt mechanisms through which SWD can form both formal and informal mentoring relationships to enable them to make social connections and acquire academic insights from their peers. In addition to enhancing perseverance for SWD, mentoring contributes to the formation of positive self images for these students, which in turn influences the way they overcome social and academic attitudinal-related barriers (Stage & Milne, 1996). Informal mentoring programs may involve pairing new SWD with those already enrolled, enabling them to connect with other students and faculty in a network that helps them adjust to college life. Informal mentoring can be encouraged through sponsored events like a sports day for SWD.

Administrative Office for SWD

Higher education institutions should set up administrative structures to handle the support for SWD. The presence of such an office will suggest to the students that the institution acknowledges the presence of SWD and is willing to commit resources for its support. However, the importance of this office will only be realized when both physical resources and trained human resources are committed to it.

Orientation Programs

Specific orientation programs should be developed to help SWD adjust to the first year of college life. Such programs should involve familiarizing students with the available resources in the college, as well as relevant faculty and administrative staff. According to Nichols & Quaye (2009), special orientation for SWD has the added benefit of helping SWD establish constructive study skills, productive routines and healthy relationships.

Revision of Institutional, National, and Regional Policies

An examination is needed of legislation and policy provisions at the regional and national level upon which individual institutional policies can be entrenched and enforced. A comprehensive policy framework should be developed that encompasses all aspects of the needs of SWD, including curriculum, examination, infrastructure and social spheres. At the university level, policy guidelines should be developed to legalize and prioritize resource allocation for SWD by students and staff members. One specific policy measure for widening access that is appropriate particularly for Kenya and Egypt would be affirmative action in the admission criteria for SWD where they can be admitted two points lower than others, as is done for female students in Kenya. Applying disability quotas for each course of study would be a related measure to ensure that SWD enter careers other than theoretically-based ones.

Special Grants and Scholarships

The study findings point to the fact that SWD face the challenge of meeting the college fee requirements due to their poor socio-economic backgrounds. In response to this, higher education institutions and loan granting bodies with the assistance of donor funding bodies should set up special grants and scholarships for SWD to facilitate their education. Work study programs used for students from impoverished backgrounds would be appropriate here, too.

Barrier-Free Infrastructure and Services

The provision of services and infrastructure, as well as quality assurance practices for SWD, should be mainstreamed in all university spheres. However, this should be done after periodical sensitization exercises are carried out to popularize the policy document guidelines. In order to determine the physical barriers that exist and hinder social and academic engagement, periodical audits should be carried out by independent monitoring and evaluation consultants. Such an exercise should incorporate generating and collecting disability data, which is useful in formulating policies at the national and institutional level, as well as developing activities and programs that enhance access and perseverance for SWD.

Campus Organizations for SWD

Students should be encouraged to form campus or national organizations that involve SWD from higher education institutions where they can meet with colleagues, share experiences and broaden their social and academic horizons. These organizations can also serve as activism and advocacy avenues for national and institutional concerns and provide opportunities for students to play an active role in ensuring they receive relevant and quality education. A starting point would be to lobby for an SWD leader position in the student union. In this study, one university with this provision had been able to push for reforms that have enhanced the infrastructure of the college in favor of SWD.

NOTES

[1] See chapter eight for a discussion of the various definitions for disabilities and the disabled.

REFERENCES

Achola, P. (1997). *Access, Equity and Efficiency in Kenyan Public Universities*, Lyceum Educational Consultants, Nairobi.

Ajayi, K. (1996). *The African Experience with Higher Education*, James Currey Ltd, London.

Assie-Lumumba, N. (1995). "Demand, Access and Equity Issues in African Higher Education: Best Policies, Current Practices and Readiness for the 21st Century." Paper presented for the donors in Africa Education Working Group in Higher Education.

Barnes, C., Mercer, G. (1997). "Breaking the Mould? An Introduction to Doing Disability Research." In *Doing Disability Research*, edited by C. Barnes and G. Mercer, The Disability Press, pp. 1 -14, Leeds.

Bogonko, S. (1992). "Special Education in East Africa: A Comparative Survey". *Basic Education Forum*, Vol. 1, May, BERC Nairobi.

Buchare, D. (2009). "A New Quality Assurance System." *University World News: East Africa Edition*, Issue 0022, 08, February, 2009.

Council on Higher Education. (2005). *South African Higher Education Responses to Students with Disabilities: Equity of Access and Opportunity?* CHE.

Cupito, E. & Sanford, R. (2008). *Inclusiveness in Higher Education in Egypt*. Institute of Public policy, Duke University, Social Science Research Center, American University of Cairo.

Government of Kenya. (2007). *Economic Survey*. Government Printer, Nairobi.

Government of Kenya. (2006). *Statistical Abstract 2006*. Government Printers, Nairobi.

Government of Kenya. (2003). *Persons with Disability Act, 2003*. Government Printer, Nairobi.

Government of Kenya. (2002). *National Development Plan 2002-2008*. Government Printers, Nairobi.

Government of Kenya. (1988). *Report on the Presidential Working Party on Education and manpower Training for the Next decade and Beyond*. Government Printer, Nairobi.

Government of Kenya. (1968). *National Development Plan 1970-1974*. Nairobi. Government Printers.

Howell, C. (2005). "Investigating Equity of Access and Opportunity for Students with Disabilities in South African Higher Education." Paper presented at FOTM Conference, October 2005, Johannesburg.

JICA (2002). Country Profile on Disability, Arab Republic of Egypt. JICA.

Kamere, I. (2005) "The Development of Special Education for the Physically Handicapped Children in Kenya 1945-2003". Unpublished Ph.D. Thesis, Kenyatta University, Nairobi, Kenya.

Kanake, L. (1997). *Gender Disparities among the Academic Staff in Kenyan Universities*. Lyceum Ed Consultants, Nairobi.

Kotb, K. and Hak, H. (2008). Hidden Disabilities: Identification and Support. Paper presented at the 15th AUC Annual Research Conference, April, 2008, American University in Cairo.

Materu, P. (2007). *Higher Education Quality Assurance in Sub-Saharan Africa: Status, Challenges, Opportunities and Promises*, World Bank.

MOHE (2004). *The Quality Assurance and Accreditation Handbook for Higher Education in Egypt*. Prepared by the National Quality Assurance and Accreditation Committee, Higher Education Advancement Programme.

Mugenda, O. (2009). Higher Education in Kenya: Challenges and Opportunities. Paper presented at AHEC meeting, Nairobi, March, 2009.

Mwiria, K., et al. (2007). *Public and Private Universities in Kenya*, James Curry Ltd, Oxford.

Ngao, G. (2005). "The Socialization of the Hearing Impaired Children: The Case of Machakos School for the Deaf." Unpublished M.Ed Thesis, Kenyatta University, Nairobi, Kenya.

Nichols, A. & J. Quaye. (2009). "Beyond Accommodation: Removing Barriers to Academic and Social Engagement." In *Student Engagement in Higher Education: Theoretical Perspectives and Approaches for Diverse Populations*, Edited by S. Harper & S. Quaye and Routledge, New York.

Oliver, M. (1990). The Politics of Disablement, Macmillan, Basingstoke.

Roth, W. (1983). "Handicap as a Social Construct" *Society*, 20 (3).

Ruto, S. (1996). "Integration of Visually Impaired into Mainstream Vocational Training in Kenya: A Comparative Study of Vocational Rehabilitation Centers and Youth Polytechnics." Unpublished M.Ed Thesis, Kenyatta University, Nairobi, Kenya.

Saint, W. (1992). *Universities in Africa: Strategies for Stabilization and Revitalization*. World Bank, Washington, D.C.

The Inter-University Council of East Africa. (2008). *Handbook for Quality Assurance in Higher Education*. IUCA.

UNESCO (2009). *The State of Higher Education in the World Today*. UNESCO, Paris.

UNESCO (1999). *Provision for Students with Disabilities in Higher Education*. UNESCO, Paris.

Shakespeare, T. (1997). "Researching Disabled Sexuality". In *Doing Disability Research*, edited by C. Barnes and G, Mercer, The Disability Press, pp. 177–189, Leeds.

Stage, F., Milne, N. (1996). "Invisible Scholars, Students with Learning Disabilities." *Journal of Higher Education*, 67 (4) 426-445.

Paul, S. (2000). "Students with Disabilities in Higher Education: A Review of Literature." *College Student Journal*, 34 (2), 200-211.

UNESCO (1999). Provision for Students with Disabilities in Higher Education. Paris, UNESCO.

UNESCO (1988). World Conference on Higher Education. Paris, October, 1988.

Chapter Eight

DISABILITIES AND THE ROLE OF DISTANCE LEARNING IN INCREASING ACCESS TO HIGHER EDUCATION

BY FELIX KAYODE OLAKULEHIN, NATIONAL OPEN UNIVERSITY OF NIGERIA

Introduction

Higher education in Africa, as in other parts of the world, is constantly changing, especially as a result of continuous and increasing demand for access, diminishing funds, rapidly evolving technology and, most recently, a global recession, which is impacting higher education in equal measure to the economies of the world. Although higher education has been popularly regarded as the driver of change and socio-economic development, current global dynamics and emerging trends are prompting a fresh look at higher education practice, with a view to ensuring its continued relevance, impact and value in a world whose view of education is moving from that of a public good to a tradable commodity. Perhaps no other set of issues confound the higher education environment as much as those of access, costs and quality. Daniel (2005) argued that these issues constitute the iron triangle of education which has affected the success of education systems over the centuries. Both developed and developing nations of the world have continued to seek ways and means of increasing access, reducing costs and improving quality of education. It is within this environment that the notion and practice of distance education or, more recently, open and distance learning has assumed a growing importance, both in terms of its inherent ability to overcome the constraints of access, quality and affordability, as well as its potential to render other socially induced boundaries invalid and irrelevant.

In terms of Africa's needs, open and distance learning is a tantalizing and viable prospect, having evolved as a potent strategy for addressing the needs of those who had been marginalized from accessing educational opportunities through the formal conventional higher education system. With the ascendancy of distance learning into the mainstream of higher education delivery, adult candidates who had previously dropped out of the conventional tertiary learning system now have a second chance. In addition, women–whether employed in the workforce or full-time housewives–may take advantage of the self-paced, flexible learning approaches of distance higher education without disrupting their other responsibilities (Olakulehin & Ojo, 2006).

While developing African nations have delved into the application of open and distance learning to reach marginalized groups, it must be acknowledged that significant and serious challenges still remain. An important sector of society is typically overlooked or has its needs underplayed. These are disabled persons who are grappling with physically challenging conditions such as blindness, deafness, lameness, quadruplexy and so on. In most countries in Africa, education provision has always been made available to the disabled at the elementary and secondary levels. In fact, there are special schools for physically challenged learners for both primary and secondary education; however, because the investment in higher education tends to be extremely high, little consideration is given to their needs when conventional higher education systems and processes are constructed. Disabilities bifurcate into two broad groups: 1) people with learning disabilities and 2) learners with disabilities (Beecher, 2005; Riviere, 1996; Moore, 2004; Burgstahler, 2006). People with learning disabilities have neurological and psychological conditions which prevent them from benefitting optimally from teaching/learning situations. Such individuals may suffer ailments like speech impairments, seizure disorders and attention deficit disorders and require special intervention from highly qualified instructors trained in special education in order to succeed. They sometimes benefit from the aid of assistive technologies to survive the learning challenges posed by their particular conditions.

The second group can be broadly categorized as physical disabilities, including visual impairment, blindness, hearing and speech impairment and lameness. Participants in higher education from these two broad groupings have been identified as *at risk*. Other learners in the at-risk category are prison inmates and those who are linguistically challenged (Moore, 2003; 2004). These learners are considered to be at risk because their identifiable conditions often cause stress beyond that experienced by members of the general population and may lead to their dropping out of the higher education system and/or failing to perform to the required standard. Yet, such individuals have roles in the stability and socio-economic development of society, provided, of course, they are given equitable access or even better access to quality higher education than is given to the able-bodied.

In this chapter, the general and specific needs of different classes of disabled learners in Africa shall be highlighted. The impact and potentials of distance learning for addressing their needs shall be examined, as well as the policy and administrative issues involved in training the disabled through distance higher education. In conclusion, recommendations are advanced for implementing strategies for overcoming generic and specific challenges of higher education for those living with disabilities. The study shows the inherent benefits which can accrue to a society with the adoption of an open and distance learning system as the single mainstream approach for meeting the higher education needs of physically disabled people and overcoming the effects of stigmatization and marginalization that they usually experience in the conventional higher education system (Ommerborn, 1998; Konur, 2006).

Conceptualizing Disability

There are numerous definitions of disability. For example, some have adopted a 'perspective method,' which suggests that writers develop definitions for the term on the basis of their orientation and experiences. If a person's ability to perform mentally deviates negatively from the norm, he or she may be considered disabled (Kranig & Ramm, 1990). Likewise, Hacker & Stapf (1987) believe that disability means the personally and socially harmful consequences of an impairment. Impairment is defined as an individual deviation from the ideal or average functional or physical norms. 'Handicap' connotes the difficulties caused to the disabled person by his or her environment, thus it is more a social construct than a biological condition. Contrary to illness, 'impairment' defines an irreversible state, like defective limb development versus broken bones. Something interesting about these definitions is their reference to the norms, notwithstanding the understanding of the term. Deviation from the norm, which refers to inadequacy or inability of a part to conform to the whole, represents the accepted definition of disability. However, this perception has an inherent weakness, as observed by Ommerborn & Schuemer (2001) who argued that:

1. Reference to a norm raises the question of who defines this norm to which end and according to which aspects and criteria.

2. The definition of disability as a deviance from a norm is linked to certain temporal and socio-cultural circumstances; setting norms (and with a claim to super-individual importance) as a rule results from a process of social and political negotiations in a concrete historical situation.

3. Defining a group of people as 'deviating from the norm' may produce the danger of a discriminating stigmatization of this group with all its possible negative consequences. This holds true even when—as in social welfare legislation—the term disability (and the disadvantages resulting from it for those concerned) is used to identify claims for compensating measures and obligations.

4. Using categories like 'disabled' or subcategories such as 'physically disabled' must not close one's eyes to the considerable individual differences or to the fact that disability always is a very individual state. Disabled people differ no less from each other than able people. Groups of disabled and able-bodied have much more in common than separates them.

5. External and internal views of a disability do in no way have to concur. Not everybody who is regarded as 'disabled' or 'severely disabled' according to the definitions of social welfare legislation necessarily sees herself or himself as impeded or impaired in his or her life. Correspondingly, not every student's disability or chronic illness means that their studies will be adversely affected (for more details see below).

Thus, while the term disability may describe a broad spectrum of physical and mental inadequacies, it is important to keep in mind always the questions and misgivings created by the term.

Dimensions of Disabilities in Higher Education

Persons living with disabilities are the least served by higher education systems all over the world. This situation becomes more acute in the case of developing states in Africa. If access and equity to quality higher education is a challenge in many parts of Africa to persons who are able-bodied and possessing all their faculties and abilities, then it should not be surprising that persons with disabilities have fared poorly. What should be surprising is the fact that issues of disabled individuals are being examined in the context of higher education. This is because in educational planning and policy making, attention tends to focus on the needs of the general population; interests of disabled persons are usually an afterthought. Even where there are clear policy positions, as in the case of Nigeria where the National Policy on Education (1977, revised 2004) addressed the interests of the disabled, there is a gap between policy and practice to the extent that existence of the policy becomes doubtful.

For the sake of clarity, the provisions relating to disability in the Nigerian National Policy on education are stated here. The Nigerian National Policy on Education (2004) provides inter alia that:

Special Education is a formal special educational training given to people (Children and Adults) with special needs (three groups were identified: Disabled, Disadvantaged and Gifted or Talented). The disabled who are relevant to our interests are identified as People with impairments (physical and sensory), and because of this impairment/disability cannot cope with regular school/class organisation and methods without formal special educational training. In this category, we have people who are:

a. Visually impaired (blind and the partially sighted);

b. Hearing impaired (deaf and the partially hearing);

c. Physically and health impaired (deformed limbs, asthmatic);

d. Mentally retarded (educable, trainable, bed ridden);

e. Emotionally disturbed (hyperactive, hypoactive/the socially maladjusted/behaviour disorder);

f. Speech impaired (stammerers, stutterers);

g. Learning disabled (have psychological/neurological educational phobia or challenges); and,

h. Multiple handicapped.

Having identified every conceivable category of disabled learner, the policy also established the aims/objectives of the Special Education Programme as follows:

(i) Give concrete meaning to the idea of equalising educational opportunities for all children, their physical, sensory, mental, psychological or emotional disabilities notwithstanding;

(ii) Provide adequate education for all people with special needs in order that they may fully contribute their own quota to the development of the nation;

(iii) Provide opportunities for exceptionally gifted and talented children to develop at their own pace in the interest of the nation's economic and technological development; and,

(iv) Design a diversified and appropriate curriculum for all beneficiaries.

In pursuance of the above aims/objectives, the Federal Ministry of Education has responsibility for coordinating Special Education activities in Nigeria in collaboration with relevant ministries and non-governmental organisations and international agencies (UNICEF, UNESCO, UNDP, WHO, etc.).

a. Education of children with special needs shall be free at all levels.

b. All necessary facilities that would ensure easy access to education shall be provided, e.g.:

    i. Inclusive education or integration of special classes and units into ordinary/public schools under the Universal Basic Education scheme;

    ii. Regular census and monitoring of people with special needs to ensure adequate educational planning and welfare programme;

    iii. Special Education equipment and materials, e.g.:

        - Perkins brailler, white/mobility cane, rallied textbooks, abacus, Braille, talking watch;

        - Audiometers, speech trainers, hearing aids, ear mould machines, etc.

        - educational/psychological toys for the educationally mentally retarded

        - callipers, prostheses, crutches, wheelchairs, artificial limbs, etc. for physically handicapped

    iv. Special Education training, e.g.:

        - Braille reading and writing

        - mobility training; use of regular typewriter for the visually impaired.

        - total communication technique: speech, sign language, the 3Rs for the hearing impaired

        - daily living activities or skills for the mentally retarded.

    v. special training and re-training of the personnel to develop capacity building and to keep abreast of latest teaching technique, for the various categories of disabilities, the gifted and talented.

    vi. Federal, state and local governments shall fund these programmes within areas of jurisdiction

c. Architectural designs of school buildings shall be barrier free, i.e.: they shall take into account special needs of the handicapped, e.g.: ramps instead of steps/stairs, wider doors for wheelchairs, lower toilets, etc.

d. Schools shall be required to arrange regular sensory, medical and psychological; screening assessments to identify any incidence of handicap (NPE, 2004: 41-44).

A cursory evaluation of the current practice and social realities reveal that the above recommendations and prescriptions of the policy did not factor into the design, development and implementation of educational institutions in general and higher education institutions specifically. The policy used words like 'disadvantaged,' 'disabled' and 'handicapped' interchangeably without focusing on the subtle differences; they are used to mean the same thing. However, Mishra (2005) states that 'disadvantaged' is used as a broader term that includes the physically, as well as mentally, challenged, the aged, patients, prisoners, women and other minorities; and 'handicap' is used only in the sense of physical and mental disability. This lack of clarity may indeed be misinterpreted by practitioners when they are attempting to implement the policy. Another issue is that the policy did not make explicit its requirements and expectations for disabled persons in higher education as it so eloquently did for those in primary and post-primary levels of education.

Contributing to the debate about lack of proper provisions for higher education learners with disabilities, Ramanujam (n.d.) argued that:

"The underlying principle behind this strange silence about the higher educational needs of the disabled is that higher education of this group is not seen as important as their school education that can teach them some vocational and technical skills through which the disabled could fend for themselves. The basic assumption behind this unstated principle is that the disabled are not really crying for higher education, and even if there is a need for it, it can wait and it is not a priority right now. Clearly, this is keeping in tune with the general attitude towards the political discourse of the education, employment, empowerment and social justice of the disadvantaged groups in general."

Distance Education in Increasing Access to Disabled

In general, education has been identified as the most potent means of empowering those living with disabilities. However, in order to ensure that they benefit optimally from economic activities and enhance their economic independence, educational provision to them must be specific, deliberate and significantly improved. Given the distinctiveness of distance learning and its open education variant, it has the potential to improve the opportunities of disabled persons. Distance education offers flexibilities in location, scheduling and course delivery formats, which may provide disabled people's first access to higher education (Mishra, 2005). After a comprehensive review of distance education for the disabled, Ommerborn (1998) answered

DISABILITIES AND THE ROLE OF DISTANCE LEARNING IN INCREASING ACCESS TO HIGHER EDUCATION the question, "Can distance study be considered a genuine alternative for the disabled?", while reporting the opinion of a disabled learner who is responsible for disabled learners at a university:

> "It certainly is an alternative. Whether it is a good one for the disabled or a bad one, or an acceptable one, this depends on many factors, not the least on the disabled person's personal circumstances, his/her inclinations, intentions and abilities. The type and degree of one's disability, whether there are more advantages or disadvantages compared to face-to-face study, the answer must be individually different and can only be given by the disabled themselves" (p. 92-93).

While no absolute statement applies to people with disabilities, the heterogeneity of distance learners and the standard features of distance education, such as flexible study time, choice of study location and autonomy in deciding the workload, can and should facilitate customization of education for the disabled. However, in spite of the possibilities to serve disabled individuals better, distance education institutions rarely provide specialized services to their disabled learners.

Increasing access to more students is a common reason given for providing instruction in a distance learning format. However, these access arguments usually focus on people separated by distance and time and rarely include consideration of the needs of people with disabilities. In fact, the design of many distance learning courses erects barriers to the full participation of students and instructors with some types of disabilities. Ensuring that individuals with disabilities can participate in distance learning courses can be argued on ethical grounds. Many people simply consider it the right thing to do, while others are more responsive to legal mandates. The Americans with Disabilities Act (ADA) of 1990 mandates that no otherwise qualified individuals shall, solely by reason of their disabilities, be excluded from participation in, be denied the benefits of, or be subjected to discrimination in public programs. The ADA does not specifically mention online courses, but the United States Department of Justice and the U.S. Department of Education's Office for Civil Rights have clarified that the ADA applies to Internet-based programs and services. Clearly, distance learning programs must make their offerings available to qualified people with disabilities (Burgstahler, 2006).

Having examined the general dimensions of disabilities in higher education environments, it is necessary to examine and discuss access issues and present design considerations for ensuring that a course is accessible to potential instructors and students with a wide range of abilities and disabilities. The field of universal design provides a framework for this discussion.

Access Barriers

Thousands of specialized hardware and software products available today allow individuals with a wide range of abilities and disabilities to productively use computing and networking technologies. If a prerequisite to a course is Internet access, administrators and instructors can assume that any student enrolled will have access to any assistive technology required. However, assistive technology alone does not remove all access barriers. Described below are examples of access challenges in distance learning courses faced by students and instructors who have access to assistive technology.

Blindness

A student or instructor who is blind may use a computer equipped with text-to-speech software. Essentially, this system reads, with a synthesized voice, whatever text appears on the screen. A user can use a text-only browser to navigate the World Wide Web or simply turn off the graphics-loading feature of a multimedia web browser. However, the user cannot interpret graphics (including photographs, drawings and image maps) unless text descriptions are provided. Printed materials, videotapes, televised presentations, overhead transparencies and other visual materials also create access challenges. These barriers can be overcome with alternative media such as audiotapes, Braille printouts, electronic text, tactile drawings and aural descriptions.

Other Visual Impairments

A student or instructor who has limited vision can use special software to enlarge screen images but may see only a small portion of a web page at a time. Consequently, users may become confused when web pages are cluttered and when layouts change from page to page. Those who require large print or rely upon enlarged electronic text may find that standard printed materials are inaccessible. Also, individuals who are color blind cannot successfully navigate web pages that require users to distinguish colors.

Specific Learning Disabilities

Some specific learning disabilities impact the ability to read, write and/or process information. A student with a learning disability may use audio-taped books. To help read text efficiently, another student may use a speech output or screen enlargement system similar to those used by people with visual impairments. And some students may have difficulty understanding websites when the information is cluttered and when the screen layout changes from one page to the next.

Mobility Impairments

A student or instructor with mobility impairment, such as the inability to move one's hands, may use an alternative keyboard and mouse or speech input to gain access to online course materials and communication tools. Another student or instructor may be able to use standard input devices, but lack the fine motor skills required to select small buttons on the screen. If one's input method is slow, the ability to participate in real-time "chat" communications may be prohibitive. If any place-bound meetings are required in a distance learning course, a participant with mobility impairment may require that the location be wheelchair-accessible.

Hearing Impairments

Most Internet resources are accessible to people with hearing impairments because these resources do not require the ability to hear. However, when websites include audio output without providing text captioning or transcription, a student who is deaf is denied access to the information. Course videotapes that are not captioned are also inaccessible. Hearing impaired students may also be unable to participate in a telephone conference or videoconference unless accommodations (e.g., sign language interpreters) are provided for that part of a distance learning course.

Speech Impairments

A student with speech impairment may not be able to effectively participate in interactive telephone conferences or videoconferences. However, modes of participation that do not require the ability to speak, such as electronic mail, are fully accessible.

Universal Design

The design of a distance learning class can impact the participation of students and instructors with visual, hearing, mobility, speech, and learning disabilities. Planning for access as the course is being developed is much easier than creating accommodation strategies once a person with a disability enrolls in the course or applies to teach it. Simple steps can be taken to ensure that the course is accessible to participants with a wide range of abilities and disabilities.

"Universal design" is defined by the Centre for Universal Design at North Carolina State University as "the design of products and environments to be usable by all people, to the greatest extent possible, without the need for adaptation or specialized design." At this Centre, a group of product developers, architects, environmental designers and engineers established a set of principles of universal design for products, environments, and communication and other electronic systems. General principles include: the design is useful and marketable to people with diverse abilities; the design accommodates a wide range of individual preferences and abilities; the design communicates necessary information effectively to the user, regardless of ambient conditions or the user's sensory abilities; and the design can be used efficiently and comfortably and with minimum of fatigue.

When universal design principles are applied, products meet the needs of potential users with a wide variety of characteristics. Disability is just one of many characteristics that an individual might possess. Others include height, age, race, native language, ethnicity and gender. All of the potential characteristics of participants should be considered when developing a distance learning course. Just as modern sidewalks and buildings are designed to be used by everyone, including those who use wheelchairs, distance learning designers should create learning environments that allow all potential students and instructors to fully participate.

Having examined the context of disabilities, it is important to attempt an analysis of the strategies for making distance learning courses accessible to persons living with disabilities.

On-Site Instruction

The interactive video sessions, proctored examinations and retreats for students in some distance learning courses require place-bound meetings. In these cases, the facility should be accessible by wheelchair, the furniture should be flexible enough to accommodate those in wheelchairs and accessible restrooms and parking should be available nearby. Standard disability-related accommodations, such as sign language interpreters, should be provided when requested. Instructors should speak clearly, face students when speaking to facilitate lip-reading, and read aloud and describe text and other visual materials for those who cannot see them.

Internet-Based Communication

Some distance learning programs employ real-time chat communication in their courses. In such cases, students communicate synchronously (at the same time) as compared to asynchronously (not necessarily at the same time). Besides providing scheduling challenges, synchronous communication is difficult or impossible for someone who cannot communicate quickly. For example, someone with a learning disability who takes a long time to compose her thoughts or someone whose input method is slow may not be fully included in the discussion. In addition, some chat software erects barriers for individuals who are blind. Instructors who choose to use chat for small group interaction should select chat software that is accessible to those using screen readers, and they should plan for an alternative method of communication (e.g., email) when not all students in a group can fully participate using chat.

Text-based, asynchronous resources, such as electronic mail, bulletin boards and listserv distribution lists, generally erect no special barriers for students with disabilities. If a prerequisite to a course is for students to have access to electronic mail, the instructor can assume that participants with disabilities already have an accessible email program to use. Email communication between individual students, course administration staff, the instructor, guest speakers and other students is accessible to all parties, regardless of disability.

Web Pages

Applying universal design principles makes web pages accessible to individuals with a wide range of disabilities. In 1999, guidelines for making web pages accessible were developed by the Web Accessibility Initiative (WAI) of the World Wide Web Consortium (W3C). W3C, an industry group that was founded in 1994 to develop common protocols that enhance interoperability and guide the evolution of the web, is committed to ensuring that the World Wide Web is fully accessible to people with disabilities. More recently, the United States Architectural and Transportation Barriers

Compliance Board (Access Board) developed accessibility standards for web pages of Federal agencies, as mandated by Section 508 of the Rehabilitation Act Amendments of 1998. The standards provide a model for other organizations working to make their web pages accessible to the broadest audience.

There are basically two approaches for making web page content and navigation accessible. Certain types of inaccessible data and features need to be avoided or alternative methods need to be provided for carrying out the function or accessing the content provided through an inaccessible feature or format. For example, a distance learning designer can avoid using a graphic that is inaccessible to individuals who are blind, or the designer can create a text description of the content that is accessible to text-to-speech software. Tips for designing specific formats or features (e.g., PDF files, forms, JAVA applications, Flash content) can be found in the AccessIT Knowledge Base at http://www.washington.edu/accessit/kb.php.

Web pages for a distance learning class should be tested with a variety of monitors, computer platforms and web browsers, including a text-only browser such as Lynx or a standard browser with the graphics and sound-loading features turned off (to simulate the experiences of people with sensory impairments). Testing to see if all functions at a website can be accessed using a keyboard alone is also a good accessibility test. Online programs (e.g., A-Prompt, Bobby, WAVE) are available to test web pages for accessibility.

Course designers using development tools, such as Moodle, ATutor, Blackboard or WebCT, can employ product accessibility tools to create accessible courses.

Print Materials

Students who are blind or who have specific learning disabilities that affect their ability to read may require that print materials be converted into Braille, large print, audiotape or electronic formats. However, making the content of print materials available in an accessible, web-based format may provide the best solution for students who cannot read standard print materials.

Video Presentations

Ideally, whenever a video or televised presentation is used in a distance learning course, captioning should be provided for those who have hearing impairments and audio description of visual content should be provided for those who are blind. If a video publisher does not make these options available, the distance learning program should have a system in place to accommodate students who have sensory impairments. For example, the institution could hire someone local to the student to describe the visual material to a blind student or to sign audio material for a student who is deaf. Real-time captioning (developed at the time of the presentation) or sign language interpreting should be provided for videoconferences when requested by participants who are deaf.

Telephone Conferences

Online courses may include small group discussions via telephone conference. This mode of communication creates scheduling challenges for everyone, and it is inaccessible to a student who is deaf. Instructors should allow alternative communication (e.g., email) that is accessible to everyone in a specific group. Or, a student who is deaf might be able to participate in a telephone conference by using the Telecommunications Relay Service (TRS), where an operator types what the speakers say so that a student who is deaf may view it on a text telephone (TTY). The operator will also translate the deaf student's printed input into speech. However, this system might be too slow to allow participation in lively conversations. Another accommodation approach involves setting up a private chat room on the web. A transcriptionist types the conversation for the student who is deaf to view. The student can also type his contributions into the chat room and they can be voiced by someone in the group who is monitoring the chat room. Various options should be discussed with the student who needs an accommodation.

Benefits of Accessible Design for People without Disabilities

People without disabilities may have temporary and/or situational constraints that are similar to those imposed by disabilities. For example, people who cannot access graphics, due to computer system limitations, are in a similar situation as students who are blind. A noisy environment that prohibits the use of audio features imposes constraints similar to those faced by students with hearing impairments. Those for whom English is a second language experience reading difficulties similar to those experienced by people with some types of learning disabilities. Individuals using monochrome monitors face limitations like those who are color blind. People who need to operate a computer but whose hands are occupied with other activities face challenges similar to those who use a hands-free input method because of a disability.

Applying universal design principles assists both people with and without disabilities. For example, using clear and simple language and navigational mechanisms on web pages facilitates use by those whose native language is not the one in which the course is taught as well as people with visual and learning disabilities. People who have turned off support for images on their browsers in order to maximize access speed benefit when multimedia features provide text alternatives for the content, as do people who are blind, and those who wish to use search tools to locate specific content. Similarly, people who cannot view the screen because they must attend to other tasks benefit from text-to-speech systems used by people who are blind. Captions provided on video assist people who work in noisy or noiseless surroundings, people for whom English is a second language, and people who have hearing impairments. Making sure that information conveyed with color is also available without color benefits those using monochrome monitors as well as those who are color blind. Providing multiple formats of information also addresses differences in learning styles.

Getting Started

Distance learning programs should be proactive in making distance learning courses accessible. They should not wait until someone with a disability enrolls in a course to address accessibility issues; rather, they should consider them from the start:

- Think about the wide range of abilities and disabilities potential students might have.
- In promotional publications include information on how to request accommodations and publications in alternative formats.
- Arrange wheelchair-accessible facilities for on-site instruction.
- Make sure media can be accessed using sight or hearing alone and online content can be accessed with a keyboard alone.
- Adopt and enforce accessibility standards (e.g., Section 508 standards, WAI guidelines).
- Establish procedures for students with disabilities to request and receive accommodations.
- Provide information about standards, training, and support to instructors and design staff.
- Use the accessibility features of development tools (e.g., Moodle, Atutor, Blackboard, WebCT).
- Review and update standards, procedures and support issues periodically.

Distance learning courses are designed to reach out to students from anywhere. If universal design principles are used in creating these classes, they will be accessible to any students who enroll in them and any instructors who are hired to teach them. Designed correctly, distance learning options create learning opportunities for students with a broad range of abilities and disabilities. Designed poorly, they erect new barriers to equal participation in academics and careers.

Employing universal design principles can bring us closer to making learning accessible to anyone, anywhere, at any time. The condescending attitude and the patronizing tone of the declarations of the governments and the mission statements of the educational institutions, however, cannot deliver the goods without coming to terms with the harsh reality. Notwithstanding the numerous debates over the strategies and methodologies to meet the educational needs of the disabled, the fact remains that it is not the question of approach and method, but the question of making the necessary resources available to both institutions and individuals. If 'special education' in the conventional, face-to-face learning environment is to be given to millions of children and adults with different types of disabilities, then enormous amounts of resources (both material and human) must be made available. This is not going to happen in the near future. On the other hand, if integrated and inclusive education is to be practiced, then educational institutions must make the necessary provision and provide appropriate facilities.

In either case, the present strength of the trained professionals is inadequate. Even if money is allocated to the institutions, they won't be able to use it purposefully. Policy makers and teachers need to be sensitized about these issues. While the efforts to make education at all levels accessible to people with disabilities should continue in the face-to-face education system, at the higher education level distance learning institutions need to make their programs and courses accessible to people with disabilities who face all kinds of difficulties in the campus-based environment. The curriculum needs to be redesigned, while the core academic content can still be retained as common to both able-bodied and disabled students.

First, the content should be presented in the accessible and useable media. Second, appropriate minimum support services must be made mandatory for the institutions of higher education. Third, methods of evaluation must be made flexible enough to accommodate the special needs and requirements of learners with disabilities. These three propositions are detailed here with a few examples.

- **Curriculum**—While designing the curriculum, special attention must be paid to the accessibility aspect of any DOL program, which is different from designing and developing special programs only for the disabled. For example, a bachelor's degree program of any distance teaching institution must be made accessible to people with disabilities, if they wish to do the program. The blind or learners with low vision, for example, will not be able to use the print medium. In such a situation, the Braille version of the courses or audio cassettes may be made available to the learners. Similarly, the mentally retarded and the learning impaired would need special considerations regarding the media of learning and support services. At the time of framing the curriculum, DOL institutions should look into these aspects. The technical aspects of these tasks must be assessed and the personnel involved in the job should be trained.

- **Support Services**—For the orthopedically disabled, the medium of instruction can remain the same as the one for able-bodied students, but the former would need assistance in their mobility, access to study centers, transport, etc. The hearing impaired will need counselors and tutors who know sign language. Blind learners may need 'readers' who would read the text materials for them. The mentally retarded might need speech modifiers and interpreters to understand their communication. One can enumerate on such special support, depending on the types of disabled learners and their actual needs. Barrier-free buildings must be chosen for setting up special study centers, and those who manage special study centers need relevant training. DOL institutions, too, must be redesigned appropriately.

- **Methods of Evaluation**—This is another area where a lot can be done. Access to examination centers, the duration to write or answer the questions, time limit to complete the programs successfully, etc. must be flexible and helpful. Attendants, scribes and interpreters must be provided to learners who need them. With a little effort the existing programs and courses of DOL institutions can be made accessible to many learners with disabilities.

Participation remains a concern. If distance education indeed provides particular benefits to students with disabilities in terms of flexibility of time, location, instructional mode, and so forth, then rates of participation higher than that in conventional campus-based programs may be expected. Such rates have yet to be reported, however. Success is also a concern. The study found that students with disabilities took courses at a much higher rate than their able-bodied counterparts: an average of four courses over the three-year period of the study compared with two courses for the general undergraduate population. However, students with disabilities experienced somewhat less success in these courses. Further study of enrollment patterns and success rates is required, particularly with regard to the different success rates that appear to exist among students with varying types of disabilities.

The removal of the requirement to be registered in three courses as a full-time student when receiving a student loan may also have a positive effect on these outcomes. Moisey (2004) stated that in her study of characteristics of disabled distance learners at Athabasca University, Canada's Open University observed that, overall, students who received more types of services tended to have more success in terms of course completions. Students with certain types of disabilities tended to receive varying degrees of services. Students received an average of 2.2 types of support services, ranging from a low of 1.8 for students with psychological disabilities to 3.0 for students with sensory disabilities.

Certain types of disabilities appear to be more amendable to assistance. For example, nearly all students with learning disabilities who received assistive technology completed their courses compared with about half of students with other types of disabilities who received this type of service. On the other hand, course extensions did not appear to be helpful for this group; whereas for students with physical or psychological disabilities, extensions to the contract date appeared to assist with course completion. Further study is required to explore the relationship between course completion and type of disability and support services received. In describing the experience of students with disabilities at Athabasca University, this study has perhaps provided more questions than answers. More answers are needed about the participation of students with disabilities in distance education, the services they access, and the success they experience in their studies. There is little doubt that distance education can enhance access to students with disabilities and that disability-specific support services can enhance success. The next step is to ensure that students with disabilities know what opportunities for distance learning exist and achieve success.

Conclusion

Open and distance learning as a strategy for expanding access to a variety of groups, both traditional and those that may be regarded as 'new learners,' holds great potentials for addressing the needs of the disabled. In terms of higher education, distance education is even more influential because students at this level tend to be mature and aware, thus they are able to relate with the nature of negotiated, self-paced or self-directed learning systems that distance education advocates.

Konur (2006) reported that surveys and statistical data show that learning disabled (LD) students account for 40 percent of the whole disabled student population. Students with chronic illnesses and injuries, which could be termed as 'medical health disabilities,' account for 30 to 35 percent (known in the UK as 'unseen disabilities'). The sensory disabilities, such as hearing and visually disabled students, and those with mental health disabilities form each a relatively small section of this population. It is also notable that generally more than 10 percent of this population has multiple disabilities such as learning disabilities and ADHD, or deaf and blind students.

As the number of disabled students in higher education has increased in recent years, teaching them in compliance with the public policies while maintaining academic and professional standards has become a crucial academic and policy issue. Their access has been facilitated in part by the anti-discrimination laws worldwide, influenced by the introduction of S 504 and then by the ADA. The access of disabled students to programs and to the curriculum in higher education—program and curriculum access—are two separate but interlinked features of such policies. The crux of this paper, however, is to place open and distance learning at the center of the strategies that are adopted for promoting access to learners living with disabilities in higher education systems.

An effective distance learning system would be designed, as proposed by Konur (2006), with curriculum modifications that include four types of adjustments: presentation format, response format, timing and setting. The research on the curriculum adjustments reviewed in this paper, building on three decades of research, has implications for academic staff in higher education and for the future research agenda. The research priorities for the next three decades could be set out as the attitudes of disabled students, attitudes of academic and other staff toward curriculum adjustments, effect of adjustments on the academic performance of disabled students, and the attitudes of non-disabled students. Adjustments to learning technologies and examinations merit particular attention. Thus, this paper identifies a crucial role for academic staff in facilitating curriculum access for disabled students, as the policy-makers have entrusted them with discretion to determine the reasonableness of disability adjustments and to decide whether they would make such adjustments.

REFERENCES

Burgstahler, S. (2006). *Real Connections: Making Distance Learning Accessible to Everyone*. DO-IT: University of Washington

Daniel, J.S. (2005). *Open and distance learning and the developing world*. Keynote at the Annual Conference of the Open and Distance Learning Association of Australia, November 11. Retrieved from www.col.org/speeches_presentations

Federal Government of Nigeria (1977, revised 2004). *National Policy on Education*. NERDC: Lagos

Konur, O. (2006). Teaching disabled students in higher education. *Teaching in Higher Education*, 11(3), 351-363.

Mishra, S. (2005). *Serving learners with disabilities in distance education*. Proceedings of the annual conference of the International Council for Distance Education, New Delhi, November 19-23.

Moisey, S.D. (2004). Students with Disabilities in Distance Education: Characteristics, Course Enrollment and Completion, and Support Services. *Journal of Distance Education*, 19(1), 73-91.

Moore, M. (2003). Editorial: Learner Support. *American Journal of Distance Education*, 17(3), 141-143.

Moore, M. (2004). Editorial: Disabilities and Other Learner Characteristics. *American Journal of Distance Education*, 18(1), 1-3.

Moore, M. (1986). *Learners and Learning at a distance*. Keynote address to 1986 summer conference: Improving Teaching at a Distance, University of Wisconsin-Madison.

Ommerborn, R. (1998). *Distance study for the disabled: National and international experiences and perspectives*, Hagen: ZIFF.

Ommerborn, R. and Schuemer, R. (2001). *Using computers in distance study: Results of a survey amongst disabled distance students, Hagen*: ZIFF.

Olakulehin, F.K. & Ojo, O.D. (2006). Distance Education as a Women Empowerment Strategy. *Indian Journal of Open Learning*, 15(3).

Ramanujam, P.R. (no date). *Staff Development: Potential and Use of Distance Mode in the Disability Sector,* retrieved from http://www.fernuni hagen.de/ZIFF/rampoten.doc

ABOUT THE CONTRIBUTORS

Segun Adedeji teaches Economics of Education in the department of Educational Management, University of Ibadan. He is the Managing Editor of the Journal of Sociology and Education in Africa. He co-edited the proceedings of a research colloquium "Education and Development in the Commonwealth: Comparative Perspectives" sponsored by the Commonwealth Scholarship Commission, June 2004. He was a MacArthur Fellow at the Center for Comparative Education Research, University of Nottingham, U.K. (2004 – 2005), and holds a PhD from the University of Ibadan. His research interests include Education for Development, Allocation of Educational Resources and Application of Information Communication Technology (ICT) for Rural Development.

Lilian-Rita Akudolu is an associate professor in curriculum and instruction at Nnamdi Azikiwe University Awka, Anambra State, Nigeria. She is a Commonwealth Fellow and completed her Fellowship at the University of Glasgow, United Kingdom in 2005/2006. She studied French-language Education and Curriculum Studies and received a PhD in computer-assisted instruction. Her area of interests includes instructional use of information and communications technology, gender issues and capacity building for women.

Pakinaz Baraka is a distinguished scholar and university professor in the field of public policy and administration. Besides her teaching at the university, she wrote several articles and published in international journals about public policies in the field of health, education, civics and sustainable development. She won two scholarships, the first by the Chevening Scholarships Program sponsored by the British Council in 1991. She studied upon this scholarship at the School of Education, the University of Manchester, and the United Kingdom and earned her Master's degree in 1992. In 2006, she won a Post-Doctoral Research-Lecturing grant by the Fulbright Commission in Egypt. She studied during her stay in the United States as a Fulbright scholar in the field of educational policies and academic standards for civics and government at the School of Education, the University of Pittsburgh, Pennsylvania. During her stay in the U.S., she collaborated and co-authored in two research projects, the first was on civic education in Egypt, and the second on quality standards in education. Besides working in research, she delivered many lectures on American universities campuses. Her lectures covered diverse topics related to politics, civic education, ancient Egyptian history, and status of women in Islam. In 2007, she was selected by Africa Higher Education Collaborative (AHEC) administered by CIES and sponsored by Ford Foundation in Egypt, and engaged in several collaborative activities to study aspects of education in African countries with a special focus on cost, equity and access to higher education. Pakinaz has traveled extensively around the world and her interests encompasses beside scholarly research novel writing as well.

Michael Cross has been teaching educational and policy studies at the School of Education, University of the Witwatersrand, since 1986. In his academic career, he has produced more than 45 refereed publications including books and scholarly articles both nationally and internationally, and has been rated as a social scientist by the National Research Foundation for his contribution to knowledge. He has served in several technical committees responsible for the development of higher education and teacher education policies in the national and provincial departments of Education. He has been awarded research and teaching fellowships in key international institutions, namely, the Johns Hopkins University, Northwestern University, Stanford University in the USA, University of Stockholm in Sweden and Picardie Jules-Verne Université in France. He is a founder and member of the South African Doctoral Consortium of Schools of Education that provides doctoral training in education policy studies, and has been an editor-in-chief of a leading education journal in South Africa, Perspectives in Education. He is currently conducting research projects on institutional culture, access and student performance in higher education.

Victor S. Dugga is Professor and Executive Director of Advancement Office, University of Jos, Nigeria. As Executive Director, he directs the central support unit that serves the entire university's alumni relations, marketing and fundraising. He has served as Monitoring and Evaluation Officer for World Bank-funded Science and Technology Education in Post-Basic Institutions (STEP-B) projects. He served as a Consultant to many state and national educational agencies and led several project implementations and carried out different types of monitoring and evaluation since 2003. Dugga is a recipient of the Commonwealth Academic Staff Fellowship and a DAAD Fellowship. He has received funding for research from the Association of African Universities (AAU). He won the Association of Nigerian Authors' Prize for Drama in 2009. He obtained a Bachelor's and Master's degree from the University of Jos, Nigeria, a Master's degree from University of Essex, United Kingdom; a PhD from University of Bayreuth, Germany, and a Postgraduate Diploma in Monitoring and Evaluation from the University of Stellenbosch, South Africa.

Nadia Elarabi works as a lecturer (for teachers) at the Right to Live Institute for Special Education, also for people with special needs in vocational training workshops. She is art supervisor and counselor psychology in developing project, in fourteen Intellectually Disabled Government Schools. She is vocational rehabilitation consultant in many developing projects for people with disabilities. She contributed in writing the book "Silent No More, Special Needs People in Egypt" published by American University in Cairo Press. Also she is the author of numerous articles about special education and art. In addition, she is considered among the first persons to organize public art exhibitions for the artists with disabilities in Egypt. These exhibitions caught the interest of the media and raised public awareness. Nadia graduated from Fine Arts College and got her PhD in Education from Education College. She is an alumna of the Ford Foundation International Fellowship Program.

Sabiha Essack, Dean of the Faculty of Health Sciences and Professor in the School of Pharmacy and Pharmacology at the University of KwaZulu-Natal, is a Welcome Trust Research Fellow who completed research towards her PhD in Pharmaceutical Microbiology at St Bartholomew's and the Royal London School of Medicine and Dentistry in the United Kingdom. She received several prestigious scholarships and grants from the Welcome Trust, Medical Research Council, National Research Foundation and the World Health Organization for Essential National Health Research investigating strategies for the prevention and containment of antibiotic resistance. Her research has been published in several journals and has been presented at a number of national and international conferences. She is president of the South African Chapter of the Alliance for the Prudent Use of Antibiotics (APUA), co-founder and chair of the South African Committee of Health Sciences Deans and a Ministerial appointee on the National Health Research Ethics Council 2010-12. Professor Essack was appointed coordinator to the Africa Higher Education Collaborative, a 4-country Ford Foundation-funded initiative run by the Council for the International Exchange of Scholars in the U.S., her leadership of which secured a £100,000 grant from the Mobilizing Regional Capacity Initiative Program of the Association of African Universities to undertake research on "Access, Retention and Success in African Higher Education".

Peliwe Lolwana is the Chief Executive Officer of UMALUSI – the Council for Quality Assurance in General and Further Education and Training in South Africa. Her past experiences in South Africa and USA include being a teacher; lecturer; psychologist; research policy director; director and executive officer. She obtained a PhD from the University of Massachusetts, Amherst (USA) in 1991. She has served in many commissions tasked with the transformation of apartheid education in South Africa. She serves in a number of Associations, Boards and Councils in education, in South Africa, Africa, and the Commonwealth. She has published and presented papers on a number of issues in education and training.

Haroon Mahomed is Director–Continuing Professional Teacher Development at the National Department of Education in South Africa since January 2005. He has worked in the education field for 30 years and has a reputation for combining scholarship, and policy-making. Prior to his current post, he served in the Gauteng Provincial Department of Education as Executive Director in the Curriculum Development Institute and as Head of Teaching and Learning. He has served on the South African Ministerial Review team for the national school curriculum. He has taught at primary and secondary levels, and worked in a range of community-based and non-formal programs. He has completed Master's Degrees in Philosophy of Education and Sociology of Development from Witwatersrand and London Universities respectively. He also holds qualifications in soccer coaching, coaches junior soccer and writes articles on the sport. His main interest is in contributing to Education for All goals.

Helen Oronga Aswani Mwanzi holds a PhD in Literature from the University of Nairobi with specialization in language. In her graduate degree, she focused on the "imagery in children's literature in Kenya". She is a professionally trained teacher, a member of the University of Nairobi Gender Committee, a creative writer, a producer and a national adjudicator of drama and music. She is also a religious scholar.

Ibrahim Oanda teaches courses in Sociology of Education and Policy Studies, Higher Education and Gender and Education, at Kenyatta University, Kenya. Besides teaching, Oanda has research interests in higher education transformations, women and gender studies in higher education and internationalization of higher education. Oanda has co-authored two books, one of which is in the area of private higher education and knowledge production in Kenya; and also has individually published several articles and book chapters and consultancy reports. He currently heads a comparative research network, finalizing a study on corporate planning and implications on higher education transformations in East African public universities, sponsored by CODESRIA, and has embarked on a project on widening access and participation to African universities for disadvantaged students; a joint project with colleagues from South Africa and Nigeria, sponsored by the UK Department for International Development (DfID), through the Mobilization of Regional Capacities Initiatives (MRCI) Program administered by the Association of African Universities (AAU). Oanda is a native of Kenya, and received a PhD in education from Kenyatta University, and was a Rockefeller Post-Doctoral Research fellow at the University of Illinois, Urbana-Champaign in 2005-2006, where he did research on women and gender studies in East African Universities.

Stephen Odebero is a Senior Lecturer of Planning and Economics of Education in the Department of Education Planning and Management, at Masinde Muliro University of Science and Technology' in Kenya. A respected author and researcher, he is well known for his expertise in equity in financing education. He has lectured in several universities and colleges in Kenya. He is the author of one text book and numerous articles, book chapters and research reports; and has developed and taught undergraduate and graduate courses on topics like demographic studies in education planning, demand and supply of education and equity and efficiency in education. He is currently the editor in chief of *Kenya Journal of Education Planning, Economics and Management* and the Deputy Chairman Education Management Society of Kenya (EMSK). He has represented his country, Kenya, in international academic for such as the African Higher Education Collaborative (AHEC). Before joining Masinde Muliro University, Odebero was a lecturer at Egerton University in the Department of Curriculum, Instruction and Education Management. He was a visiting lecturer at Laikipia and Chuka University College. Administratively, he serves his university as the Coordinator, Bishop Sulumeti Study Center. He sits in University Senate and PSSP Directorate

Board. Dr. Odebero is also keen on community service. He was appointed by the Minister for Education to serve on the Board of Governors, Sigalame Boys High School where he was eventually elected chairman of BOG, a position he holds to date. He is currently contracted by SID to identify asymmetries that exist in education system in East Africa Community with view to recommending the curriculum and employment policy for the region. He is a native of Kenya and received a PhD in Education Planning from Egerton University.

Dr. Sabine O'Hara is the Managing Director and Vice President of Professors Beyond Borders and Principal of Global Ecology, LLC. A respected author, researcher and higher education executive, she is well known for her expertise in sustainable economic development, global education and executive leadership. She has lectured around the globe, is the author of three books and numerous articles and research reports and has taught courses and professional development workshops on topics like: sustainability and education; preparing for success in a global economy; linking teaching and research through community based economic development; solving complex problems through collaborative research; and cultural perspectives on valuation and stakeholder processes.

Dr. O'Hara was the Executive Director of the Council for International Exchange of Scholars (CIES) and Vice President of the Institute of International Education (IIE). Before joining CIES/IIE, she was the 10th President of Roanoke College in Salem, Virginia and held faculty and administrative leadership positions at Concordia College in Moorhead, Minnesota, at Green Mountain College in Poultney, Vermont, at Rensselaer Polytechnic Institute in Troy, New York, and was a visiting scholar at Harvard University.

A native of Germany, O'Hara completed her undergraduate and graduate studies at the University of Gottingen, where she also earned a doctorate in environmental economics. She serves on the board of directors of several national and international organizations, including as president of the United States Society for Ecological Economics, as secretary of the Council of Scientific Society Presidents, and as editorial board member of several academic journals.

Felix Kayode Olakulehin is a Research Fellow at the Regional Training and Research Institute for ODL, National Open University of Nigeria. He holds degrees in Educational Management and Distance Education. He was a recipient of the Rajiv Ghandi Fellowship for ODL under the Commonwealth of Learning (2005-2008) and he was a Scholar of the Africa Higher Education Collaborative (2008-2009), a project of the Council for International Exchange of Scholars. He is a member of the Free and Open Source Software Foundation of Africa, European Association of Science Editors, and the Global Research Management Network. His research interests include: educational planning & policy, open, distance & eLearning, open educational resources, ICT in Education & Training, as well as lifelong learning. He is currently a doctoral student at the University of Leeds, United Kingdom.

Gerald Wangenge-Ouma teaches higher education studies at the University of the Western Cape, South Africa, where he is a Senior Lecturer. He holds a Ph.D. from the University of Cape Town for a thesis entitled, "Reducing Resource Dependence on Government Funding: The Case of Public Universities in Kenya and South Africa". He has published extensively, mainly in the area of higher education finance. He is also developing a research interest in the relationship between higher education and development.

Violet Wawire is lecturer and researcher in the Department of Education Foundations at Kenyatta University, a position she has held for the last fifteen years. Her research and teaching interests are in the areas of elementary and higher education with an equity and development perspective. She has been granted numerous research grants and scholarships to conduct research in the field of education that have resulted into several co-authored books chapters and journal papers including, *Public and Private Universities in Kenya*, published by James Curry. She was a visiting scholar at University of London, School of Oriental and African Studies (SOAS). She has a PhD in Education from Kenyatta University.

IIE INFORMATION AND RESOURCES

OPEN DOORS REPORT ON INTERNATIONAL EDUCATIONAL EXCHANGE

The Open Doors Report on International Educational Exchange, supported by the U.S. Department of State, Bureau of Educational and Cultural Affairs, provides an annual, comprehensive statistical analysis of academic mobility between the United States and other nations, and trend data over 60 years.

WEBSITE: www.opendoors.iienetwork.org

THE CENTER FOR INTERNATIONAL PARTNERSHIPS IN HIGHER EDUCATION

The IIE Center for International Partnerships in Higher Education assists colleges and universities in developing and sustaining institutional partnerships with their counterparts around the world. A major initiative of the Center is the International Academic Partnerships Program, funded by the U.S. Department of Education's Fund for the Improvement of Postsecondary Education (FIPSE), and the U.S. Indonesia Partnership Program for Study Abroad Capacity (USIPP), funded by the U.S. Department of State, Bureau of Educational and Cultural Affairs (ECA).

WEBSITE: www.iie.org/cip

ATLAS OF STUDENT MOBILITY

Project Atlas tracks migration trends of the millions of students who pursue education outside of their home countries each year. Data are collected on global student mobility patterns, country of origin, as well as leading host destinations for higher education.

WEBSITE: http://atlas.iienetwork.org

IIE STUDY ABROAD WHITE PAPER SERIES: MEETING AMERICA'S GLOBAL EDUCATION CHALLENGE

An IIE policy research initiative that addresses the issue of increasing capacity in the U.S. and abroad, in order to help pave the way for substantial study abroad growth.

- Expanding Study Abroad Capacity at U.S. Colleges and Universities
- Promoting Study Abroad in Science and Technology Fields
- Expanding U.S. Study Abroad in the Arab World: Challenges & Opportunities
- Expanding Education Abroad at Community Colleges
- Exploring Host Country Capacity for Increasing U.S. Study Abroad
- Current Trends in U.S. Study Abroad & the Impact of Strategic Diversity Initiatives

WEBSITE: www.iie.org/StudyAbroadCapacity

IIE/AIFS FOUNDATION GLOBAL EDUCATION RESEARCH REPORTS

This series explores the most pressing and under-researched issues affecting international education policy today.

- Innovation through Education: Building the Knowledge Economy in the Middle East (January 2010)

- International India: A Turning Point in Educational Exchange with the U.S. (January 2010)

- Higher Education on the Move: New Developments in Global Mobility (April 2009)

- U.S.-China Educational Exchange: Perspectives on a Growing Partnership (October 2008)

WEBSITE: www.iie.org/en/Research-and-Publications/

IIE BRIEFING PAPERS

IIE Briefing Papers are a rapid response to the changing landscape of international education, offering timely snapshots of critical issues in the field.

- International Education as an Institutional Priority: What Every College and University Trustee Should Know (September 2010)

- Attitudes and Perceptions of Prospective International Students from Vietnam (January 2010)

- Attitudes and Perceptions of Prospective International Students from India (December 2009)

- The Value of International Education to U.S. Business and Industry Leaders: Key Findings from a Survey of CEOs (October 2009)

- The Three-year Bologna-compliant Degree: Responses from U.S. Graduate Schools (April 2009)

- Educational Exchange between the United States and China (July 2008)

WEBSITE: www.iie.org/researchpublications

IIE Web Resources

HIGHER EDUCATION IN AFRICA

The purpose of AHEC is to identify strategies for increasing equity and access to higher education in Africa. AHEC seeks to accomplish this task by serving as a think tank and source of information for policy makers, practitioners and the interested public. AHEC is a project of the Council for International Exchange of Scholars (CIES), part of the Department of Scholar and Professional Programs at the Institute of International Education (IIE).

WEBSITE: www.africahighered.org

IIEPASSPORT.ORG

This free online search engine lists over 9,000 study abroad programs worldwide and provides advisers with hands-on tools to counsel students and promote study abroad.

WEBSITE: www.iiepassport.org

STUDY ABROAD FUNDING

This valuable funding resource helps U.S. students find funding for their study abroad.

WEBSITE: www.studyabroadfunding.org

FUNDING FOR UNITED STATES STUDY

This directory offers the most relevant data on hundreds of fellowships, grants, paid internships and scholarships for study in the U.S.

WEBSITE: www.fundingusstudy.org

INTENSIVE ENGLISH USA

Comprehensive reference with over 500 accredited English language programs in the U.S.

WEBSITE: www.intensiveenglishusa.org

IIE RESOURCES FOR STUDY ABROAD

IIE offers a single point of entry to access valuable study abroad information, including policy research, data on study abroad trends, news coverage of new developments, fact sheets for students, and dates and deadlines for major scholarship and fellowship programs.

WEBSITE: www.iie.org/studyabroad

INTERNATIONALIZING THE CAMPUS

IIE administers a wealth of programs and provides a variety of services and resources to help U.S. colleges and universities develop and implement their strategies for greater campus internationalization.

WEBSITE: www.iie.org/internationalizing

FULBRIGHT PROGRAMS FOR U.S. STUDENTS

The Fulbright U.S. Student Program equips future American leaders with the skills they need to thrive in an increasingly global environment by providing funding for one academic year of study or research abroad, to be conducted after graduation from an accredited university.

SPONSOR: U.S. Department of State, Bureau of Educational and Cultural Affairs

WEBSITE: http://us.fulbrightonline.org

FULBRIGHT PROGRAMS FOR U.S. SCHOLARS

The traditional Fulbright Scholar Program sends 800 U.S. faculty and professionals abroad each year. Grantees lecture and conduct research in a wide variety of academic and professional fields.

SPONSOR: U.S. Department of State, Bureau of Educational and Cultural Affairs

WEBSITE: www.cies.org